CW00798973

ALLENBY

Figure 1 Allenby as rendered in chalk by Eric Kennington in 1926. Commissioned by T. E. Lawrence for the subscribers' edition of *Seven Pillars of Wisdom*, the original of which hung over the stairwell at Clouds Hill until his death.

Also by C. Brad Faught

Kitchener: Hero and Anti-Hero
Clive: Founder of British India
Into Africa: The Imperial Life of Margery Perham
The New A–Z of Empire: A Concise Handbook of British Imperial History
Gordon: Victorian Hero
The Oxford Movement: A Thematic History of the Tractarians and Their Times

ALLENBY

Making the Modern Middle East

C. Brad Faught

I.B. TAURIS
LONDON • NEW YORK • OXFORD • NEW DELHI • SYDNEY

I.B. TAURIS
Bloomsbury Publishing Plc
50 Bedford Square, London, WC1B 3DP, UK
1385 Broadway, New York, NY 10018, USA

BLOOMSBURY, I.B. TAURIS and the I.B. Tauris logo are trademarks of
Bloomsbury Publishing Plc

First published in Great Britain 2020

Copyright © C. Brad Faught, 2020

C. Brad Faught has asserted his right under the Copyright, Designs and
Patents Act, 1988, to be identified as Author of this work.

For legal purposes the Acknowledgements on p. xii constitute an extension
of this copyright page.

Cover design: Charlotte James
Cover image © Liddell Hart Archives/King's College London

All rights reserved. No part of this publication may be reproduced or transmitted
in any form or by any means, electronic or mechanical, including photocopying,
recording, or any information storage or retrieval system, without prior
permission in writing from the publishers.

Bloomsbury Publishing Plc does not have any control over, or responsibility for, any
third-party websites referred to or in this book. All internet addresses given in this
book were correct at the time of going to press. The author and publisher regret any
inconvenience caused if addresses have changed or sites have ceased to exist,
but can accept no responsibility for any such changes.

A catalogue record for this book is available from the British Library.

A catalog record for this book is available from the Library of Congress.

ISBN: HB: 978-1-7883-1240-0
PB: 978-1-3501-3647-2
ePDF: 978-0-7556-0058-8
eBook: 978-0-7556-0059-5

Typeset by Deanta Global Publishing Services, Chennai, India
Printed and bound in Great Britain

To find out more about our authors and books visit www.bloomsbury.com
and sign up for our newsletters.

In Memoriam Michael Bliss

CONTENTS

FIGURES

PREFACE

I am still puzzled as to how far the individual counts: a lot, I fancy, if he pushes the right way.[1]

T. E. Lawrence, 1930

The geopolitical map of today's Middle East bears the imprint in a significant way of the actions taken by both Britain and France immediately before, during and after the First World War. Although it is true that 'The Making of ...' has become a well-used (over-used?) trope of historians in recent years, one of the places where indeed it can be deployed accurately is in relation to the Middle East. And one of the most important names in this regard is that of Edmund Allenby. Viscount Allenby of Megiddo and Felixstowe, as he became later, was the principal British military figure in the region from 1917 to 1919. He then fulfilled a similar proconsular role in Egypt from the latter year until 1925. In these two roles Allenby's eight years in the Middle East were of great impact both then and long afterwards, and in probing his life an especially revealing window can be found through which to observe closely and understand more fully the history that has resulted in the terminal roil afflicting the·Middle East and international affairs today. To paraphrase the words of the writer Saki, the Middle East has always produced 'far more history than it could consume locally'.[2]

Born into the Nottinghamshire squirearchy in 1861, Allenby came of age in the mid- to late Victorian era and was shaped therefore by the prevailing British imperial verities of the day. Educated at the East India Company's Haileybury College, the young Allenby aspired initially to a career in the Indian Civil Service. But after failing the entrance exam twice, the prospect of life as a member of the so-called 'Heaven born' cadre of Raj administrators came to an abrupt end and he looked instead for what was understood to be a more prosaic career in the British Army. In this way, success at the Royal Military Academy Sandhurst would soon follow, and after passing out in 1881 Allenby served as a cavalryman, spending much time in South Africa, culminating in service in the Second South African, or Anglo-Boer, War fought from 1899 until 1902. Later, as a major general upon the outbreak of the First World War in August of 1914, Allenby was given command of the British Expeditionary Force's Cavalry Division. Stellar, though undistinguished, service on the Western Front followed until, in 1917, he was put in charge of the British-led Egyptian Expeditionary Force and sent to Palestine to do battle against the occupying Ottoman Turks.

Dogged, aggressive and stentorian – a skein of qualities that were reflected in his nickname, 'The (Bloody) Bull' – Allenby found his leadership feet in the Middle East. Tasked with defeating the German-bolstered Ottomans in the region and thereby usurping their rule and ultimately substituting it in part with Britain's own, he won several indispensable military victories, usually by employing various modes of attack that presaged a modern twentieth-century style of combined operations warfare. Beginning with a stunning victory in October of 1917 at Gaza in Palestine, Allenby continued his winning ways by taking Jerusalem that December, and then Megiddo in October of 1918. In the aftermath of this latter victory came a triumphantly climactic entry into Damascus. Shortly thereafter the 400-year-old Ottoman Empire in the Middle East would come to an end. Throughout the campaign Allenby had depended significantly upon the field intelligence and fighting success provided by a number of key operatives, many of whom were under the purview of the Arab Bureau such as its leading figure, the increasingly influential T. E. Lawrence. Intrinsic to the campaign's military achievements was the dependable fighting character of Allenby's British, Australian and New Zealander (Anzac), and Indian regular troops, as well as the determination and aspirations for freedom of the Arab Army, bolstered by its irregular comrades.

Once victory in Palestine and Syria had been achieved, Allenby was transferred in due course to Cairo as British (special) high commissioner for Egypt, a post he would hold for six years until 1925. As such, he would preside over Egypt as it pushed relentlessly for independence in the wake of its revolution of 1918 and the surge in political activism occasioned by the founding of the nationalist *Wafd* party, the first of its kind encountered by the British anywhere in the Middle East.[3] Later, in 1922, Allenby would be successful in recommending that Egypt be declared independent, which, in practice, granted it a significant measure of national autonomy. Throughout his years as proconsul he faced both real and threatened nationalist uprisings, a chronic feature of Egyptian society since at least as far back as Colonel Urabi's army rebellion in 1881 and the British armed intervention at Alexandria that would follow the next year. Indeed, until the day Allenby left Cairo in June of 1925 for retirement in England he would remain at the centre of Egyptian political affairs.

Long considered by historians, as well as by many others, to be a kind of modern 'Crusader', or simply as an average general who got lucky in command in a peripheral theatre, or even as a mere accomplice of the more daringly heroic Lawrence, Allenby, it may be argued, is viewed best as a hard-headed man of war who combined – like his near-contemporary Lord Kitchener had done very successfully not so many years earlier in both India and Egypt – a pronounced quality of command with considerable skill as a government administrator and diplomat. In the aftermath of his military victories in Palestine and Syria, Allenby's voice was critical in influencing the controversial political outcome of them for both Arabs and Jews. His six years in Cairo would see him grapple further with the very essence of modern Arab (Egyptian) nationalism, based in large measure on the geopolitical decisions made by his immediate predecessor, Sir Henry McMahon, as well as by the major diplomatic events of the period, the Sykes–Picot Agreement, the Balfour Declaration, the Paris Peace Conference and the San Remo and Cairo Conferences. It is the purpose of this book to show that Allenby's impact on Palestine and Egypt was both decisive and positive. Had his legacy been acted upon by a subsequent generation of British administrators in a wise and timely manner, it could have been even more far-reaching than it was and, arguably, helped to prevent much of the political violence and dysfunction that continues to disfigure the region today.

This biography of Allenby, therefore, aims to be modern, nuanced and concerned with capturing the totality of the man, most especially in relation to the years that he spent in the Middle East. In the aftermath of the Arab Revolt and its romantic portrayal first, in the 1920s, at the hands of the American publicist Lowell Thomas, and then later those of the celebrated British filmmaker David Lean in his award-winning 1962 epic *Lawrence of Arabia*, Allenby as a figure of vital importance in helping to create the modern Middle East became overlooked to some extent. The two best biographies of him, Field Marshal Archibald Wavell's *Allenby: A Study in Greatness* (two volumes, 1940 and 1943) and Lawrence James's *Imperial Warrior* (1993), though published over a half-century apart, nonetheless both lean towards the conventionally heroic, especially Wavell's, a view that I seek to modify in certain respects.[4] The attempt here therefore, by way of contrast, is to probe deeply and dispassionately the events and actions of Allenby's life, as well as to examine his thinking on both the British Empire and the post–First World War international order. The goal is to bring maximum clarity to Allenby's deep impact on British imperial policy in the making of the modern Middle East, and thereby on the long arc of the region's continuing and controversial place in world affairs.

Note: In spelling peoples' names, as well as that of place names, I have used the form common today – for example, Aqaba, rather than Akaba; Sharif Faisal, rather than Sherif Feisal. However, I have left untouched the spellings given to such names and places by contemporaries at the time that the events in this book occurred, unless doing so were to obscure their correct identification.

ACKNOWLEDGEMENTS

Over the past twenty-five years I have been privileged both to teach history and to write books. I have tried never to take either one for granted, and when putting the finishing touches on this book, I was reminded of such a happy vocational intersection by seeing in the newspaper the name of Northrop Frye, the late great Canadian literary critic. Not long before he died in 1991 I attended one of Frye's lectures at the University of Toronto. By the time I saw him in action, he was approaching the end of his brilliantly accomplished career. During the question and answer period at the conclusion of Frye's lively and learned lecture he was asked, after all these years, how he was able to remain so keen about both his teaching and his scholarship. He replied simply that he had always treated the lecture hall as his 'engine room'; that is, he explained, teaching was the act that energized him for the work of research and writing. I was deeply and, I think, rightly impressed by what Frye – a master teacher and scholar – had to say that day, and since then I have tried to treat both these facets of my work as an historian with equal devotion, viewing them ideally as an integrative whole.

Still, writing a book – unlike teaching, for the most part – is dependent significantly on the help, expertise and resources of others, and for all of those who have helped me with this biography I am grateful. Therefore, first, I should like to thank the archivists and staff at the following institutions for their ready and superb assistance: the Liddell Hart Centre for Military Archives at King's College London, especially Lianne Smith, Archives Manager; the National Archives at Kew, London; the National Army Museum, London; the Parliamentary Archives, Westminster; the Imperial War Museum, London; Cambridge University Library; St. Antony's College, Oxford, Middle East Centre Archive; the Bodleian Library, Oxford; the National Records of Scotland, Edinburgh; the American Colony Archive Collections, the American Colony Hotel, Jerusalem; the Be'er Sheva Anzac Memorial Centre; and the Museum of the History of Jerusalem. For historians, such places as these are treasure houses from which the words necessary to tell the story of their subjects are drawn, and I for one never tire of working in their pleasant and thoroughly professional surroundings. As well, I would like to acknowledge Abraham Tours and guide Abdallah As'ad for an outstanding trip to various sites in Jordan connected to Allenby and T. E. Lawrence.

Second, my home institution, Tyndale University, has been unstinting in its research grant support, as well as in the provision of a sabbatical, without which this book could not have been written. I should like to thank in particular Dean Barry Smith and President Gary Nelson for continuing to support the vital work of faculty scholarship in an era of increasing budgetary pressure in higher education that would militate against it. I would like also to acknowledge my colleagues in the Department of History and Global Studies at Tyndale, Professors Eric Crouse and Ian Gentles, as well as the students whom I teach, for their continued interest and support. In particular, my thanks to Sam Wachob, who as a student summer research assistant ably prepared comprehensive bibliographies of the works written both on and by Allenby and T. E. Lawrence.

Third, I should like to thank Sophie Campbell, Rory Gormley, and James Tupper at Bloomsbury and its imprint I.B. Tauris, as well as IBT's former history editors, Joanna Godfrey and Lester Crook.

As usual, however, I save my best thanks for my wife, Rhonda, who has always tolerated my historical obsessions – including the need to stop and read just about every historical plaque we come across! – with indulgence and good humour. My research trips abroad – which sometimes include the need simply to 'walk in the footsteps of …', have been supported always too, and for this I am very grateful. The same thing can be said of our daughter and son, Claire and Luke.

I have dedicated this book to the late Michael Bliss, one of the all-time great historians of Canada. As a doctoral student in the Department of History at the University of Toronto at the height of Michael's career, I was privileged to work for him as a teaching assistant. But much more than that, his high skill and dedication as a teacher were married to surpassing ability as a scholar and writer, evidenced by his winning a passel of awards over the course of his professional life too numerous to itemize here. In all ways he was a model and inspiration. His practical help too, from the very outset of my career, was always appreciated greatly including, just a few years ago, his very kind introduction of me when launching my biography of Kitchener. Thank you, Michael. RIP.

Chapter 1

BOY TO MAN
BECOMING AN OFFICER AND A GENTLEMAN, 1861–99

In 1861, the year in which Edmund Henry Hynman Allenby was born, Prince Albert, Queen Victoria's beloved husband and consort, died. Albert's death that December from typhoid fever, aged just forty-two years, would plunge the Queen into what came to be an almost interminable period of mourning, at the end of which she would emerge, among other things, as a resolute, Tory imperialist. The British Empire over which the queen presided during the last quarter of the nineteenth century would become, for Allenby, the imaginative landscape that provided him with the main contours of his military vocation. And even though his signature feat of arms would not occur until many years later in 1917, and with it a triumphant entry into the holy city of Jerusalem after having vanquished the Ottoman Turks, what had occasioned it was the continuing geographical capaciousness of Victorian-era imperial Britain. In many respects Allenby would be the last in a lengthy line of leading British imperial commanders. But long before any of that would take place, Edmund Allenby was born on 23 April 1861 at his mother's Midlands home of Brackenhurst, in Nottinghamshire.

Edmund was the second child and eldest son of Hynman Allenby and his wife, Catherine Anne (Cane). Today, Brackenhurst is part of Nottingham Trent University and appropriately, given Allenby's lifelong love of flora and fauna nurtured as a child, houses the School of Animal, Rural and Environmental Sciences on a substantial tract of 200 hectares of land a short distance outside Nottingham near the town of Southwell. Catherine was the daughter of a Church of England parson, the Rev'd Thomas Coats Cane, and his wife Mary (Brettle). One of the leading men of the county, a 'sqarson' with a comfortable private income, Cane shot, bred livestock and lived well, while presiding over a large family of twelve children, Catherine being the third eldest.

Hynman Allenby himself was the second son of a prosperous solicitor and country gentleman, Hinman Raddish Allenby, and his wife Elizabeth (Bourne). He and Catherine were married in 1859. They then went to live at Dartmouth in Devon where their first child, Catherine Mary (known as Kitty), was born the next year, and where Hynman could pursue his passion for sailing. Edmund's birth would follow in 1861. Four more children – Elizabeth, Claude, Helen (called Nell) and Alfred – would be born, the last of whom arrived in 1871. By that time the Allenbys had removed themselves to live permanently in the Suffolk coastal town of Felixstowe, which would remain the family seat until the death of Catherine at the age of ninety-one in 1922.[1]

Life at Felixstowe Hall (or House, to which it is sometimes referred) for the growing family and the young Allenby was nothing less than idyllic.[2] In those days, Felixstowe was a tiny town – nothing like the bustling coastal city of over 25,000 people today, which contains the largest container port in Britain – and Allenby spent much of his childhood outside dirtying his hands in the abundant natural world that lay at his doorstep. To add to the wide-eyed wonders of birds, small animals, insects and plants of the meadows and streams of his immediate surroundings, his father also had purchased an estate of about 2,000 acres near West Bilney in the neighbouring county of Norfolk, to which the family removed regularly, especially in autumn and winter. Apart from a few childhood maladies – including an especially bad bout of whooping cough – Allenby grew up strong of body. His first education lay in the hands of a governess, Miss Simpson, and then, at the age of ten, in those of an obliging vicar of the High Anglican variety, the Rev'd Maurice Cowell, of Ashbocking, a village located some 15 miles from Felixstowe. Beginning therefore in 1871, Allenby was educated in the rudiments of the classics, along with mathematics and botany. Altogether, he seems to have been a singularly happy and well-adjusted child: dutiful, content and confidently Christian. 'Whatsoever thy hand findeth to do', his devout mother read to him in the cadence and language of the Revised Standard Version, 'do it with thy might' (Eccl. 9.10).[3] No words were ever more thoroughly inwardly digested – as any properly catechized young Anglican was enjoined to do, and it would appear that Allenby lived by them for the rest of his life.

From the age of ten until fourteen Allenby's life was spent under the amiable tutelage of the Rev'd Cowell, and within the bosom of his family and its varied country pursuits. Riding, shooting, sailing – Hynman Allenby's sailboat, the *Water Witch*, figured prominently in their recreation – and rambling, all were engaged in readily, as was skating in wintertime. Notwithstanding these recreational and sporting endeavours, however, the young Allenby himself was never much inclined to participate in formal games. The full-flower of Dr Arnold's influence emanating from Rugby School was just beginning to transform the English public school sporting ethos, only to be skewered later by Kipling as 'oafish' in light of the manifest disaster of the Second South African War.[4] But neither at Ashbocking nor later at Haileybury College would Allenby go in much for team sport. That said, he was always 'painstaking and thoroughgoing' and demonstrated a 'high ideal of duty', according to James Welldon, a frequent visitor to Ashbocking vicarage and very much the sportsman who later would become Winston Churchill's headmaster at Harrow, and then later still, bishop of Calcutta.[5] In other words, Allenby might well be considered the embodiment of the Victorian 'muscular Christian', a type that until Lytton Strachey's satirical demolition of it in *Eminent Victorians* published in 1918 at the end of the First World War, had been lauded as a cultural ideal.[6]

In the spring of 1875, having just turned fourteen, Allenby was enrolled by his father in Haileybury College in order to complete his adolescent education in a more formal setting. Haileybury, while not in the front rank of public schools such as Eton, Harrow and Winchester, was considered nonetheless to be entirely respectable and had been re-founded just thirteen years earlier as a modern successor of its original iteration as the training ground for servants of the East India Company. In most respects, Haileybury was a perfect setting for the adolescent Allenby. He breathed deeply of its imperial service-oriented air, a feature that would long remain a part of the Haileybury experience, as the future prime minister Clement Attlee recalled admiringly of his own days at the school a generation after Allenby's.[7] And while the sporting ethos was pronounced, it was not (yet) pervasive. Dutifully, Allenby would play rugby for his house, but apart from that he was not an athletic 'hearty'. But in other respects he was the ideal anvil upon which to hammer home the principles of duty, service and loyalty that, altogether, spoke of the character-building necessary for imperial responsibility and stewardship to come. Haileybury belonged to Tom Brown's world and Allenby's own aspirations came quickly to intersect squarely with its main features.[8]

To this service-oriented end, nothing in full-orbed school experience matched being appointed a prefect. And Allenby was duly made one in the Sixth Form, his last year of three at Haileybury. According to one of his prefectorial peers, he was 'sane, simple, and direct in all he did; he had no difficulties with discipline, which he exercised without harshness and with absolute justice'.[9] Indeed, as a thumbnail description of Allenby, this one is near perfect. And as a supervisory training ground for someone who would eventually become a career military man, a year as a public school prefect lording it fairly benignly – 'he was always noble and fair' – over his younger peers was equally ideal.[10] However, in the midst of this rather halcyon period of Allenby's young life sadness and disruption made an unwelcome entry upon the death of Hynman Allenby in February of 1878. In his sixty-seventh year, Allenby's father was not especially old, even by the standards of the latter nineteenth century when life expectancy first began to lengthen significantly. But at seventeen years of age, Allenby's character was not yet fully formed, and with his squire-arch father now gone, and as the eldest son, it fell immediately to him to think more clearly about a professional career. In light of Hynman Allenby's death, the family was forced to retrench financially, meaning that the Norfolk properties at West Bilney were sold and more than ever Felixstowe House became their focal point.

One of the main ways in which Haileybury continued to embody its former educational ethos was in setting before the boys the possibility of a career in British India, especially as a member of the augustly regarded Indian Civil Service (ICS). The ICS believed itself to be – and certainly was considered by most to be – the elite of the British colonial services. The ICS's relatively small membership – only some 1,200 at its late Victorian, Edwardian-era height – its esprit de corps, which was pronounced, and its sense of superiority were supreme.[11] Upon Hynman Allenby's untimely death the young Allenby was in the Lower Sixth Form with a year left to go in the Upper Sixth in order to complete his full time at Haileybury. He was not to stay on, however. His father's passing provided an unwelcome but necessary impetus to start to make his way in the world, and this meant an attempt to enter the ICS and with it the potential establishment of a comparatively well-paying, prestigious and covenanted career. Of course these were the very features of life among the so-called Heaven born that made the entrance examination so highly, even legendarily, competitive.

Accordingly, at the conclusion of the summer term in 1878, Allenby departed Haileybury and was duly enrolled at an ICS crammer's called Wren's, located in London's Bayswater, in order to study intensively for the daunting entrance examination. Using a crammer was standard practice for a service exam, and Allenby did so, accompanied by his close Haileybury friend, Henry McMahon. He will, as we shall see, come to figure prominently in Allenby's later life in the Middle East. Together, they and a number of other students sat under the tutelage of Mr Wren in Greek, Latin, French, English composition, mathematics and chemistry.[12] The course of preparation was highly demanding, the other boys were equally bright and driven and the chance of examination success was minimal. Allenby duly took the examination in the summer of 1879, and failed. Not to be put off he tried it again during the following summer, but failed once more.[13] In both years the ICS admitted just 50 candidates out of 356 who wrote the examination, a stringency akin to the rate of undergraduate entrance at Oxbridge today.[14]

Allenby's initial acute disappointment over his failed attempts to join the ICS was softened by what was all along, however, probably the better option for a young man of his disposition and talents: the prospect of a British Army career made possible by admission into the Royal Military Academy Sandhurst. Consequently, he enrolled in a different London crammer, this one run by a Mr Adams who specialized in readying candidates for the Sandhurst examination, which is recognized widely as considerably less demanding than that of the ICS. In December 1880, aged nineteen and after another intensive experience of cramming, a determined Allenby proceeded to ace the examination, passing fifth into Sandhurst out of a class of 110.[15] Easier the Sandhurst entrance exam may have been, but no matter for the prospective young cadet. Allenby had found his vocation and he duly went off to the academy, arriving for his first day on 10 February 1881, feeling both happy and relieved.[16] So likewise did his family welcome this success, especially his mother, who had wondered about her eldest son's future from the moment her husband had died almost exactly three years earlier. Now, thankfully, the answer had been found in the form of Queen Victoria's Army.

The Royal Military Academy Sandhurst had been founded in 1801 under the auspices of Major General John Le Marchant in order to train 'Gentlemen Cadets' for the infantry and cavalry regiments of the British Army, as well as for the East India Company's presidency armies that were stationed in Bombay, Madras and Calcutta.[17] Located initially in Buckinghamshire, it had relocated to Sandhurst, Berkshire, in 1812. Together with the Royal Military Academy Woolwich, which trained artillerymen and engineers, Sandhurst provided for the professional needs of Britain's Victorian-era military. Sandhurst was a physically rigorous, if not especially intellectually challenging, place, although Allenby was being over-modest when he remarked later that he had gone there in light of his ICS examination failure 'because he was too big a fool for anything else'.[18]

The young Allenby's ten months on course at Sandhurst were unremarkable in that he was not a high-flyer, set apart necessarily for greatness as some of his comrades might have been. He made good friends – his best one, Henry McMahon, many years later to precede him as the top British official in Egypt – accompanied him there from the crammer's, and he participated fully in cadet life. But his natural seriousness of mind, together with his full adult height of 6' 2" and strong physical bearing combined to give him a presence more greatly pronounced than that of many of his peers. Still, he was in no way the centre of attention. As one of them recalled much later in life, Allenby was a 'very handsome, quiet young man, retiring in his ways. Probably he did apply himself to the Science of War, whereas I was more interested in polo and games.'[19] And while it could not be said that his upbringing had been cosmopolitan, Allenby just then had begun to travel on the Continent with both family and friends, and his increased exposure to the world in this way had had an important impact on his cultural maturation. Most especially was this true after he had spent a couple of months in provincial France learning to speak French. Altogether, by the time he passed out of Sandhurst in December of 1881 – having done so 'with honours' and ranking twelfth in his class – the twenty-year-old Allenby was an ideal subaltern, ready to find his way in the newly reformed British Army.[20] Just a short time later, therefore, in May of 1882, he was gazetted a commission in the 6th (Inniskilling) Dragoons, an Irish regiment stationed then in South Africa. A storied, if not especially fashionable (but therefore also less expensive to join) regiment, the Inniskillings had been founded in 1689, just before seeing action at the soon-to-be legendary Battle of the Boyne the next year.[21] As a regiment of heavy cavalry, that is, cavalry of the line, it would fight at Waterloo, as well as during the Crimean War at the Battle of Balaclava and in India at the time of the Mutiny (or Rebellion) in 1857. Later, in the aftermath of the Anglo-Zulu war of 1879 in South Africa, the regiment would be sent to Natal as part of a reinforced British garrison stationed there, which is where it was serving when the young Allenby arrived at the port city of Durban in the late summer of 1882.

In joining the Inniskillings, Allenby had become part of a fighting regiment with a strong record of British imperial service and in that world there were few places more roiling than southern Africa in the closing years of the nineteenth century. Allenby's arrival in 1882 occurred between the two great mineral discoveries that did more than anything else to set the British on a final collision course with the resident Afrikaners, their chief rival for European dominance in the region. The discovery of what came to be called the 'Eureka' diamond in 1867 in the interior district of Griqualand had occasioned an onrush of mining, speculation and economic development, exacerbating the pre-existing cleavages between Boer and Briton. Into that volatile mix was added the presence of a number of indigenous African populations – principally the Zulu and the Xhosa peoples – who were scrambling to maintain their ethnic and territorial integrity against galloping and pervasive Europeanization. In 1886, four years after Allenby had joined his regiment at their camp located just outside Durban, gold was discovered to the northwest at Witswatersrand in the Transvaal, one of two Afrikaner republics, the other being the Orange Free State where diamond mining was now well underway.[22] The republics' stubborn existence – at least to the British – had been fought over twice, the most recent occurrence of which had been just a few years earlier during 1880–1. In the aftermath of that war, an uneasy truce had settled over the Anglo-Boer relationship, the maintenance of which was a large part of the reason for the presence of the Inniskillings in southern Africa.

Prior to the mineral discoveries, the Boers and the British – the first having arrived at the Cape in 1652, and the latter in 1806 as a weigh-station on the route to India during the Napoleonic Wars – lived in an uneasy share-out of the territory. Neither the Transvaal nor the Orange Free State was wealthy or especially attractive to the British whose sea power was demonstrated and reinforced amply by its own colonies of the Cape and Natal. Both of these colonies contained excellent harbours, as well as thriving nodes of commerce and settlement, especially their leading cities of Cape Town and Durban respectively.[23] The two Boer states, on the other hand, were impoverished, almost wholly agricultural, and under the control – again as far as the British were concerned – of a stubborn Calvinist religious leadership verging on the theocratic.[24]

Meanwhile, the various indigenous African peoples existed within this disputed European paramountcy in a kind of suspended state, occasionally resorting to armed resistance – such as had occurred recently in 1879 at Isandlwana when a British force was badly defeated by Zulu *impis* – but more usually giving ground to the almost irresistible advance of European colonial settlement and military power.[25] Thus it was that no one was surprised when just six months after their defeat at Isandlwana in January of 1879, the British firmly vanquished independent Zulu power at the equally lopsided Battle of Ulundi, a defeat from which the Zulu nation would not soon recover.[26]

Indeed, following the British victory at Ulundi the Zulu would cease to be a territorial rival in any real sense and the focus of geo-strategic concern for the British became almost wholly the two Boer republics. The British had annexed the Transvaal (South African Republic) in 1880, sparking a war with the Boers which lasted until the following year.[27] This First Anglo-Boer War, as it would come to be called, proved to be both brutal and surprisingly difficult for the British whose superiority in weapons and tactics they had assumed were theirs. In particular, the decisive Boer victory at Majuba Hill in Natal in February of 1881 made it clear to the British that the Boers were not be cowed in the way that the pre-industrial Zulu had been. Accordingly, in the aftermath of the war the Transvaal's formal independence was restored. But its position in this regard was always temporary as far as the British were concerned, especially once gold was discovered later in 1886.

The situation in South Africa therefore was both fluid and tense at the time of Allenby's arrival in 1882. The Inniskillings were sent out as one part of what was required to reinforce the British military presence in the region. Based in Natal Allenby adapted quickly to the regimental life he found there. Thus he rode and shot; he drank, though moderately, and socialized infrequently. Characteristically, as we shall see, he was 'a bit brusque' in his treatment of the younger subalterns, but altogether gained invaluable formative service along a challenging imperial frontier that was in constant flux.[28]

Bechuanaland (today's Botswana) was the contested area of the frontier that would draw in Allenby and the Inniskillings during their first sustained period of service. An enormous tract of southern African desert, plain and swamp, which teemed with game, Bechuanaland was sparsely populated by the San people (the so-called Bushmen of the Kalahari), among others. The territory was coveted by both Boer and Briton, but for different reasons. For the Boers, Bechuanaland was seen as a natural northern extension of the Transvaal. Indeed, there was a rump Boer population of perhaps a thousand settlers living there already under the nominal suzerainty of two new covenanted statelets, the Boer republics of Stellaland and Goschen. For the British, on the other hand, the prospect of Bechuanaland becoming a beachhead for the extension of Afrikanerdom was in itself enough of a provocation for them to act in order to prevent such an eventuality.[29]

But there was more to the situation for the British than just an attempt to check Boer expansion. Another consideration was that expressed by John Mackenzie, a resident Scottish missionary, who feared that an increasing influx of Boer settlers into Bechuanaland would have a seriously deleterious impact on indigenous Tswana society. The best thing to do in light of this sure eventuality, he argued, was for the British to proclaim a protectorate over the territory.[30] Of equal import too, but taking a different form, was the persistent expansionism of the increasingly powerful and insistent Cape Colony politician Cecil Rhodes, whose grand vision of a strip of British-controlled territory in Africa stretching from 'Cape to Cairo' was fast taking shape. Bechuanaland was included in this vision as it lay on the old 'Missionaries' Road' – pioneered by David Livingstone in mid-century – to what was then called Zambesia, but would later take the name of Rhodes himself.[31] The fact that Rhodes called this road the Suez Canal of the South African interior gives an idea as to what he thought of its importance, and therefore of the necessity of a British protectorate being extended over the region.[32] Finally, complicating the picture even further was the recently established German presence at Angra Pequena, or Luderitz Bay, on the Namibian coast. The expectation that this tiny colony, which German trader Adolf Luderitz had founded in 1883 and then turned over to the German government the following year, would serve as the egg from which a broader German southern African territorial presence would be hatched was a lively one for the British. Altogether, with Bismarck having subsequently proclaimed Luderitz-Angra Pequena and the surrounding territory to be a German protectorate in August of 1884, there was much to be concerned about in geo-strategic terms in London.[33] Enough, indeed, that in November of that year the Gladstone government – notwithstanding its chief's earlier rejection of the 'prevailing earth-hunger' of late Victorian British imperialism – decided to check Germany's provocative move in southern Africa by calling for the creation and deployment of what would be called the Bechuanaland Field Force.[34]

Accordingly, in late November, Allenby and the Inniskillings sailed out of Durban bound for the Cape in order to form the required cavalry regiment of the newly established BFF. The force was commanded by Lieutenant Colonel Charles Warren, a career engineer officer whose various commissions, commands and appointments would make him a remarkable Victorian type. He would be appointed, for example, commissioner of police for London in 1886 and in that short-lived role preside over the gruesome Jack-the-Ripper case of 1888. But on 22 January 1885, however, Warren and his 4,000-man BFF marched out of Cape Town heading north. Warren was determined to succeed in this sensitive venture in imperial expansion. Little could he have known that at that very moment almost 5,000 miles to the north his fellow Royal Engineer Major General Charles Gordon was about to make his last fatal stand against the jihadist imprecations of the Mahdi.[35] That unmitigated disaster – which is how it would be understood by most of the country – would not be duplicated in Bechuanaland, however.

Cautious by nature and prescient in his meticulous planning, Warren ensured that the BFF would have enough water and be dressed in such a way as to resist the extremes of heat that the march through the high *veldt* and desert entailed. Equipment for drilling wells and piping water therefore was brought along. Sanitation in camp was insisted upon, as was the fact that the men would be dressed in corduroy or cotton khaki rather than in the usual scarlet woollen tunic and breeches. As well, in place of the traditional pith helmet the required headwear on the Bechuanaland Campaign would be a broad-brimmed slouch-style hat, excellent for reflecting the penetrating rays of the sun. In addition, the presence of three observation balloons – the first time they had ever been used by a British armed force on campaign – contributed to a state of comprehensive readiness by the BFF.

Three days into the march on 25 January, and with Allenby in command of the troop of cavalry that was escorting Warren, they met for a conference with the crusty and dogmatic president of the Transvaal Republic, Paul Kruger, at an outpost called Fourteen Streams. The gruff Boer leader's reputation preceded him, and his deep distrust of the British was virtually an innate feature of his character. He would, of course, have much more about which to complain in the near future in his dealings with the British, but on this occasion he told Warren simply that he was responsible for law and order in Bechuanaland and therefore neither the presence of the BFF nor the extension of a formal British protectorate were required. Cecil Rhodes – in the capacity of recently appointed Deputy Commissioner for Bechuanaland – was present for these discussions also. Neither he nor Warren agreed with what Kruger had to stay, however. In the event, Kruger's position was weak. He had no force of his own to call upon and no active engagement by resident Boers. Accordingly, he was in no position to do anything other than concede reluctantly that the British position was simply stronger than his own and therefore that he would have to submit to their plans. The moment of tension thus passed without recourse to violence by either side, but it was clear who the victor had been. Similarly, once the BFF moved on from Fourteen Streams and had arrived at Vryburg, the capital of the putative Boer state of Stellaland, the Boer settlers there chose not to resist either. Indeed, during the whole of the campaign, which included the occupation of Mafeking in March, scarcely a shot was fired, except for those heard during off-duty hunting by officers such as Allenby who went after the abundant game. In due course in September of that year the British claim of protectorate status was made official.[36]

For Allenby, a witness to high politics as well as to the mundane requirements of moving a force of men across unforgiving country at speed, the Bechuanaland experience was useful if not overly taxing introduction to active military service. Making and breaking camp; handling an armed force on the move; ensuring the health and efficacy of horses in the field. As skills necessary to his chosen vocation, Allenby could not have done better than the few months he had spent marching around southern Africa. And as a kind of bonus – although of course not to be recognized as such until later – was his making the acquaintance of the irrepressible Rhodes and even good-naturedly competing with him for a shared blanket while encamped on campaign.[37] As remembered by one of Allenby's colleagues, and in a style typical of the man, Rhodes pushed 'him [Allenby] out [of the tent] quite unconsciously, and it was merely the man's guiding instinct to push everyone else out of his way, which asserted itself even when asleep!'[38] By the end of the year, however, and with the campaign well-over Allenby had returned to Natal where he would remain until the summer of 1886, at which time he shipped out for England and a two-year regulation posting at the Canterbury cavalry depot. At twenty-five years of age, with promising prospects and a period of stellar African service of which to boast, Allenby settled happily into a brace of years enjoying the life of a young officer.

Thus it was that for the next two years Allenby fulfilled his regimental duties, engaged regularly in fox-hunting and was promoted captain. In the summer of 1888, he returned to Natal and shortly thereafter was named regimental adjutant, the latter a reflection of his natural leadership ability and gravitas when in command. Allenby's life during this period was rather uneventful, however, even if all-around him the turmoil in South Africa continued to build. In 1889, the ever-voracious Rhodes founded the British South Africa Company, which he would use to spearhead the penetration of Zambesia, as the territory north of the Limpopo River was called.[39] The BSAC's Pioneer Column to come would set in motion the delimitation of that territory, which in 1896 became known as Rhodesia. For Allenby, these and other large-scale geo-strategic events came at several removes, of course, and by the time he sailed for home with the rest of the Inniskillings in October of 1890 the machinations of Rhodes and his fellow 'Gold Bugs' would be left behind – at least for the moment.

Once having arrived in England, Allenby was quartered initially at Preston Barracks, Brighton, where he continued to serve as adjutant until 1893 when the Inniskillings were transferred to Shorncliffe, thence briefly to Manchester, and finally to Edinburgh.[40] Compared to much of his service in South Africa these years were quiet – 'I occupied myself peacefully in sunbathing & golf, at which game I improved a bit,' he wrote to his always attentive mother in August of 1893.[41] He followed dutifully the events of the day, especially in the late winter of 1894 when the six-decade-long career of W. E. Gladstone, the Grand Old Man (GOM) of British politics, finally was coming to an end: 'It seems pretty certain that Gladstone is resigning,' he wrote home.[42] Like most conservative military men in the years following the death of Gordon at Khartoum, Allenby had little time for Gladstone, who was blamed for having caused it. Indeed, Allenby met the GOM's resignation on 2 March with approbation, not unlike that displayed by the Tory Party itself, as well as by the Liberal Imperialists whose party-political machinations had helped engineer it.[43]

Perhaps, however, because of the relative somnolence of the period, which had not been made enjoyable by 'the great many balls & festivities on down here', as he informed his mother somewhat sourly, Allenby's aspirations for career advancement came into sharper focus.[44] Consequently, after a period of cramming in London – much like what he had experienced in advance of the ICS and Sandhurst exams – Allenby attempted to win entry into the Army Staff College at Camberley in Surrey, which just then was beginning to assert itself as the embodiment of what a modern army required by way of the specialization of its leadership. Allenby's first attempt in 1895 resulted in a narrow failure, but he took the examination again, this time passing it successfully by coming twenty-first out of sixty-eight candidates.[45] He was the only cavalry officer to do so, and the first Inniskilling ever to gain admission to what rapidly was becoming a gold star appointment. In January of 1896, therefore, Allenby began what would be two years of close instruction in the finer points of modern warfare, as well as in those of military command. As might be expected, the role of cavalry in the swiftly changing environment of waging contemporary (industrial) war was of especial interest to him.

At Camberley one of Allenby's classmates was the young Douglas Haig, then a captain in the 7th Hussars. Haig was the same age as Allenby, and like him had failed at his first attempt to enter the Staff College. The two young officers were amiably competitive over the following two years. Allenby, better liked than Haig by his contemporaries, was elected by them to be Master of the Staff College Draghounds. Astride his trusted mount, 'Chisel', Allenby won the annual point-to-point, 'Heavy Weight Cup' race, even though it was conceded by most that Haig was the better horseman.[46] Still, Allenby and Haig respected each other and many years later would emerge as probably the two most famous British generals of the First World War (Figure 2).

Promoted major in January of 1897, Allenby's increase in rank came just after he had got married on 30 December of the previous year. His wife was named Adelaide Mabel Chapman. She was twenty-eight years old and hailed from the Wiltshire gentry. They had met first in 1895 and, despite the initial misgivings of her father who was unimpressed both by Allenby's social position and career prospects, agreed with their wish to marry. The fact that Allenby was said to be 'the handsomest man in the Army in his time' had cut absolutely no weight with Horace Chapman.[47] But presumably the imprecations of the daughter convinced the father to relent and the ensuing marriage was to be warm and loving, made even more so by the birth of their only child, a son they named Horace Michael Hynman, in January of 1898. By that time Allenby had passed out of Camberley – 'he has energy, good judgement and rapid decision making … the man I should choose to lead the Forlorn Hope,' stated his final report – in anticipation of taking up the post of brigade-major (or adjutant, as it was formerly called) of the 3rd Cavalry Division at the Curragh in Ireland.[48] For the next two years, therefore, the Allenbys would live a rather idyllic military life in the rural surroundings

THE STAFF COLLEGE, 1896

Allenby is second from the left in the second to last row. Haig is last officer on the right, three rows from the back.

Figure 2 Allenby as a young officer at Camberley Staff College (second row from top, second from left) with an equally young Douglas Haig (third row from top, far right), 1896.

of the base at the Curragh in County Kildare. Happiness reigned, if punctuated occasionally by professionally mandated travel to the Continent: 'We do the Waterloo battlefield tomorrow … I long to see you again,' he wrote to Mabel, who went by her middle name, in the spring of 1897. But soon enough this quiescence would come to an abrupt end when war, long anticipated by both Boer and Briton, broke out in South Africa in October of 1899.[49]

Chapter 2

THE SECOND SOUTH AFRICAN WAR
AND BEYOND, 1899–1914

In October of 1899, when the long-simmering feud between the British and the Afrikaners finally boiled over into war in South Africa, Allenby was ensconced happily at the Curragh in Ireland. Few, however, least of all Allenby with his many years of service in South Africa and his advanced understanding of the geopolitical situation there, could feign surprise at the descent into war. The various figures involved Paul Kruger and Cecil Rhodes, of course, but also Alfred Lord Milner, the provocative British high commissioner to the Cape, and Joseph Chamberlain, the equally provocative colonial secretary, had plumped for war and now they had got it. The Jingo spirit was alive and well among the Imperial British – 'Make us masters of the situation in South Africa', Chamberlain had written to the prime minister, Salisbury, in January of 1896, just weeks after the debacle of the Jameson Raid, which was the ill-advised adventure that attempted to overthrow Kruger's Transvaal government.[1] Dreamed up by Rhodes and executed disastrously by one of his chief henchmen, Dr Leander Starr Jameson, it had everyone running for cover in its tawdry aftermath. Henceforth, Kruger was under no illusions about the grand plans harboured by Rhodes, Milner and Chamberlain for supreme British paramountcy in South Africa: 'It is my country you want. I am not ready to hand over my country to strangers,' he had said scornfully to Milner in a face to face meeting between the two men in May of 1899.[2] The dogged and realistic Transvaal president was right about that perception. And in October of that year, after having been cornered by the relentless jingoistic diplomacy of Chamberlain and Milner, Kruger could see no way forward other than to act on the war ultimatum that he had given to them earlier. In a calculated move designed to provoke war the British government let the ultimatum expire, and as a consequence Kruger was left with little choice but to authorize a column of Boer mounted infantry to cross the border between the Transvaal and Natal. As of the 11 of October, therefore, the war in South Africa was on.

Immediately following upon the war's outbreak, Allenby's regiment, the 6th (Inniskilling) Dragoons, were mobilized for service. He would be going back to South Africa, now for the third time in his career, but on this occasion with the assured prospect of concerted military action. At the time very few people in Britain, or indeed anywhere throughout the empire, had a nuanced view of who bore the responsibility for the coming of the war. The linked issues of gold, diamonds, *uitlander* (foreigner) rights in the Transvaal, the Anglo-German imperial rivalry, and Rhodes's 'big idea' of British control of South Africa and concomitant world dominion remained essentially unprocessed by most observers.[3] The result was that 'Brother Boer', as a racial and political type, was seen by many in Britain and elsewhere as being both wholly inferior and routinely dishonourable, and as such had manoeuvred the British into having no option but to go to war. The investigative journalism of the crusading J. A. Hobson, which would yield both *The War in South Africa: Its Causes and Effects*, and *Imperialism: A Study*, in 1900 and 1902 respectively, began later to provide reasons for some people to dissent from the British imperial project as it had unfolded in South Africa.[4] But in the meantime, the empire's peoples marched into battle against the recalcitrant Boer, and that of course included Allenby. 'Kruger and his gang', as he wrote disparagingly to Mabel in October, were 'totally responsible for this war'.[5] As such, upon his departure for South Africa at the end of the month Allenby was firm in his conviction that the Boers would be vanquished thoroughly and South African geopolitics settled once and for all in Britain's favour. 'Anchored tonight near Queenstown,' he wrote to his wife on 28 October. 'Very comfortable. Sail early tomorrow. … Goodbye. Take care of yourself and Michael.'[6]

Allenby's passage aboard the S.S. *Persia* to South Africa took considerably longer than expected, however, which gave him ample time to brood about this not entirely welcome return to active service. He wrote plaintively to Mabel that as a family man and therefore no longer the carefree subaltern, 'I am coming to the conclusion that I have too happy a life at home to make a really good soldier.'[7] In the meantime, the weather had turned rough – 'most annoying' – as Allenby termed it, and the journey was complicated further by shipboard mechanical troubles. 'Our screw shaft', he opined to his wife, has become 'practically unrepairable'.[8] The result was an almost three-week delay in port at St. Vincent in the Cape Verde Islands off the northwest coast of Africa, then under Portuguese control. Finally, almost a month after departing Ireland – 'I catch myself often half hoping that the war may be over by the time we arrive, so that I may get back quick to my old woman!' – St. Vincent was left behind on 24 November and without further incident on board a replacement ship, the *Goth*, Allenby and the other Inniskillings arrived safely at Cape Town on 11 December.[9]

Ironically, shortly after Allenby's arrival at the Cape, it was thought by many that the war indeed might well be very nearly over because of the comprehensive beating that the British had taken at the hands of the Boers from 10 to 17 December. In three successive battles at Stormberg, Magersfontein and Colenso, the British had been outclassed completely in the field and beaten badly. So comprehensive was this trio of defeats, which included almost 3,000 total British casualties, that it was summed up as 'Black Week' and the generals responsible for it blamed wholly for the debacle. 'Bad news, yesterday', Allenby reported to Mabel as soon as he had disembarked at Cape Town, '[Major General William] Gatacre had had a real licking [at Stormberg]. … I hear that nearly the whole Dutch population of the Colony's against us, & that the colonists are joining the Boers by hundreds.'[10]

Allenby's initial reading of the prevailing situation was essentially right and at home the sobering, if not shocking, news of the serial nature of these defeats prompted the Salisbury government to revise its war-making strategy. Part of this effort at revision involved a reinvigoration of British military leadership. Accordingly, an immediate call went out for the prosecution of the war henceforth to come under the command of Generals Herbert Kitchener and Frederick Roberts, two unimpeachable sentinels of empire, and in the former's case, just a year removed from the re-conquest of Sudan. Kitchener and Roberts thus duly arrived together at the Cape on 10 January 1900 aware keenly that the trajectory of the war must be changed swiftly if a British victory were to be achieved.[11] The two commanders had spent their joint voyage to South Africa in earnest discussion about what had gone wrong in British operations thus far in the war, and what might remedy the situation. To that end, quickly after arriving at Cape Town, they put in motion the way in which the British would begin to fight the war anew. Key to this change was a rapid improvement in transport and supply (to oversee it they imported Sir Percy Girouard, the brilliant French-Canadian railway strategist behind Kitchener's ultimate victory at Omdurman in 1898) and a swift enlargement of manpower, including thousands of Imperial troops, especially Canadians and Australians, some of whom had arrived already.[12]

As a measure of the urgency the British felt about the way the war had progressed thus far, and within three days of their arrival at Cape Town, the Inniskillings had boarded a train for the northeastern Cape, bound for a location very near the fighting front. 'I am off at last,' wrote Allenby to Mabel on 15 December. 'We are now in the midst of the Karroo, a barren undulating plateau, with rocky hills. … It is hot & very dry … 107 [degrees] in the tents today.'[13] Allenby's usual acuity when describing the natural world would serve him well over the next few years because he would spend a great deal of time out on the land, much of it in the 'Great Karoo', which indeed is as he described it, a vast swathe of semi-desert lying between the Cape and the high *veldt* of the South African interior. After five stultifying days on the troop train Allenby and his men arrived at Arundel Camp, located near the town of Colesberg, an important junction on the Port Elizabeth to Bloemfontein railway line. Already, with barely a week spent in the country, the fact that the war was not going to be a 'victorious procession' had become clear to the always-practical Allenby. 'I personally expect it will be a long job,' he wrote presciently to Mabel on 19 December, '& that we shall need many more troops.'[14] To that end, Allenby soon predicted that 'we shall want quite 300,000 men to lick them', which was not far off the number that eventually would be required in the form of British regulars by war's end in 1902.[15]

In the field Allenby and the Inniskillings were attached to a unit commanded by Major General John French, a cavalryman destined for great prominence in the First World War, but just then tasked with harassing a large contingent of Boers who were threatening Colesberg. The job was hot, dirty and unconventional, as the Boer style of fighting was hit and run, or guerrilla, not something to which the British were readily adaptive, although over the next few years the need to change their approach would make them so. The Boer was 'crafty' and 'tough as nails',

Allenby wrote home in grudging admiration of the enemy, but most of the time for him and his colleagues was spent in reacting to wherever the Boers chose to strike.[16] Fighting in the Karoo also meant that Allenby was 'covered day & night with red dust. ... Most fellows have their faces so cracked by the sun that they can't shave. We always sleep in our boots & breeches, & saddle up the horses at 3 a.m. every day, in case of an alarm at daybreak.'[17] For Allenby, as well as for his colleagues, taking on the Boer enemy in his natural element was a protracted exercise in hard soldiering, made even less palatable by the fact that 'I don't think there are any signs of their weakening ... they will see it through to the bitter end now they have started'.[18]

December passed in this way and for Allenby Christmas was celebrated in an unremarkable and lonesome way. He attended an officers' dinner, which included his old Staff College colleague, Douglas Haig, which was enjoyable. But, 'I wish I was going to be with you all,' he lamented to Mabel. Christmas Day itself was unusually hot, with whirlwinds of dust – 'sand-devils' – 'spinning through the camp' and everyone 'sitting tight, waiting for more troops'.[19] In this apprehended state the New Year 1900 passed, but with the announcement made shortly thereafter that 'Bobs & Kitchener' had arrived at Cape Town, the spirits of the men in camp rose. Still, Allenby remained sure that 'I wish this business was over, & that we were back at the old Curragh'.[20]

The day after penning these words to his wife Allenby engaged in his first concerted action of the South African War. A few weeks earlier, just before Christmas, he had gone out on patrol and engaged in a brief firefight with 'about 30 Boers' who had 'come out along a rocky ridge, & just then began to snipe at us'.[21] But on 14 January Allenby, in command of a small detachment of men, was sent on a secret raid designed to blow up the Colesberg Bridge that straddled the Orange River and was vital to the Boers' supply network. Rudyard Kipling's *Bridge-Guard in the Karroo* – 'We slip through the broken panel of fence by the ganger's shed; we drop to the waterless channel and the lean track overhead' – would later come to capture poetically the sort of fighting in which Allenby now found himself engaged regularly (Figure 3).[22]

In the event, the element of surprise was lost, however, according to Allenby, by the presence in camp of a Boer spy. 'The whole place is full of spies', he had complained to Mabel a few weeks earlier, and he believed the Boers had been alerted to their arrival in just such a fashion.[23] Consequently, they were not successful in blowing up the bridge. But what this brief foray behind Boer enemy lines had succeeded in demonstrating to the British was that the Boers were vulnerable to penetration. Consequently, Allenby was sure that any such forays in the future would yield the welcome result of making the Boers 'nervous for their communications'.[24] At the conclusion of this first operation Major General French was pleased with the outcome, even if the bridge itself had not been demolished. Indeed, his commanding officer's praise was so extravagant that Allenby reported to his wife that 'I may get a D.S.O or Brevet or something'.[25] In this instance there were no such awards for Allenby, but there would be plenty of time for the winning of so-called gongs in the future.

Figure 3 Allenby in repose during the otherwise rigorous South African War, Bloemfontein, 1900.

By late January Kitchener and Roberts were now fully in harness and had begun to operationalize their plans to relieve Kimberley, the diamond capital of the Transvaal. These plans included a cavalry and mounted infantry force of about 8,000 men, to be augmented by the main infantry force of nearly 40,000 troops, which together was intended to take the fight directly to the besieging Boers at Kimberley. The Mounted Division would be under the command of French, and to it was attached Allenby's squadron of Inniskillings. Allenby, emboldened by his recent 'secret enterprise' to take out the bridge, was hopeful, as he explained to Mabel, that now 'Roberts has come … he will concentrate all his force on one line, either here, Modder River, or Natal, & drive through while the rest sit tight.

It's no use trying to be strong everywhere'.[26] Allenby's Napoleonesque thinking in this instance was right, although as events transpired in what came to be called the Battle of Paardeberg the British victory there would leave much to be desired.

But for Allenby and his squadron another long train journey first would ensue. On 10 February, therefore, they reached Modder River Station and were ready to advance on Kimberley, which was now into its fifth month under siege. The next week would prove to 'very hard', wrote Allenby, and 'the longest week I have ever spent', he reported home.[27] At its outset Roberts had addressed his British generals, as relayed home by Allenby, that they were about to embark on 'one of the biggest enterprises that had been attempted, & that we would remember it all our lives'.[28] And so it would be for Allenby. Not only was Kimberley duly relieved on 15 February, but in the process he became reacquainted with Rhodes, whose constant imprecations to Roberts to relieve the town had at last been heeded. In the event, Roberts had thought some of these demands impertinent, admitting nonetheless that Rhodes had done 'excellent work during the siege ... but he desires to control the military situation. I have refused to be dictated to by him'.[29] As far as Allenby was concerned, however, the South African Colossus was 'behaving very well. He sends our men soup, firewood, etc., as well as forage for the horses'. Indeed, a few days after the relief of the town Allenby took the opportunity to dine with Rhodes, finding him to be 'much the same as I remember him 15 years ago. He lives in a huge hotel. ... There he keeps open house'.[30]

Following this welcome social interlude for Allenby, however, it was back to hard campaigning. Across the hard ground and up and over the undulating *kopjes* surrounding Kimberley, Allenby and his mounted squadron tracked bands of resistant Boers with tireless determination. At last, success at this kind of fighting now was beginning to be achieved by the British, and Allenby was in its vanguard. Meanwhile, a more conventional battle was shaping up a few miles south along the Modder River near the town of Paardeberg. Here, Piet Cronje, the 'crack Boer General', as Allenby informed Mabel, was holding out with a small number of men against a far larger British force.[31] The British, under Kitchener's command (Roberts just then had taken ill and was lying fevered and prostrate in his camp bed), had superior numbers and better position, but as always the Boers were absolutely dogged in resistance. In trying to break them Kitchener had insisted on launching a series of exposed 'frontal attacks across the open', which in Allenby's view was a useless and costly manoeuvre, he complained privately.[32] Allenby attributed these attacks to Kitchener's simple 'pigheadedness', a criticism made often of him, although not always, it would seem, fairly.[33] In this case, indeed, as I have suggested elsewhere, Kitchener's instinct was more that of the 'predatory general' in search of a decisive victory in order to raise morale both at the fighting front and back in Britain, than it was about pig-headed intransigence.[34] Still, by that day's blood-soaked end, Cronje's laager remained intact, and owing in large measure to a vainglorious cavalry charge ordered by Kitchener, some 300 British and Canadian troops lay dead. In fact, the butcher's bill that day marked the highest death toll for British and Imperial troops in the whole of the South African War.

The battle at Paardeberg would go on for a brutal ten days until at last an exhausted and over-matched Cronje surrendered finally: 'We saw a white flag go up & the Boers trekking out of the river bank & sitting down,' Allenby wrote home. 'The stink of dead horses & oxen is quite pestilential.'[35] By this point, indeed, the war had become an interminable slog for Allenby. 'Personally, I'm sick to death of it,' he wrote despairingly to his wife at the end of February.[36] Of course, the way forward for Allenby and the British was to continue to force the Boers to retreat. And such is what they did in a campaign of methodical and relentless fighting until they had reached Bloemfontein – 'at last!' – on 14 March.[37] After Paardeberg, despite its heavy losses, the British had found their marching stride under a recovered Roberts and had begun to roll eastwards, before turning north in order to penetrate the Boers' Transvaal heartland. The Inniskillings were a small but key part of this serially effective offensive. By now, Allenby had become highly proficient in the required form of warfare. He was spending an enormous amount of time in the saddle of his trusted Bay gelding, 'Pirate', scouting the locations of Boer commandos who, usually from a concealed position, would fire upon approaching British cavalry or infantry. Allenby's job became one of riding out in advance of the main body of troops in order to find such hidden pockets of Boer resistance and to eliminate them, or at least force them to fall back. The task was relentless, as well as dangerous, and it demanded all of his skills and concentration. Allenby's understanding of the natural world and his years of experience on the land made him a quick study in this terrain of scrub, rock and *kopje*. But it was wearying work nonetheless. 'This is my 11th consecutive day of active campaigning,' he wrote to Mabel in a complete state of exhaustion on 1 April.[38]

Despite Allenby's dogged work in pursuit of the elusive Boer, it was not clear yet that the overwhelming force the British were bringing to bear now on the enemy was having the impact that both he and others in command had anticipated. 'I can't make out', he wrote home, 'that the Transvaalers are losing heart much. I wish they'd throw it up.'[39] To that end, the British continued to push forward relentlessly, however, and took Johannesburg at the end of May. But a bigger prize lay in store when a week later on 5 June, after being 'steadily on the march to Pretoria', as reported home by Allenby, the Transvaal's capital city fell.[40] At last the British had prevailed, or so it seemed. A relieved and victorious Allenby arrived in town shortly thereafter, riding in triumph with one of his officers, Captain J. W. Yardley, in order to view the heart of conquered Afrikanerdom and to enjoy a celebratory lunch at the Pretoria Club. During the meal Allenby happened to strike up a conversation with two other officers; he would report later to Mabel, who had helped relieve the just-concluded 217-day siege of the beleaguered city of Mafeking: but were now 'a little sore, as they say that Baden-Powell thinks he did it all himself'.[41] These two officers would not be the only ones to complain in this way about the Hero of Mafeking's self-aggrandizement. Nevertheless, Allenby respected 'B-P', the future Chief Scout, and they would meet up later in Johannesburg to celebrate victory.[42]

Now that Pretoria had fallen and Kruger had fled east to Delagoa Bay (and from there to Europe) would not the Boers be on the verge of a general surrender?

But a month later, with Pretoria firmly under British control, neither Allenby nor anyone else knew the answer to that question. 'I can't prophesy anything yet as to when the war will be definitely over', he wrote to Mabel on 5 July, 'or when anyone, or who, will be sent home.'[43] Indeed, by that time the war had begun to transform itself into something substantially different – that is, into a war in which the Boers would be able to utilize fully their guerrilla expertise and thereby force the British to stay in the field despite the expectation that the taking of Pretoria was a prelude to its ending. Little did Allenby know that the war would carry on, in fact, for almost two more years and in the process become even costlier and a good deal more controversial than it had proved to be already. Such an eventuality would mean also that he would not see his wife and child again until mid-1902.

Over the balance of the summer of 1900, therefore, as it became clear that the Boers would not be quitting the field anytime soon, Allenby's life on mounted patrol continued in earnest. These Boers, led by the elusive General Christiaan De Wet and various other excellent field commanders such as 'Koos' de la Rey and Marthinus Steyn, were so-called *bittereinders* (bitter-enders) committed to fighting the British to the last man. In conventional military terms, the war may have come to a symbolic end with the fall of the Boer capital of Pretoria, but to those who had believed always (such as the bitter-enders) that the only way for the inferior Boers to win the war was to take on the British guerrilla style, it was really only the beginning. Accordingly, for Allenby, the war had come now to enter a second phase, one that would prove to be as intense and all-consuming as anything that he had experienced so far.

At the end of November, Lord Roberts, his task now complete as he understood it, turned over supreme command of the war to Kitchener and sailed for home in order to become commander-in-chief of the British Army. Before leaving South Africa, however, Roberts had initiated two linked measures designed to counteract the ability of the Boer guerrillas to live off the land while at the same time engaging in their signature acts of sabotage and sneak attack that continued to frustrate mightily the British. Roberts's first order was for the British to undertake farm-burning on a wide scale.[44] They proceeded to do so, and the result was that by the end of the year some 600 Boer farms had been put to the torch. Their inhabitants, whose sympathy for their Afrikaner commandos was complete as manifested by their steady support of them in the field, were then placed systematically into what were called by the British 'camps of refuge'. As Roberts's successor, Kitchener inherited both of these policies and executed them enthusiastically for the simple reason that he, like most everyone else on the British side, thought that such measures would help speed up the end of the interminable war. Cutting off the Boers' ability to sustain themselves while on commando was a sensible response to a guerrilla-style war, which at that time remained an essentially unknown species of warfare. For Kitchener, however, fighting this kind of war would prove to be both extraordinarily difficult and philosophically objectionable. The Boers' guerrilla warfare, in his view, was both a 'puzzle' and not 'straight', as he put it, but yet had to be both solved and fought.[45] Kitchener's answer to it was to turn the map of the Transvaal into a grid, divided by manned blockhouses and linked by barbed cable wire, and in this networked fashion funnel the Boer commandos into inescapable capture. 'Bag' them, as he put it bluntly to his officers, using the language of the hunter.[46] The sharp end of the stick to bring this plan to fruition, according to Kitchener, was to use the flying column, something that the Irish revolutionaries of twenty years later would use to perfection in their struggle against the British themselves after the First World War. Here, in South Africa late in 1900, the British began to use it themselves to great effect against the Boers. And in executing this new style of warfare Allenby himself became extremely proficient.

Beginning therefore in January of 1901, and now in command of the Inniskillings, Allenby spent an increasing amount of time on the land pursuing Boer commandos. Rarely felled by ill-health – although a nasty case of flu would land him in the Yeomanry Hospital in Pretoria for a week's stay in May – Allenby thrived on a diet of rough country and hard riding.[47] Still, the daily grind in the service of 'Lord K' took its toll. 'We have been on the trek, steadily since 26th January', he reported to Yardley in September, 'I'm getting a bit tired of it all; but I take great care not to say so, out here; the example is bad.'[48] Allenby, like his peers, was under the firm control of Kitchener, no bad thing considering that the commander-in-chief was hoping equally for a soon end to the war. But Kitchener's relentless drive – that single-mindedness of purpose that had earned him the sobriquet 'Sudan machine' during the recent re-conquest of that bleak territory – was clearly in evidence in South Africa.[49] 'K. of K. tries to run the whole show himself; that accounts for much,' Allenby complained to Yardley.[50] Running the show meant high expectations of success combined with very little leave for officers. The fighting men too, of course, paid a high price, as did their mounts and remounts – 'our waste of horses is appalling' – Allenby wrote to his father-in-law, the Rev'd Thomas Cane, in October.[51] But Kitchener's swift-victory imperative ruled nonetheless. Still, over lunch in Pretoria with Kitchener three days after this letter was sent, Allenby decided to broach the topic of necessary rest, for both his men and their horses, and the commander-in-chief, 'in high good humour', reported Allenby, promised him both.[52] But Kitchener's 'high-pressure' desire to win and go home remained constant and rest for either men or beasts would remain a casualty of war.[53]

Although as we have seen he was not an easy man to please, Kitchener was impressed strongly by Allenby. Unlike many of his fellow officers, Allenby's height was exactly that of Kitchener's own (6'2"), something Kitchener respected especially. But more than that of course it was Allenby's moderate temperament, at least with fellow senior officers (with juniors, he was starting to develop a reputation for stentorian prickliness, which later would see him given the (not wholly) uncomplimentary nickname of the 'Bull'), and the dogged effectiveness that most impressed Kitchener. Indeed, Kitchener would mention Allenby's name in despatches, and throughout the balance of the war they met together on a number of occasions, including once when he good-naturedly and with evident irony chided Allenby for not having taken a very long leave.[54]

As the war reached its penultimate phase the Roberts-ordered camps of refuge, or 'concentration' camps as they were starting to be called in the press, had grown into a political scandal in Britain. Emily Hobhouse, as head of the Distress Fund for South African Women and Children, had come out from London in order to visit some of the camps and then had written a scathing public report on their dire condition. The issue was taken up in Parliament first by David Lloyd George of the opposition Liberals, and then by the party leader Sir Henry Campbell-Bannerman. The camps were condemned by both men as evidence that the British government was using 'methods of barbarism' in executing the South African War.[55] The criticism was powerful and emotive and it damaged the Salisbury Conservatives severely.[56] Clearly and regrettably the camps, after having been constructed hastily and without proper provisions for sanitation, had quickly become nests of communicable disease, which had had an especially devastating impact upon children. Later comparisons of these camps to the Nazi concentration camps of the Second World War infamy, however, is inaccurate.[57] But there is little doubt that the camps were both conceived badly and administered faultily, and they would only improve once taken out of military hands, as they were early in 1902. For Allenby, however, as for most of his colleagues, the camps themselves were a necessary means of trying to break the Boers' willingness to continue to fight: 'All stubborn, no-surrender Dutchmen,' as he put it in a letter home.[58] Nevertheless, he recognized clearly the appalling conditions of the camps, even if he thought that the health of their inmates could be improved if the directives issued by camp doctors were adhered to more closely than often was the case. At Standerton in the Transvaal, for example, Allenby visited a camp in which 'a great epidemic of measles' had broken out. Children were dying in droves. But according to Allenby in a letter to Mabel, it was 'partly the fault of the mothers. They won't do what the doctors tell them. One covered her child with green paint; another covered the child with cow dung. In neither case did the child recover!'[59] To contemporary readers Allenby's observation might well come across as heartless under the circumstances as it speaks much more of a loving mother's desperation than it does to disobeying a doctor's professional imperative. The concentration camps were a blight on the war and would come to cast a long shadow over the British record in it. Still, Allenby's view reflected a real problem in the camps that would be overcome only near the end of the war in the spring of 1902.

By the time that the war finally came to an end officially with the signing of the Treaty of Vereeniging on 31 May 1902 Allenby was thoroughly exhausted. He had fallen ill again with flu just before Christmas 1901, which had required yet another hospital stay in Pretoria.[60] Although he relished the time that he spent there as constituting a form of much-needed rest – 'grand' is how he described his time in hospital – the war itself continued to drag on interminably.[61] And this state of affairs continued in spite of regular predictions about the war's imminent conclusion: Lord Milner's firm prediction was that it would occur in July, for example.[62] For Allenby, therefore, once having been released from hospital he was obliged to return immediately to the hard riding and bitter fighting that had characterized for him the whole length of the war. Optimistic that the war simply must end soon, however, he encouraged Mabel to come out to Natal or to the Cape and wait in hopes of it coming to pass.[63]

Allenby's responsibilities throughout the war had been heavy. Beginning in January 1901 he had had some 80 officers and almost 2,000 men under his command, including an Australian cavalry regiment, the New South Wales Lancers, a foretaste of his command of Anzacs in Palestine during the First World War. His letters and diary entries are replete with references to many 'night marches' and 'sharp attacks'.[64] In the end, the protracted nature of the war and his long separation from Mabel meant that they decided she should indeed come out to South Africa for a visit, which she did, arriving at Durban in March of 1902. However, continuing offensive operations prevented their seeing one another until near the end of May.[65] But by then the war was finally almost over, as the treaty signing at Vereeniging would signify shortly. In June at Pretoria, therefore, Allenby bade farewell personally to Kitchener – who unexpectedly had been both magnanimous and skilful in negotiating the treaty with the Boers. A short holiday for Allenby and Mabel at the Cape, which included a visit to Rhodes's hillside mansion, 'Groote Schuur', would follow.[66] At long last, on 9 July they duly departed South Africa, boarding the *S.S. Briton* for the voyage home.[67] After an uneventful passage, on 26 July they were back in England and on their way home to Felixstowe.[68]

The return to England was well earned and joyous, especially Allenby's reuniting with his five-year-old son Michael, whom he had not seen since 1899. A similar feeling was experienced also upon seeing his ageing but still spry mother, Catherine, with whom he had corresponded constantly while in South Africa. She continued to be an emotional and moral pillar in his life. A good rest for Allenby would follow, of course, but next steps in what was now a highly promising military career were of immediate interest to him. 'I can't say yet what will become of me,' he had written to his mother just before leaving South Africa, but, as we have seen, Allenby had acquitted himself extremely well in the war.[69] As the culminating act of service in Africa that stretched back twenty years, the war had given him a legitimate claim to be 'an old Africa hand'; but even more than that his consistently superior leadership and readiness in command – as the admiring Yardley had put it to Mabel: 'he is a splendid fellow – everyone looks up to him and he always does magnificently' – meant that he had arrived home as one of the coming officers in cavalry circles.[70]

Very soon that status would mean promotion for Allenby to a brevet lieutenant-colonelcy and the awarding of the Companion of the Bath (CB) in recognition of his excellent service across the full duration of the war. Indeed, he would be duly named to command the 5th Lancers, signalling his sure rise. Promotion to full colonel would follow in 1903, and then two years later to that of brigadier general, at which time Allenby was given command of the 4th cavalry brigade. In 1909, he received yet another promotion, this time to the rank of major general, and in 1910 he became inspector general of cavalry, the top post for a cavalryman. This appointment was met with approbation by a number of newspapers, including the *Manchester Dispatch*. 'A New Face at the War Office', headlined its report of 27 April. 'General Allenby has had a distinguished career in the cavalry … has seen considerable active service, and held the command for some time of the 5th (Royal Irish) Lancers, a regiment that he brought to an extremely high condition of efficiency.[71] Not yet fifty years old, Allenby had risen steadily, if not spectacularly, over the preceding decade. As a result, he found himself now in a position of high authority and engaged in both serious war planning and military reform, twin features of the early twentieth-century British Army's response to what Kipling had suggested was the 'no end of a lesson' given it by the unexpectedly long and costly Second South African War.[72]

But for Allenby, in as much as the first decade of the new century revolved around the consolidation of his own career, it was also about raising his adored son, deepening his abiding marital relationship and – in what came to be seen later as the halcyon days of Edward VII's reign – enjoying the life of a respected military professional. Therefore, beginning in 1906, the Allenbys took up residence at Roman Hill House near Colchester in Essex. Purchased by the War Office in 1898, it was an impressive Georgian mansion situated amid 14 acres of lush parkland and came complete with coach house, stables and a paddock. Ownership of the property also came with the courtesy title, lord of the manor of East Donyland. Although as Roman Hill's occupant rather than its owner Allenby could not assume the title, his natural gravitas and evident habit of authority bespoke otherwise. Moreover, as befitted the cool-headed cavalry commander who still enjoyed his boyhood pastime of sailing, he had had occasion to save three people from drowning in the sea off Cowes during the summer of 1905. 'I think it shows how fitted he must be', wrote one of those he had rescued, a Miss Cicely Papillon in a letter of unbridled praise sent to the Royal Humane Society, 'as a soldier to command others, when I tell you that for 20 minutes he was able to make 3 people in such great peril obey him in every detail. There are few men who would have such powers of command.'[73]

During these rather leisurely years Allenby and his wife also travelled extensively, especially while Michael attended boarding school, mainly at Wellington College in Berkshire.[74] One of these journeys took them to East Africa in the spring of 1908, then at the very outset of the period that would yield the onrush of British and European settlement and its legendary personalities such as Lord Delamere, Galbraith and Berkeley Cole, Denys Finch Hatton, and Bror and Karen Blixen. Just as they would be also, Allenby and his wife were duly smitten with the natural beauty and grandeur of what would later turn into the colonies of Kenya, Tanganyika and Uganda. The prospect of going on an 'expedition' – as Allenby termed what would shortly become known as 'safari' – and then seeing 'hundreds of animals', the spectacular Rift Valley, and the majestic mountains of 'Kilima Njaro and Kenia', was breathtaking. Afterwards, leaving behind the comforts of the recently opened and fashionable Norfolk Hotel in Nairobi, the Allenbys then journeyed northwest to Kampala in Uganda and on to the Ripon Falls. Altogether, after three memorable weeks, he wrote to his mother, 'we were both very loath to leave East Africa.'[75]

Once back in England from this journey, Allenby's military duties took over immediately. One of the results of his professional position was that the authority and pressures of high command continued to have a small but apparent altering effect on his personality, at least when in uniform. As was suggested by his South African experience, Allenby had developed gradually a more pronounced peremptoriness when dealing with both his peers and subordinates. Along with an overbearing manner had come an increasingly sharp tongue. In short, to a number of his colleagues, Allenby had begun to become an officer to avoid. This was the period when the nickname 'The Bull' was attached to him permanently. In the future, its use would only intensify.

Over the next few years Allenby would continue to carry out his duties as inspector general of cavalry. These included participating in detailed discussions about the evolving role of the cavalry within contemporary warfare. He pushed for a more modern understanding of the cavalry as constituting mounted infantry with rifles, rather than the traditional but antiquated view of them sporting sabre and lance. Such a view was favoured, nonetheless, by his South African War colleague, Douglas Haig. Then, not long before the outbreak of general European war in August of 1914, Allenby was caught up briefly in what came to be called the Curragh Incident in which some sixty British officers stationed at Allenby's old haunt in Ireland determined that they would not act against anyone in Protestant Ulster who chose to oppose the recently introduced third iteration of the Irish Home Rule Bill. Even though Allenby's personal sympathies lay with the officers over this highly explosive issue, and present briefly at the Curragh during the controversy for his annual inspection of cavalry, he wisely kept clear of it by returning to London immediately afterwards.

A few months later in the spring of 1914 the government resolved the Curragh Incident just in time for all attention to turn towards continental Europe.[76] The assassination of Archduke Franz Ferdinand, the heir to the Austrian throne, on 28 June by a Serbian nationalist terror group called the Black Hand, augured war. The prospect of a major European war meant conflict on a scale that would dwarf anything that Allenby had witnessed before, and indeed would be the first significant war on the continent since France and Prussia had fought one another beginning in 1870. Notwithstanding the clearly anomalous size of the South African War, the era of Queen Victoria's so-called 'little' wars had come to an end.[77] 'The lamps are going out all over Europe,' as the British Foreign Secretary Sir Edward Grey would put it memorably, and as they were duly extinguished Major General Allenby waited now in London in anticipation of being called into the War Office in order to help set a course for the major conflict to come.[78]

Chapter 3

ON THE WESTERN FRONT, 1914–17

The protracted run-up to the outbreak of war on 4 August belied the swiftness with which Britain plunged into the conflict immediately thereafter. The thirty-seven days that elapsed between the assassination of the Austrian Archduke, Franz Ferdinand, in Sarajevo on 28 June and the declaration of war by Great Britain against Germany on 4 August had seen steady, if unhurried, diplomatic activity at the great chancelleries of Europe.[1] Whitehall, under the long-time direction of the Foreign Secretary Sir Edward Grey, was at the centre of British diplomacy, but when war at last was declared resignation about its seeming inevitability turned instantaneously into action. Lord Kitchener, just then on his way back to Cairo to resume his post as British high commissioner to Egypt, was called back from Dover in order for him to assume (however reluctantly) the position of secretary of state for war. The British wheels of war were now in motion and Allenby, along with his fellow generals, was summoned to the War Office on 6 August in order to be given instructions as to what was expected of them. There was little doubt that Allenby would be given command of the Cavalry Division, and the due confirmation of such that came on 8 August meant that he and his men would be shipping out for France within days in accordance with Plan XVII, a strategy designed by the French to interdict the Germans at the French-Belgian-German border.[2] Lord Roberts, now eighty-two years old and retired, but still spry and beloved always of the British Army, was quick with his congratulations for Allenby. He sent him a note on 11 August praising him for having been given 'such a splendid command, and I shall look with intense interest to the doings of the cavalry in the war'. And just as he had done in South Africa, Roberts enjoined Allenby also to ensure that the men, in order to conserve both their own strength and that of their mounts, 'be made to understand that they should never be on their horses when they can be off them'.[3]

From London, Allenby proceeded quickly on 13 August to Aldershot, home base for the Cavalry, and then two days later departed Southampton for France. 'I have five good horses to start with,' he wrote to Mabel. 'You were so plucky on the platform; I love you very much. ... The Solent's full of big steam yachts. God bless you, my dear love, & Michael too.'[4] And with that hurried farewell Allenby was on his way to France for what would turn out to be almost three years of steady service on the Western Front.

In August of 1914 the British Army remained yet a small force, although highly professional and well experienced. Still, the prospect of its going up against the gargantuan, million-man-plus German Army made potentially for a David versus Goliath situation about to unfold in France. All told, approximately 90,000 men only were then available to move across the Channel, a 'contemptible little army' in the disparaging words of Kaiser Wilhelm II, although once there it would converge with the ten-times larger French force.[5] Together, they would face very soon and very directly the full weight of German military might. The four British infantry divisions along with Allenby's Cavalry Division were headed to Maubeuge, the guiding Plan XVII's agreed destination in northeastern France and the hinge-point for the imminent Anglo-French stand against the expected onrush of the Germans. Accordingly, under Commander-in-Chief Sir John French, Allenby's old South African War colleague, the British Army began its march towards the Franco-Belgian border. Being that it was high summer meant a sunny and beautiful passage was had by the men, a quiet interlude that would prove to be utterly out of step with the carnage that was to come shortly. But the incongruity of it did not have a discernible impact on Allenby. After 'a dead smooth crossing', he had informed Mabel, 'we are very well & fit and full of keenness. The country receives us enthusiastically; and shower flowers on us as we pass through the villages.'[6] But a mere three days after this sanguine note was sent, on 23 August, Allenby and his men were plunged into ferocious fighting with the Germans, and with it any sense of summertime reverie disappeared immediately.

The occasion for this momentous change was the advent of what would become known later as the First Battle of Mons, named for the small Belgian town destined to become one of the best-known sites of the First World War. After just a few days of fierce fighting the French Fifth Army found themselves driven back from their position at Charleroi. In desperation, an appeal was made for the British Expeditionary Force to launch an attack on the western flank of the rapidly advancing German 1st Army, which was attempting to carry out the precepts of its Schlieffen Plan by rolling in a northeasterly direction towards the Channel.[7] Owing to a 3:1 differential in size of force favouring the Germans, however, General French wisely withheld attack. Nevertheless, he did assure his desperate French allies that he would continue to hold fast along the Mons Canal in order to prevent the Germans from outflanking them, which was the enemy's intention. Accordingly, beginning on 23 August the Battle of Mons erupted, fast becoming a violent and sustained fight during which the badly undermanned British fought doggedly to hold the line.[8] Soon enough, however, the overwhelming numbers and superior firepower of the Germans won sway and the British were left with no choice but to retreat. The fact that they had held on as long as they did, however, came as a surprise to the Germans, especially to their commander, General Alexander von Kluck. Still, forty-eight hours into the battle the British were in full retreat even though they had held the Germans off for a time and in the process inflicted twice as many casualties on the enemy as they had suffered themselves. For von Kluck, these casualty figures were a bitterly unwelcome and unexpected development in the first days of the war.[9]

Meanwhile for Allenby, the retreat from Mons meant employing his Cavalry Division to provide cover for the infantry.[10] The job of doing so was complicated and the situation remained fluid as British soldiers – many of whom had been fighting over two days without respite and now were exhausted – began a pell-mell retreat south towards the Marne River, some 250 miles distant. The nature of this retreat resulted in Allenby struggling to keep the four brigades of the Cavalry Division together.[11] The path of the hurried British retreat covered a width of about 20 miles and often was little short of chaotic. Allenby, as was his way, endeavoured to remain steady in command throughout it all, even while some of his subordinates, especially General Sir Hubert Gough, chose to defy him.[12] But the intense stress of the retreat was clear, even if by 30 August Allenby could write to Mabel and state calmly that 'we've had a strenuous time, & have been fighting every day for a week. Very short of food & sleep.'[13] By the time of writing the British retreat had been punctuated by the Battle of Le Cateau, commanded by another of Allenby's colleagues from the South African War, Sir Horace Smith-Dorrien. As a rearguard action Le Cateau was a pyrrhic victory, but it achieved enough to repulse von Kluck and therefore allow time for the retreating British to regroup and continue marching southwards. Tactical successes such as Le Cateau, the growing myth of divine assistance rendered by the 'Angel of Mons', and a flying visit to Paris by a highly concerned but greatly determined Kitchener during which he spoke very strongly to the shaken Commander-in-Chief French about the absolute necessity of fighting on, meant that after two weeks in the field the BEF were able to coalesce along the Marne. Although precariously close to Paris, the British now were in a position to launch a counter-attack.[14] And on 5 September they did exactly that by launching the Battle of the Marne.[15]

After a month in the field, some 1,500 casualties, and with morale having plummeted, the commencement of the Battle of the Marne was met with ready approbation by the beleaguered British. And as if to symbolize this welcome shift in fortunes, 5 September was also the day on which the periodical magazine *London Opinion* published a recruiting illustration designed by the graphic artist Alfred Leete featuring the stylized face and gloved finger of Kitchener pointing imperiously towards the reader. In bolded letters the caption read: 'Your Country Needs YOU.'[16] The first weeks of the war had pushed the BEF to the brink of being chased from the field and now, with the tide turning slightly and the whole country awakened to the cross-Channel peril, the war had been well and truly joined. Thus less than a week after the battle had begun, Allenby could write with confidence to his wife that 'we have turned round now; & after a fortnight of being hunted, are now on the hunt; & are giving the Deutschers a bit of their own back.'[17]

Able finally now to go on the offensive, Allenby was in his element, fighting a mobile war (if only for a short time), cajoling and sometimes hectoring his men to take the fight to the enemy and throw them back. Doing so was not easy, however, and indeed the war turned swiftly into a kind of forward and back match. 'There is perpetual attacking and counter-attacking,' he informed Mabel near the end of September.[18] The use of artillery, especially by the Germans, was intense. 'Incessant shelling' is how Allenby described it in yet another letter sent home to Mabel then resident in the contrasting quiet of Belgrave Mansions in London's Grosvenor Gardens. By the end of the month it was clear that the allied counter-attack had saved Paris – and indeed France itself – and Germany's Schlieffen Plan rendered ineffectual.[19] In the process, Allenby's cavalry had become essentially mounted infantry and soon, as the frontlines congealed and as the soldiers' mobility lessened, the place of the horse in the war – at least on the Western Front – would change from being an offensive force to that of defensive stalwart.

Throughout this period Allenby was in command of the 1st, 2nd and 4th Cavalry Brigades, guarding the advancing right flank of the 1st Corps of the British Army, while on the left the still-shaky and insubordinate Hubert Gough commanded the 3rd and 5th Brigades. Given this configuration it was decided that the Cavalry Division should be split into two, with Allenby in command of the 1st Cavalry Division, and Gough the 2nd.[20] As both commanders approached the Aisne River, which lay about 75 miles north of the Marne, mobility began to lessen even further however, and then would cease altogether. 'We are engaged in a big battle,' Allenby wrote his wife, but the Marne counterstroke which had yielded the Battle of the Aisne was turning the war into an exercise in entrenchment along the now fast-forming Western Front.[21] Allenby's usual stoicism in the face of enemy fire meant that on at least one occasion amid the surrounding thunder, as one of his officers recounted later, he casually finished reading his newspaper, put away his reading glasses and strolled out of a barn just moments before the shells that were destined for it found their mark.[22] Perhaps with this episode in mind Allenby wrote home to say that the Germans had 'failed everywhere' and were now faced with a resurgent Anglo-French force which was determined to resist their residual onslaught and to set the pace offensively. From the Admiralty in London First Lord Winston Churchill had come out to the front for a brief visit at the end of September just as Allenby was directing his men to gather entrenching tools for the job ahead.[23] 'The battle here continues', he reported to Mabel on 30 September – and he thanked her for the recently arrived care package of socks and handkerchiefs – but the prospective face of war was stasis, something that did not auger well for Allenby's training and temperament as a lifelong cavalryman.[24]

As the calendar passed into October the prospect of a static frontline meant that both sides began to engage in a frantic competition to outflank each other in what came to be known as the 'Race to the Sea'; that is, was it still possible for the Germans to right-hook their way around the Anglo-French forces in a last-ditch effort to salvage control of the Channel ports as a small victory in the name of their almost-failed Schlieffen Plan? To this end therefore, the Germans fought desperately along a line running northwest from the Aisne River, culminating ultimately at Ypres in Flanders and towards the Channel coast. For Allenby, the month of October would prove to be one of the most strenuous of the whole war, with almost daily sustained fighting with the Germans – 'the Deutschers attacking hard' – much of it ferocious.[25] His letters of the time offer a constant reprise on the theme of ferocity: 'hard & bloody fighting today'; 'we have had two busy days of fighting'; 'we have been engaged with the Germans all day'; altogether during October Allenby crisscrossed the battlefield, as he noted to Mabel and without exaggeration, commanding 'the largest force of cavalry ever … by a British officer'.[26] Casualties on both sides were high, and occasionally the name of one of the fallen in particular would stand out such as on 13 October when, as reported by Allenby, 'we killed Prince Max of Hesse, a near relation of the Kaiser, an officer in a cavalry regiment'.[27]

At the end of each of these long days of fighting, Allenby would retire to his headquarters, usually a country estate offered up by its grateful French owner – 'I am tonight in a huge chateau, in a forest. It belongs to a Baroness La Grange. She is an elderly widow; talks English perfectly' – and there regroup in anticipation of entering the fray again the following morning.[28] By early November the intensity of the race to the sea had begun to dissipate however, as the Germans appeared to Allenby to be 'drawing off'.[29] Indeed they were. On 18 October Ypres had been re-captured from the Germans and for the next four weeks both armies had thrown themselves at one another in a final frenzy in the Ypres Salient, a 50-square-mile bulge of killing ground in which more than 5,000 British and the same number of German soldiers lost their lives in the span of a few weeks. After all this killing had taken place, the 1st Battle of Ypres came to an end in a stalemate on 22 November. And with it both armies, along with the French, hunkered down in the mud. Soon, trenches serrated the ground in an almost unbroken line that would stretch for almost 500 miles from the North Sea to the Swiss Alps.[30]

As the year drew to a close with no end of war in sight those who had suggested that 'it would all be over by Christmas' could only look on ruefully at what had transpired during these first few months of fighting. There were some in positions of authority, principally Kitchener, who had never thought this way, assuming that once a general, mechanized European war had got under way it would be extraordinarily difficult to stop.[31] And now, indeed, an interminable war seemed to be at hand. By Christmas, Allenby, like almost all of his officer colleagues, had been in the field for some eighteen weeks with no respite. From time to time such protracted service at the front had been broken by the arrival of certain august visitors from England: 'The Prince of Wales called to see me today, but I was out', wrote Allenby to Mabel on 18 November. Just over two weeks later he received a similar visit from King George, having come to inspect Allenby's now full Cavalry Corps.[32] But despite these moments of encouragement by royal visitors, the daily grind remained grim. Adding to the gloom that autumn was the news that after having arrived in theatre on tour Lord Roberts had taken to his bed almost immediately with pneumonia and had died shortly thereafter. Allenby grieved for his old commander. But at least, he wrote to Mabel that Roberts had died 'quickly in the centre of the Army in the field, at a ripe age, with all his work finished'.[33]

In the meantime, Allenby's sixteen-year-old son Michael had joined the Royal Horse Artillery and was training at the Royal Military Academy Woolwich, otherwise known as the Shop. 'Don't worry', about him, he wrote to reassure his wife, although it may have had the opposite effect, 'the artillery subalterns don't get killed any more than others. As a matter of fact, I think they lose fewer'.[34] For Allenby, after four hard months in the field, a short rest therefore would be welcomed greatly, and when it came finally early in January of the New Year 1915, he returned to London for first time since August to savour the pleasures of four days of well-earned leave.[35]

Allenby's brief time at home that January was occasioned mainly by the war's having become firmly entrenched and the consequent move of the cavalry into a static position to the rear of the frontline at Ypres, near Hazebrouck. There it would recover from its four-month-long exertions, and act as a reserve force. On 12 January, just two weeks after the famous short-lived Christmas 1914 truce between British and German troops along the line at Ypres, Allenby's brief leave was over and he had returned to France.[36] 'Here, the situation remains about the same as usual', he informed Mabel soon thereafter, in a style of reportage that would come to characterize the tedium of life on the Western Front.[37] Allenby's first months of the war had demonstrated those features of his command and leadership that had been established long before at Camberley, as well as on the *veldt* in South Africa. Imperturbability, stamina, and aggressiveness were its hallmarks, and his August to December baptism of fire at the hands of the Germans on the Western Front had consolidated them. Notwithstanding his stellar performance during that first autumn of the war, however, it fell now to Allenby simply to wait for subsequent action. And that he did, grimly, along with the Cavalry Corps, for the duration of the winter of 1915. A brief and unremarkable entry along the line by the corps was made in February, but otherwise it essentially lay dormant. The most significant event of the period was the German offensive of late April in which chlorine gas was used for the first time in the war, in a clear contravention by Germany of the Hague Conventions of 1907. The use of gas at Ypres against French colonial (Algerian) troops spurred panic among their ranks and they fled the line, while alongside them the newly arrived Canadians had held firm. During the Second Battle of Ypres, as it would be called, Allenby was back in London, however, this time recovering from a severe case of influenza. He was able to return to France early in May, however, just as the battle was coming to an end, only to find that his life was about to change significantly by being put in command of a full army corps.

Throughout the First World War the great maw of the Ypres Salient would prove to be a quagmire, sucking down men, horses and materiel into its grimy depths. Like his fellow commanders, Allenby found it and other similar battle-fronts an interminably soul-destroying place, in large part because it inhibited battlefield movement. The appalling cost in men's lives in exchange for little or no territorial gain was the terrible by-product of such stasis. On 8 May General French decided to install the trusted Allenby into a position of command at Ypres by handing him control over V Corps, replacing Lieutenant General Sir Herbert Plumer who had been reassigned and then promoted. For Allenby, this move was a clear step up the ladder of command as he had never before overseen an army corps, and immediately he was thrown into action by ordering its deployment at Frezenberg Ridge. The battle there, designed to prevent the Germans from taking control of the Ypres Salient, raged initially from 8 May until 13 May. During these hellish days over 9,000 British soldiers lost their lives, including some 430 officers, and there was little Allenby could do except attempt to plug holes along the badly damaged line and try to maintain a semblance of morale among the stricken troops.[38] The Germans, sensing an opportunity to push the British (and Canadians) back, kept up the pressure incessantly at Frezenberg. 'I shall go down in History as "The Man Who Lost Ypres!"' Allenby despaired in a letter to his schoolmaster brother-in-law, Thomas Porter, who was married to his youngest sister, Helen (Nell).[39]

Within days of Allenby taking up his new command at Frezenberg, the Germans launched a fresh assault at nearby Bellewarde Ridge, which proved to be similarly costly in British lives.[40] Moreover, as they had done in April, the Germans used chlorine gas again. Altogether, these first days of commanding infantry were exceptionally challenging for Allenby. As a consequence, his characteristic abruptness and short temper were displayed regularly. One of his officers, Major General Aylmer Haldane, took an intense dislike to the hard-driving Allenby, complaining in a letter home that 'Everyone hates being in Vth Corps'.[41] Haldane's animus would continue, complaining again shortly thereafter that Allenby could not be held in 'check when he plays the bull'.[42] Perhaps. There's little doubt that when in the field Allenby was fiercely determined and singular in his thinking, attributes that understandably could readily cause offence, even among battle-hardened officers, not to mention ordinary troopers. But the horrors of and losses at Ypres weighed heavily upon Allenby; so too, the endless stultification of the front, and in response he decided to launch a small counter-attack at Bellewarde Ridge, close to the town of Hooge, on 16 June. The attacked failed. By the time the attack was made the Germans had regrouped and with their usual superior firepower won the day. This small operation, while unsuccessful, was certainly not a 'debacle' however, as has been suggested by one of Allenby's biographers. Rather, it had offered at least the prospect of a limited advance by the British and therefore a change in the narrative of serial retreat.[43] Still, losses at Bellewarde were heavy, not unlike many other operations along the Western Front, large and small, for the duration of the war. Accordingly, in its aftermath Allenby took what little satisfaction he could from it, as he wrote to his wife, and moved on psychologically.[44]

Moving on for Allenby meant that the summer of 1915 also saw a continuation of trying to hold the line at the Ypres Salient, although, given events of the preceding months, the Germans had pushed forward there a distance of about 2 miles. These days were tediously immobile and unhappy ones for Allenby, a period of time that gave vent to his caustic temper. Certainly for those who knew him only by reputation they confirmed his nickname of 'the Bull' – or 'the Buffalo', as C. S. Forester later used the term in a thin disguising of Allenby in his novel, *The General*.[45] Not everyone saw him in this way, however. For example, Allenby's chief staff officer, Lieutenant General Hugh Jeudwine, remarked later that Allenby was usually 'unruffled' in command.[46] On balance, of Allenby's manner while in command it might be said that even though he surely knew the biblical passage, 'a soft answer turneth away wrath: but grievous words stir up anger', he was not necessarily disposed at all times and in all places to heed it.[47] In any event, the pressure on Allenby remained intense in the face of what was 'almost incessant warfare. The Germans are determined to get through', he wrote to his mother at the end of August, 'and I have got to stop them. The Krauts have been using a lot of this gas, whenever there has been a favourable wind; and it has done us a lot of harm.'[48]

In October, Allenby's time in command of V Corps came to an end – just as his son Michael was being gazetted as a second lieutenant in the Royal Horse Artillery – because at that particular moment General French hoped that he might be used to better effect as commander of the 3rd Army, then located just north of the Somme, rather than continuing in his current position.[49] Allenby's doggedness in command was well known to French, an attribute he respected greatly, and in anticipation of what would become the Big Push of 1916 – otherwise known as the Somme Campaign – he had decided that he wanted Allenby to be in command of one of Britain's quartet of armies now fighting in France. Hence Allenby's fresh appointment, which took effect on 23 October, just days after the conclusion of the Battle of Loos, which saw another sharp victory for the Germans who suffered just half the number of casualties there as did the British.[50] For Asquith, the prime minister, as well as for Kitchener, the defeat at Loos would spell the end for French as commander-in-chief. Too much battlefield failure had been compounded by the so-called Shells Scandal of earlier that year during which a newspaper campaign undertaken by the Fleet Street magnate Lord Northcliffe and abetted by French and Lloyd George was used to try and force the prime minister to remove Kitchener from office.[51] Now, a few months later, the tables had been turned, and French himself was headed for home, although his return to England would come with a soft landing. The post of commander-in-chief, home forces, was created for him, and in January of 1916 he was raised to the peerage as Viscount French of Ypres.

In the event, Allenby was both well pleased – 'there were not a few senior generals available' – and relieved – 'the new locality is not such a storm centre as this has been; & there has been little doing there, of late,' he informed his mother in October – to be moving 60 miles south to the environs of the Somme.[52] Indeed, for his first six months there in theatre all would be rather quiet. Allenby said farewell to French personally and was pleased to hear that his successor would be Douglas Haig, his old colleague.[53] He was able to visit Michael too, whose RHA battery was part of the 7th Division and therefore attached to Allenby's new army. 'He looked very well & smart … [and] is not in the firing line, just now,' Allenby reassured those at home. Michael, now eighteen years old and having impressed at Woolwich – especially in riding – was in France to stay.[54] Indeed, given father and son's new proximity to one another they were able to meet together on a number of occasions during this period of the war.[55]

During that February stormy winter weather bore in hard upon Allenby and his men: 'snowed under … & the wind is blowing drifts on our roads'. But as the season turned to spring anticipation of the coming major offensive meant that Allenby's 3rd Army was moved in order to allow the 4th Army under the command of Lieutenant General Henry Rawlinson to shift into position to lead the projected assault at the Somme, which would commence in July. In March, the French government made Allenby a grand officer de la Legion d'Honneur, which was small comfort for having not being chosen by Haig to be in the British vanguard at the Somme. To be sure, after having poured over strategic plans for weeks and discussed intermittently and never satisfactorily with Commander-in-Chief Haig the objectives of the Somme Offensive, the choice of Rawlinson and the 4th Army to lead it was keenly disappointing to Allenby.[56] But Haig's plans were ever-evolving, and it suited his projected deployment of troops to have Rawlinson's Fourth Army lead the offensive, the design of which was to effect a demoralizing breakthrough of the German lines. Meanwhile, Allenby's 3rd Army was to provide a diversionary action at Gommecourt, while the main Anglo-French attack would come just north of the River Somme.

The Big Push at the Somme duly commenced on 1 July and by the end of the day the disastrous results were a portent of things to come for the British throughout the balance of 1916. Almost 60,000 British casualties were suffered on that dark day, which spoke volumes about the spectacular futility of the assault against which the Germans had stood strong. Likewise, at Gommecourt German resistance had been stout, based on their advance knowledge of the attack gained by several reconnaissance flights, as well as by the deep dugouts that protected their men from British artillery attacks. Characteristically, Allenby had pushed his men hard at Gommecourt but to no avail, and by late afternoon on 1 July the fight was given up. The British had suffered almost 7,000 casualties, some 5 times the German number, a defeat in microcosm of the cataclysm playing out simultaneously at the Somme.[57] The Gommecourt action, alas, had had no bearing on the outcome of the Somme, its diversionary role proving to be useless.

For Allenby, the Gommecourt assault had come as yet another in a tedious and costly series of actions promising some measure of success but delivering nothing of the kind. Indeed, 1916 itself was turning into an annus horribilis for Allenby, as well as for the British Army altogether. Attrition was the watchword, and a grim one it was throughout what would prove to be the middle year of the war. During this period Allenby's 3rd Army was absorbing about 400 casualties per week, suffered from a combination of trench raiding, wastage, artillery fire, sniping and skirmishing, an unending harvest of suffering and death for the men involved.[58] For Allenby, however, no other large-scale actions were undertaken during this period and accordingly he spent considerable time at his Saint-Pol headquarters residing as usual in a commandeered chateau. At one point that summer a bad water source made him ill, and later on he received treatment for neuritis at a clinic in Boulogne, but day over day he lived in considerable comfort. However, despite the quotidian comforts of his well-appointed headquarters, and apart from a notable visit for lunch in September by H. H. Asquith, the soon-to-be-deposed prime minister, these were not sanguinary times for Allenby.[59] His son's exposure to enemy fire was a constant concern; his relative impotence as a commander in the face of the intractably static nature of the war was wearisome; and his never-smooth relations with Haig added to the depressive atmosphere. Indeed, for Allenby nothing on any of these scores would change until the spring of 1917 when the Battle of Arras came firmly into view.

The year 1917 proved to be a singular turning point in the war, as it would be for Allenby personally. The United States at last would join the Allies in declaring war against the Axis powers, although American troop strength along the frontlines in France would not be felt until the following year; the Bolshevik Revolution in Russia would take that country out of the war altogether; the Arab Revolt against the Ottoman Turks in the Middle East, having begun tentatively during the previous year, would begin to demonstrate a measure of success; and on the Western Front, Allied High Command would launch a Spring Offensive that began to push back the German lines in a way that had not been achieved during the first three years of the war. This ultimately successful offensive would be centred on Arras, which was located north of the Somme about halfway to Ypres.

Initial planning for the Arras offensive had begun in the autumn of 1916, as the Somme Campaign ground on in its remorseless and discouraging way and following the Allied strategy conference at Chantilly in November. While the British suffered through the Somme, at much the same time the French were having an almost equally appalling time of it in their defence of Verdun. Even more than the British, the French were intent on finally moving forward against the Germans in 1917 rather than remaining locked in what seemed to be a constant state of inertia. In Britain, Lloyd George as prime minister was keen to change the narrative of defeat and loss for the public – as well as to give the French a clear assist in reversing a growing trend in their soldiers' willingness to mutiny – and did not agree with Haig's devotion to attrition as constituting the road to ultimate victory.[60] Hence he had impressed upon the commander-in-chief a need for a fresh offensive, which would be coordinated with that of France's own new C-in-C, General Robert Nivelle, who had taken over from the exhausted Marshal Joseph Joffre in December.

During the early winter of 1917, therefore, the French under Nivelle had devised their own plan of attack, one that would take place on a large scale (some twenty-seven divisions) south of the Somme.[61] Similarly, the British would attack the German line further north, centred on Arras but extending above it as far as Vimy Ridge, as well as below it to Monchy. To effect this three-pronged attack the British 1st, 3rd and 5th Armies would be deployed, corresponding in the field to the locations listed earlier. For Allenby, this configuration meant some hard thinking for himself and his staff throughout January of 1917 as he was assigned the task of readying a battle plan for delivery to General Headquarters during the next month. The key component of the plan – in which Allenby's staff artillery expert, Lieutenant General Arthur Holland, was equally responsible – was to begin the proposed attack on the Germans with a ferocious and constant artillery bombardment that would last for forty-eight hours only, much less than was conventionally believed necessary to commence a great battle. But Allenby and Holland believed that it could be done and – in the service of surprise – should be done in order to disorient and overwhelm as rapidly as possible the German enemy, just before throwing at them the combined force of 350,000 men the 3 armies had at their disposal. For Allenby, after almost three enervating years on the Western Front, here was a clear plan for a war of movement and a potential breakthrough, a plan that owed something at least to the traditional thinking of a cavalryman.

From the moment that the plan was delivered to Haig's GHQ, however, it met with resistance, if not outright hostility. By the received standards of the time the plan was deemed to be unorthodox and unlikely to succeed on account of its proposal for an abbreviated initial bombardment. For Allenby, on the other hand, such a bombardment was the *very element* of the plan that was key to its success. If the intensity of the bombardment could be maintained over two days of unrelenting hellfire then the Germans, he argued, might not be able to adjust to it effectively, bring up their reserves and launch a counter-attack, which is what had happened usually in the past, especially at the Somme. Alas, for Allenby, he was not able to win the argument. Ultimately, Haig vetoed the plan and replaced it with the traditional five-day bombardment. Allenby responded with fury at the inability of Haig and the others at GHQ to grasp the need for a plan that was even mildly unorthodox.[62] In a number of other ways, however, and these Allenby recognized readily, the prospects for success were good. Men were plentiful in numbers, as were artillery, munitions, airplanes, tanks and gas shells. In addition, tunnelling companies had dug a dozen subways, some of which were linked with pre-existing caves, cellars and sewers. Therefore, despite Allenby's personal disappointment over having had the central element of his plan jettisoned, otherwise all seemed in readiness. Moreover, in the midst of this intense preparatory period in February came the immensely gratifying news that Michael had been awarded the Military Cross 'for conspicuous gallantry in action', while serving in a battery of the Royal Horse Artillery in September of the previous year.[63]

On 20 March the opening barrage of the Arras Offensive began to cascade down on the German lines defending the hitherto impregnable Vimy Ridge. Two weeks later on 4 April, the guns opened up on the other two sectors along a 25-mile-wide front. The thunder and crash all along the line was cacophonous. Over the next five days – Zero-Day had been changed from the 8th to the 9th – almost three million shells fell on the German lines, and their effect was exactly what Allenby had predicted.[64] Indeed, it is likely that his planned two-day barrage would have done enough damage to achieve what the British and Canadians did with their onrush beginning five days later in the dark, cold and snow of Easter Monday, 9 April. The artillery pounding – with the fillip of a 'hurricane' bombardment just five minutes before the men started to move forward at 5.30 am – had destroyed the German trenches and ripped up the attendant barbed wire. The disoriented Germans scrambled backwards and were pursued quickly, especially at Vimy, where the four divisions of the Canadian Corps advanced at speed across some 4,000 yards of deeply scarred former farmland. By one o'clock that afternoon they were in control of the Ridge. Meanwhile, success was had also at Scarpe just east of Arras, if of a less spectacular kind. Still, the 3rd Army had reached its initial objectives nonetheless and the signs augured well for continued success.

Allenby's response to the early achievements of the offensive throughout the Arras sector was little short of ecstatic. 'We have had a big battle today, gained a lot of ground, & taken a great many prisoners,' he wrote in haste to his wife late on 9 April.[65] And so it would continue. The next day he penned another such missive, elaborating on what he had written earlier, by telling her that 'I had really a very big success yesterday. I won, all along the line; killed a host of Boche, & took over 7,000 prisoners. Also, I have captured anything between 30 & 60 guns

– but they have not yet been counted.'[66] Allenby, despite his clear effusiveness, was not exaggerating. Indeed, if the British and their allies had been able to maintain this kind of momentum throughout the Battle of Arras – especially of the kind represented by the Canadian breakthrough at Vimy Ridge – it would have counted as an unalloyed victory. However, its early success would soon be mitigated, in part because German intelligence had been made aware of British preparations.

Still, on 12 April Allenby's view of the situation remained positive, though it was now properly tempered. 'We gain ground gradually,' he informed Mabel.[67] Indeed, the swift Allied advances of the first forty-eight hours had slowed and would stop altogether within a few days. The Battle of Arras, however, would continue to be fought for another month before petering out by the middle of May. In shoring up their line of defence, the Germans had been able to reassert the Hindenburg Line thus stopping the Allies from pushing forward any further. Although a certain kind of victory at Arras was claimed by the Allies, once again, as so often in the First World War, the casualty numbers make for extremely grim reading: 158,000 for the British (including 11,000 Canadians) and some 125,000 for the Germans.[68]

The whole experience of early success at Arras followed by a return to quotidian hammering against an implacable foe with little scope for movement left Allenby frustrated to a degree not yet seen in the war.[69] Thus prompted, a week into May Allenby told Haig that the 3rd Army simply was no longer in a fit condition to continue the fight. Allenby believed that in the aftermath of the Battle of Arras his men were well and truly exhausted and in need of recuperation. Moreover, the battlefield initiative that had marked the Allies so impressively in April had been lost. A breakthrough, in Allenby's view therefore, was now little more than a chimera. Better to save the troops to fight another day, he advised Haig, than to continue to pile up unsustainable casualties in a campaign that was devolving once again into attrition.[70] Haig disagreed strongly with Allenby, however. Despite praising him later for the 'great initial success' of the Arras battle plan, he read Allenby's position just then as constituting a form of mild insubordination.[71] Consequently, a short time later, Haig relieved him of his command of the 3rd Army and replaced him with Lieutenant General Julian Byng. He, along with the Canadian General Arthur Currie, had enjoyed the most conspicuous success during the Arras campaign by leading the Canadian Corps (reinforced by the British 1st Infantry Division) in taking Vimy Ridge.[72]

Surprised, angry, but also somewhat relieved by Haig's decision, an understandably emotional Allenby chose this moment to unburden himself to a sympathetic Byng.[73] After doing so, on 6 June the otherwise characteristically stoical Allenby then departed France for London.[74] Although angry and resentful, Allenby's relief in leaving behind Haig and the Western Front after thirty-four months of nearly uninterrupted service was clear nonetheless. His peremptory return home also brought with it an interregnum in command. But it would be momentary only, however, because by the time Allenby had left France he had been informed that he was going to be transferred immediately to the Allied fighting front in the Middle East. For Allenby, June of 1917 therefore would be marked not only by his loss of command on the Western Front but also by the provision

Figure 4 Allenby in uniform as he appeared in the years immediately after being transferred from the Western Front to command the Egyptian Expeditionary Force.

of what would be a fresh start in the First World War. As we shall see, the events of that month would set him up for over a year of outstanding battlefield victories that then would yield seven more years of deep proconsular influence over what remains still the modern world's thorniest thicket of war and diplomacy. Indeed, exiting the Western Front at the time that he did would prove to be a stroke of very good fortune for Allenby, the best of his military career so far (Figure 4).

Chapter 4

'WITH ALLENBY IN PALESTINE AND LAWRENCE IN ARABIA', 1917[1]

Upon Allenby's return to London from France on 6 June 1917, he found both a city and a country in thrall to the spectre of defeat by the Central Powers. As much as he felt a sense of relative freedom and relief at having departed the command struggles, immobility and daily carnage of the Western Front, Allenby was keenly aware that the war had not yet turned in the Allies' favour. The recent, on 6 April, and long-awaited announcement of the entry of the United States would not, he knew, result in an increase in manpower for many months so the interminable nature of attrition warfare would continue unabated for the foreseeable future.

Upon becoming prime minister just six months earlier in December 1916, David Lloyd George had begun an attempt to reinvigorate the British war effort that had stalled, he argued, under the indecisive leadership of his predecessor, H. H. Asquith. Others thought so too, of course, including his admiring ministerial colleague, Winston Churchill, who remarked that Lloyd George was the only man in the government who demonstrated 'any aptitude for war or knowledge of it'.[2] The former attribute alone was considered enough by some commanders such as Allenby to mark a departure from the careful, perhaps even timid, leadership of Asquith. Allenby was sanguine, therefore, about both the war's future and his own when he arrived at Number 10 Downing Street on the warm late spring morning of 8 June for a meeting with the prime minister.

Allenby's sanguinity had not been there a few days earlier on 5 June, however, when during his last full day in France he had been informed that he was being transferred to Cairo in order to take command of the Egyptian Expeditionary Force (EEF) and its sputtering campaign against the Ottoman Turks in Sinai. Indeed, the stentorian 'Bull', according to his sympathetic colleague General Julian Byng, became 'desolate' upon hearing the news as he considered the appointment to be an ignominious exile to what was thought of then as being little more than a sideshow.[3] Contributing to Allenby's initial 'desolation' was the knowledge that sideshow or no, he had not even been the prime minister's first choice. That choice, in fact, had been one of Allenby's old battlefield enemies in the South African War, the Boer General Jan Christiaan Smuts. He had turned it down based upon the belief – influenced by General Sir William Robertson, chief of the imperial general staff (CIGS) – that the Middle East indeed was a sideshow and that nothing 'first class' could be accomplished there. Smuts's rejection of the offer at the end of May meant that it would fall to Allenby. Cabinet approval for the appointment had come on 5 June, and now three days later Allenby was at Downing Street being given his marching orders by Lloyd George. The prime minister, impressed immediately by Allenby's considerable physical bearing and his usual habit of authority, encouraged him to ask for all the men and materiel that he needed in order to succeed: 'If you do not ask it will be your fault,' he stated. And then Lloyd George told Allenby bluntly that it was expected of him to deliver 'Jerusalem before Christmas' as a gift for the war-weary British nation.[4] These things were said intentionally by the prime minister in the presence of Robertson in order to counter the view that if Palestine was a 'sideshow' it would necessarily be a drain on scarce resources that were otherwise needed on the Western Front. As far as the prime minister was concerned, however, Palestine was no sideshow, but rather was the site of a potential signal victory: the sooner, the better! And in Allenby he was convinced that he had the man who could deliver it. The meeting then came to an end. As a parting gift, Lloyd George – well steeped in the Scriptural and geographical traditions of the Middle East compliments of his Welsh Chapel upbringing – handed Allenby a copy of *The Historical Geography of the Holy Land* by Sir George Adam Smith, a well-known book in the growing field of biblical geography and archaeology.[5] And with this final gesture, Allenby left Downing Street in order to ready himself for a soon-departure for Cairo to take up his new command.

Accordingly, just ten days after Allenby's memorable interview with Lloyd George, he departed London for Cairo. Travelling via Brindisi, he sailed into Alexandria on the cruiser HMS *Bristol* on 27 June and on the next day took command formally of the EEF at British General Headquarters in Cairo. Once having arrived in Egypt and taken command, Allenby wasted little time in imprinting his forceful style on his new complement of staff officers; nor did he hesitate immediately to undertake an inspection tour of the EEF's fighting front. Consequently, shortly after arriving in Cairo Allenby boarded a special train laid on for the occasion, which took him to Gaza and then to within a few miles of Beersheba, a hinge-point in the campaign to come and to which he would therefore soon return. His journey to 'the land of the Philistines', as he readily reported in a letter to Mabel, had brought him into territory that was 'parched and dry, covered with scanty grass, sandy and dusty … . Water is none too plentiful; but we have pipelines from the Nile – 150 miles away'. Indeed, Allenby's 'tour of inspection on my Palestine front' had helped to acquaint him well with the nature of the two recent defeats endured by the EEF at the hands of the Ottomans.[6] Allenby's predecessor in command, General Sir Archibald Murray, another of his former colleagues from his first tour of duty in South Africa, as well as a stint together at Staff College, Camberley, in 1897, had proven incapable of achieving success in the desert. Having arrived in Egypt in January 1916 to take command of the EEF, Murray had started well, however. Securing the Suez Canal was his main task, and this he did in August by defeating the Turks at Romani and then driving them out of the Canal Zone altogether. Murray then followed up this signal victory by pushing across the Sinai Peninsula via a newly laid railway line, which was accompanied by the equally swift construction of a water pipeline. By year's end the EEF thus had achieved its main initial objectives.

But early in 1917 the War Cabinet decided that a further advance by the EEF should take place, into southern Palestine, in order for a more comprehensive victory to be achieved in the Middle East that would stand in stark contrast to the protracted stagnation on the Western Front. The first attempt by Murray's forces to do so occurred on 26 March, and while initially successful the line of advance was not held and losses for the participating British, Australian and New Zealand troops were high, some 4,000 killed, wounded or missing. Notwithstanding this dire result Murray's relatively positive report of the fighting spurred the government to direct him to carry on in order ultimately to take Jerusalem, a prize pregnant with all sorts of propagandistic, geo-strategic and diplomatic prospects. Murray, however, protested that to do so would require considerably more men than he had at his disposal currently. Nevertheless, he decided to attack Gaza for the second time on 17 April (during which phosgene gas was used against the enemy to little effect), only now to be repulsed decisively over three days, and again with high casualties. Some 6,500 of his troops were killed or wounded this time around, almost three times the number suffered by the Turks. In the aftermath of this stinging defeat a disheartened Lloyd George deemed that a change of command was necessary if the Palestine campaign were to be continued with any hope of achieving ultimate success. Hence the call that had gone out first for Smuts, which he had rejected at length, and then for Allenby who had accepted it immediately.

The earnestness and insistence displayed by Lloyd George in pursuit of victory in Palestine were of a piece with general British wartime strategy in the region. The 'Middle East', a term coined in 1902 by the American naval strategist, Alfred Mahan, had entered the language of international affairs quickly and by the time of the First World War was being used as shorthand for the region that lay between eastern Europe and India. Certainly, British officials at the Foreign, War and India Offices had adopted the term, none more enthusiastically than one of its keenest proponents, Sir Mark Sykes.[7] Born in 1879 into the Yorkshire squirearchy as the only son of a rich and eccentric father, Sir Tatton Sykes, and his even grander-in-social-station wife, Jessica Cavendish-Bentinck, Sykes had turned a childhood and youth of inveterate travel throughout India, Egypt and the Middle East into a key government advisory position come the outbreak of war in 1914. Earlier, Sykes had served in the South African War and then as parliamentary secretary to George Wyndham, chief secretary for Ireland in the Conservative government of Arthur Balfour. The young Sykes's good relationship with Balfour would come into play later, but between 1903 and 1914 he had served in Parliament, married Edith Gorst – whose brother, Eldon, was consul general in Egypt from 1907 to 1911 in succession to the legendary Earl Cromer – and fathered six children.[8]

As war descended upon Britain during that summer of 1914, Sykes began immediately to make his expertise on the Middle East more widely known to the Asquith government. Towards the end of the tension-wracked month of August, Sykes – by then colonel commanding of the 5th Yorkshire 'Green Howards'

Regiment – sent a letter to the first lord of the Admiralty, Winston Churchill, offering his services and those of his regiment for use in the Middle East whenever war should break out there, as he expected it would soon. The peremptory and self-confident letter – 'I might be of some use on the spot' – was indicative of Sykes's manner, and even though Churchill did nothing with the letter other than to offer its writer a courteous reply, the die had been cast for Sykes's keen and close participation in the next few years of increasingly important and fraught Middle Eastern British diplomacy and warfare.[9]

But Sykes's participation, while fundamental, was just one part of a complicated kaleidoscope of persons and events that would draw all of the leading political figures of wartime Britain into the irresistible geopolitics of the Middle East. The year 1915 is seen rightly as when these persons and events began to coalesce, although Britain of course had maintained a clear interest in the Middle East for a very long time indeed. If one chooses to do so, the crusading Richard the Lionheart might be said to be the twelfth-century progenitor of such long-term interests. But in a more modern frame, Horatio Nelson's victory at the Battle of the Nile in 1798 in defence of British India inaugurated a century's worth of British geo-strategic concentration on the Eastern Mediterranean. The construction of the Suez Canal between 1854 and 1869, and the controlling shareholder's interest in it purchased by the British government under Benjamin Disraeli in 1876 in the name of safeguarding the route to India, all but guaranteed that Britain's late Victorian Imperial policy would revolve around Egypt and the Middle East.[10] Indeed, it did so, spawning all manner of professional, private and humanitarian interpolations, from Richard Burton and John Hanning Speke's search for the source of the Nile, to David Livingstone's intrepid African continental peregrinations, to Charles Gordon's epic defeat at Khartoum in 1885, and Lord Kitchener's re-conquest of the Sudan thirteen years later in 1898, followed immediately by his thwarting of rival French regional imprecations at Fashoda.[11]

Beyond the geo-strategic heartland of North Africa, Palestine, Syria and Arabia, the British interest manifested itself in additional anthropological and archaeological forms through the travels and writings of, notably, Charles Montagu Doughty, Wilfrid Scawen Blunt and Gertrude Bell.[12] Altogether, and when taking into consideration also the wider ramifications of Anglo-Ottoman-Russian relations as they related to the so-called Great Game, the Middle East had developed into a key British strategic interest by the early twentieth century, one which from 1914 the unfolding European war would bring into very sharp and unrelenting focus.[13]

The anticipated participation of the Ottoman Empire in the First World War came to pass near the end of October 1914 when the Turks entered the war on the side of the Central Powers. In turn, one week later on 4 November, the Allies declared war on the Ottomans, and battle was joined. By the early twentieth century, the Ottoman Empire had ruled over the lands now increasingly being referred to as the Middle East for some 400 years, and with its direct participation in the war those lands were now about to be put into contest in a way that had not occurred since the Middle Ages. In the vanguard over this potential contest was Britain, led into war by the Asquith Liberal government and now, owing to the exigencies of war, required to think about and plan for a new configuration of interests and power in the Middle East. If Ottoman Turkey, the so-called Sick Man of Europe, was indeed as sick as some British and other European observers believed it to be, then what better opportunity was there for geopolitical re-configuration in the Middle East than through the anticipated upheavals of war?[14]

Certainly, such thinking was top of mind for Mark Sykes, and scarcely less so for a number of his governmental and military contemporaries. The long-range catalyst for this way of thinking was the changing nature of the thirty-two-year-old 'veiled protectorate', as Britain's continuing occupation of Egypt that had begun in 1882 was called. This three-decade-long period had commenced with the Gladstone government's decision to bombard Alexandria in the summer of 1882. Bombardment and subsequent occupation was the considered British response to the Egyptian nationalist rebellion led by the disaffected army officer, Colonel Ahmed Urabi ('Arabi') – 'put down Arabi & establish Khedive's power' – as the prime minister had instructed General Garnet Wolseley to do. Afterwards, the Khedive as the Turkish Sultan's representative in Egypt had been retained by the British.[15] Egypt's status as an autonomous province of the Ottoman Empire may have been nominal, therefore, but constitutionally the system was defensible. However, an increasing national debt load and the serial financial crisis that it had spawned meant that over time Britain had come to control Egypt through the figure of the British agent general, rendering the Khedive essentially powerless. For most of this period that all-powerful person was the estimable Sir Evelyn Baring, Earl Cromer, whose supervision of Egypt was close to absolute, supported by the *Sirdar*, the British head of the Egyptian military.[16] Sir Edward Grey, as British foreign secretary, had long advocated for Egypt's formal annexation in order to remove the ambiguity that existed in her constitutional status. Consequently, in the state of war that existed between Britain and the Ottomans as of November of 1914, Grey got what he wanted.[17] The 'veiled protectorate' was duly removed in favour of a full, constitutional one. The sitting Khedive Abbas Hilmi II, the Ottomans' representative, was therefore replaced by a new Sultan of Egypt, Prince Hussein Kamel. Constitutionally, Kamel was responsible solely to the British.

For the Ottomans, having their long-time suzerainty over Egypt undercut in this way meant that such British effrontery could be met only by force. Accordingly, they decided to invade the Suez Canal zone in order to strike at the so-called spinal cord of the British Empire. Indeed, the move was nigh unto automatic, spurred by the Caliph's provocative issuing of a fatwa in Constantinople in November demanding that the British be both defeated and expelled from Egypt.[18] Subsequently launched in February 1915, the Ottoman attack on the Suez Canal was meant to signal a universal Islamic jihad against the infidel. In the event, as noted earlier, the attack proved a failure, and no such general rising occurred. But resistance along the vital Suez spine nonetheless became part of Britain's wider strategic plan to reinforce its interests throughout the Middle East, especially at the Dardanelles, as well as in Mesopotamia. Both of these campaigns of course would culminate in the spring of 1915 at Gallipoli, and a year later at Kut, respectively, where the British would suffer heavy defeats. But these losses in turn would help to catalyse the hope for decisive British victories in Egypt and Palestine. As much as a change of narrative from the chronic 'chewing of barbed wire' – to paraphrase Churchill's comment – on the Western Front was desired, an even stronger impetus for action was an understanding of the integrated nature of Britain's strategic plan in the Middle East.[19] Since the Ottomans were busy constructing railways in Syria and Palestine in order to funnel troops into that part of their eastern empire, the British would believe themselves to be compelled to enlarge their own field of vision also and do likewise.

For Sykes, the increasing roil in the Middle East was both predictable and potentially productive because it meant that his view of the necessity for British intervention in the region would now likely gain firm traction at Westminster. One of those in high government office who shared Sykes's expansive view of what was possible in the midst of the emergent centripetal forces of the Middle East was secretary of war Lord Kitchener. In office from the day after Britain had declared war against Germany, Kitchener was highly cosmopolitan, even 'oriental' in his outlook, as the (usually pejorative) term was then understood. Fluent in both French and Arabic, he had spent considerable time in the East, including stops in Cyprus, Palestine, Egypt and India, the last assignment in that list as commander-in-chief of the Indian Army from 1902 until 1909. Afterwards, for three years, he had served as British agent general in Egypt.[20] Indeed, the call from Asquith for Kitchener to come to London and direct the British war effort had meant his being snatched off a ship at Dover just prior to his departure for Cairo in August of 1914. Since that time Kitchener had put his inimitable footprint on the war's execution, engendering the New Armies, disavowing anyone of the misguided idea that the war would be 'over by Christmas' and searching for ways in which to break the stultifying stranglehold of the Western Front. 'I don't know what is to be done', he had remarked in great frustration in the autumn of 1914, 'this isn't war'.[21]

The possibilities of what might be accomplished on a wide and mobile Eastern warfront, therefore, were ones that appealed greatly to Kitchener, although it is not the case that he can be categorized as being either an 'Easterner' or a 'Westerner', to invoke contemporary British wartime strategic parlance. But what Kitchener did want, as surely as did Churchill, was to inject some clear movement and strategic possibility into an otherwise turgid war. For Churchill at the Admiralty this meant, initially, pondering a naval attack via the Baltic. But when that idea did not appeal to the War Council of the Cabinet, a switch to advocating for an attack against the Ottomans at the Dardanelles became central to his strategic thinking. As the spearhead of what was understood to be an emergent 'Eastern Strategy', the Dardanelles campaign was predicated upon the idea that the Ottoman defences of the Gallipoli Peninsula, the Narrows and Constantinople could be forced open by a naval bombardment followed by a ground invasion. Once having captured the Ottoman capital, the British believed, the Black Sea would be opened up to the Royal Navy in collaboration with the allied Russian fleet. An unimpeded supply line to Russia then would be established; the Ottomans would be driven from the war; Bulgaria – a recent, October 1915, addition to the Central Powers –

would become isolated and rendered impotent; similarly, the Austro-Hungarians too would become more vulnerable; altogether, as Maurice Hankey, the cabinet secretary, put it, such a campaign would have the effect of 'knocking the props from under' Germany.[22]

Gallipoli, as the broader Dardanelles campaign came to be called, would prove to be a disaster of course, especially for the Australians and New Zealanders – the Anzacs – for whom it yielded a blood sacrifice on a massive scale. The historiography on the Gallipoli campaign is equally massive, and a retelling of that sad story here is unnecessary other than to say that along with Churchill, the campaign was heavily supported also by Lloyd George, and to a lesser degree by Kitchener. When the full magnitude of the failure of the Dardanelles began to become clear in the spring of 1915 it had the effect of smashing – temporarily at least – the main plank of the British War Council's Eastern strategy. But despite the intense disappointment of Gallipoli's aftermath – which, of course, cost Churchill his ministerial appointment and sent him by his own choice to a junior officer's command on the Western Front – the strategic plan further afield in the East did not die. Indeed, for some, particularly Kitchener, the prospect of causing damage to, or even overthrowing, the Ottomans in the Middle East remained highly appealing and achievable, although obviously such a prospect could no longer be centred on Gallipoli. And having been made aware of Mark Sykes's expertise in Britain's wartime strategic aspirations in the Middle East, Kitchener's thinking in this regard became that much more telescoped.

The secretary of war's long service in the region, especially the years from 1911 to 1914 in Egypt, had left him in no doubt as to the centrality of the Middle East to Britain's strategic interests. In general, the War Council agreed with him, which meant that the destruction of the Ottoman Empire now was a shared British goal of the war. How this goal might be accomplished, however, remained inchoate at this stage of the war, both to Asquith and Lloyd George. To Kitchener, on the other hand, who had stated flatly in a memorandum to the War Council in March of 1915 that Egypt, the Suez Canal and Persian oil were 'essential to Britain', the right way forward was to settle on war aims in the region as quickly as possible. Earlier, such aims – especially that of securing oil supplies – had been advocated also by Churchill, who in 1914 as first lord of the Admiralty had purchased a controlling interest for the British government in the Anglo-Persian Oil Company. Thus convinced, Asquith decided to strike a government committee on Middle Eastern affairs in April chaired by the undersecretary of state at the Foreign Office, Sir Maurice de Bunsen.[23] The 'De Bunsen Committee' got to work immediately, its leading voice fast becoming Sykes, whose membership on it was ensured by Kitchener who had had him placed there in order to act as his eyes and ears. Indeed, Sykes would remark later that Kitchener was the chief inspiration for his work as a member of the committee.[24]

For the next few months the De Bunsen Committee worked through the various configurations of what the Middle East might look like, from a British perspective, once the Ottomans had ultimately been defeated and the war had come to an end. Key both to its deliberations and to its subsequent report, published on 30 June, was the necessity for Britain to hold a central role in both Arab and Zionist nationalist aspirations. Sykes endorsed this view, intrinsic to it he believed, the necessity of regional territorial partition (to include the French). Shortly after the committee's deliberations ended, therefore, he was despatched by Kitchener on a tour of the Eastern Mediterranean, Middle East and India in order to take soundings to this end from the various men on the spot. Sykes – pleased as always to be setting out on an Eastern journey – fulfilled his task happily within a month or so. After that, from July he ensconced himself in Cairo from which he ran a kind of politico-strategic salon out of Shepheard's Hotel – long the unofficial headquarters of British expatriate life in Egypt – as he sought to push European territorial partition as the centrepiece of British strategic thinking for the post-Ottoman Middle East. His initial task in this regard complete by the end of 1915, Sykes returned to London in anticipation of the government's next steps.

For Sykes as well as others, events began now to move rapidly towards a climax, which would of course have both military and diplomatic implications. Encouraged by the work of the De Bunsen Committee, the Asquith government decided in February of 1916 to make the committee's mandate permanent by creating a successor body to it called the Arab Bureau. Carved from the long-standing Cairo Intelligence Department, the Arab Bureau's remit moved the British from a position of theorizing about the potential re-configuration of the Middle East, to one of operationalizing a plan for its achievement. Specifically, as a first step, the Bureau was to 'harmonise British political activity' in the region so that the 'general tendency of Germano-Turkish policy' could be understood.[25] Even though such wording made the nascent Arab Bureau sound benignly bureaucratic in intent, over the next two years in particular (operations would continue until 1920) its work can be described as near-revolutionary, and the long-range impact of the Bureau remains profound on the Middle East of today.

For Sykes, meanwhile, the New Year 1916 saw him directed by the British government to enter into close negotiations over the future of the Middle East with the French diplomat, Francois Georges-Picot. A career civil servant, Picot had served in Copenhagen, Berlin and Beirut, and shortly after war was declared in August of 1914 he had been sent by the French government to Cairo. Picot, like Sykes, saw the Ottoman Middle East as ripe for an eventual Allied victory, followed by a concomitant partition of its constituent territories. French interest in the Eastern Mediterranean – or the Levant as the region was referred to usually in France – was as equally long-standing as Britain's. Specifically, the French occupation of Egypt under Napoleon in 1798, though unsuccessfully held owing to Nelson's destruction of the French Fleet at Aboukir's Battle of the Nile that year, planted a seed that took root both there and in nearby Syria and Lebanon. Accordingly, the rupture of Ottoman suzerainty that was anticipated to occur because of the war left open the prospect that France might enlarge its empire over lands to which it claimed an historic connection and mandate. For their part, the British – especially Sir Edward Grey at the Foreign Office – were of the opinion that any long-term solution to the wartime iteration of the chronic 'Eastern Question' would need also to include the Russians. Hence the negotiations that would yield in short order the 'Sykes–Picot Agreement' were necessarily tripartite, although they were driven mainly by the British and led by the irrepressibly 'ebullient' Sykes.[26]

In the event, a significant part of the backdrop to the Sykes–Picot negotiations – as they proceeded in London in January of 1916 (they had begun formally a few weeks earlier in Paris) – was an understanding arrived at recently by the British high commissioner in Cairo, Kitchener's successor, Sir Henry McMahon, and Sharif Hussein, the Arab Hashemite tribal leader and Emir of Mecca. On the recommendation of Kitchener who had known McMahon in India, he had been appointed high commissioner for the Sultanate of Egypt (such terminology now denoting Egypt's new status as a British protectorate owing to the war), and had taken up the appointment in January of 1915 following the interim commissionership of Sir Milne Cheetham. McMahon may have been an 'Old India Hand' owing to his birth and long imperial service there – it will be recalled that he had been a schoolmate of Allenby's at the ICS incubator, Haileybury College – but the internecine world of Anglo-Arab politics that he had entered now was of a complexity that would come to tax his navigational ability. Nevertheless, in these negotiations McMahon was sure of Kitchener's support, both personally and from the broader perspective of Britain's strategic interests in the Middle East. Meanwhile, for his part, Sharif Hussein had long been growing in distrust and hatred of the Ottomans, represented especially by what he regarded as the impious secularist movement led by the modernist reform group the Young Turks and dating from 1908. To that end, if and when the right time presented itself for an Arab Revolt against the Ottomans, the fight would be at least as much about their violations of traditional Islam as it would be about modern Western-style political nationalism and aspirations for self-determination.

Beginning in July 1915, therefore, McMahon and Hussein had opened what became a ten-letter detailed correspondence about the political status of the historic Arab lands long under Ottoman control, and what the disruptions of the First World War might portend for their future in this regard. At this point, band or tribal division militated against anything other than a nascent 'pan-Arab nationalism', at least as far as the British were concerned, although as Ali Allawi points out persuasively the inevitable disintegration of the Ottoman Empire was an accepted fact in the Arab world from the early 1880s onwards.[27] Following the outbreak of war in 1914 and within the ruling Hashemite royal family, discussions of what Arab independence – centred in the first instance on the Hijaz region of western Arabia, as well as in Syria – might look like were lively and ongoing. Indeed, while Hussein and the eldest and third-born of his four sons, Princes Ali and Faisal, respectively, were cautious in their view of launching an Arab Revolt against their Ottoman overlords, the second-born son, Prince Abdullah, was much more confident of a potential revolt's positive outcome.[28] Accordingly, during yet another heated Hashemite royal family meeting on the topic in July 1915 a date – June of 1916 – was decided upon for such a nationalist uprising to commence.[29]

Sharif Hussein's provisional decision at this meeting to sponsor an Arab Revolt was the event which had sparked his extensive correspondence with McMahon.[30] At first, and unsurprisingly, coming as it did after a long period of silence between

Hussein and the British, McMahon's responses to Hussein were cautious and revolved mainly around what the borders of a potential Arab state might look like. Such borders, Hussein believed, should stretch in a unified whole from Aleppo in Syria, south to the Hijaz and east to Aden in Yemen. Essentially, he saw these potential borders as constituting the revival of a historically identifiable caliphate. The quid pro quo, of course, for the British recognizing such an expansive Arab state – which at first seemed to them to be far beyond what might have been either desirable or achievable – was the raising by the Hashemites of an Arab military revolt against the Ottomans. In engaging in this correspondence, McMahon naturally began to draw into its deliberations a circle of advisers who had much longer and deeper experience in British Middle Eastern affairs than did he. Accordingly, Gilbert Clayton, the director of British Military Intelligence at Cairo, and Ronald Storrs, the oriental secretary, became key figures in influencing and shepherding this correspondence as it extended over the next several months until its eventual conclusion in March of 1916.[31]

The question of potential Arab borders, of course, was cardinal to the correspondence and would be at the heart of the Arab Revolt as it developed over the next few years, which meant too that the position of France in the region was of constant concern to the British. In the event, the McMahon-Hussein correspondence and the discussions leading up to the Sykes–Picot Agreement, as well as the establishment and remit of the Arab Bureau, while concurrent, were not of course transparent, which would lead later to a host of problems, as we shall see. But in the short term, by the end of October 1915, the British and Hussein had come to an understanding – to the latter, indeed, it would constitute an agreement – that in exchange for an Arab Revolt against the Ottomans, Britain was 'prepared to recognize and uphold the independence of the Arabs in all the regions lying within the frontiers proposed by the Sharif of Mecca'.[32] In making this pledge McMahon and the British – especially Storrs – were extremely careful about the expected implications for France of that to which they had agreed. Nevertheless, henceforth Britain found herself allied with the Arab nationalist cause, something that would become clearer still with the Sykes–Picot Agreement, and then ultimately with the commencement of Arab hostilities against the Ottomans in June of 1916.

In mid-1916, as all of these diplomatic machinations were proceeding, Allenby remained ensconced on the Western Front, oblivious to them and a full year away from his appointment to command the EEF. But as was noted earlier, by that time the EEF had resisted the Ottomans' incursion of the Suez Canal zone and was pushing them back towards the Sinai Peninsula and Palestine. On 10 June at Mecca when Sharif Hussein initiated the Arab Revolt by authorizing an attack on the city's Turkish garrison he did so thus in the full knowledge of British support for his actions: McMahon's final letter to Hussein in March had agreed to his requests for the furnishing of L50,000 in gold, as well as for weapons, ammunition and food.[33] Hussein declared the Revolt also to be in response to what he believed were the impieties committed against Islam by the Young Turks and their sympathizers. In keeping with the Arab Bureau's understanding of the Revolt's motivations, therefore, they were less nationalist than jihadist, at least at this early stage. Still, regardless of which motivation was dominant, the Arab Revolt had begun and from Cairo's perspective its operations in the Arabian Desert and beyond would open up a new and valuable fighting front that just might reverse the EEF's current disappointing deployment in Sinai.

In addition to money, weapons, ammunition and food, the British also sent out to the Hijaz a number of officials from the Arab Bureau in Cairo. They were put into the field by Gilbert Clayton. As director of British Military Intelligence in Egypt, Clayton was the key figure in orchestrating the Arab Bureau's wartime intelligence and military activities. An artilleryman like Kitchener his chief, under whom he had served in 1898 in Sudan, Clayton had stayed on there afterwards. Later having moved to Egypt, at the time of the outbreak of the war he was positioned well to fulfil an important organizational role in British Middle Eastern affairs. Clayton had encouraged Kitchener strongly to approach Sharif Hussein about whether or not he would raise an Arab force to assist the British against the Ottoman Turks. Earlier, he had interviewed Muhammad Sharif al-Faruqi, a young Ottoman Arab officer, who had come across to the British at Gallipoli in 1915 in order to report that there was strong support for Arab independence among his peers. Clayton's interviews with Faruqi had convinced him that the possibility of an Arab Revolt was real and that the British should exploit it rather than leave the field open to such an advantage falling potentially to the Germans.[34]

As secretary of war, Kitchener in fact needed little encouragement to court Arab support in attempting to overthrow the Ottomans. As early as April of 1914, not long before returning to England for a summer holiday from which he was destined not to return, Kitchener had interviewed Prince Abdullah in Cairo and then had passed him on to the oriental secretary, Ronald Storrs, for further talks along these lines. Storrs was likewise impressed with the possibility of a successful Arab uprising, followed by the potential for the creation of a British-Arab protectorate. In September 1914, therefore, and with the war now well underway, Storrs had reacquainted Kitchener with the nature of his earlier discussions with Abdullah. Emboldened by Storrs's report, Kitchener authorized him to send a mission to Mecca in order to interview Sharif Hussein directly as to whether or not he 'would be with us or against us' should the Ottomans declare war on Britain, which, of course was poised to happen and then did so in November.[35] Following the Ottomans' declaration of war, a second British diplomatic mission was sent to Mecca and Hussein, while not willing 'to break with the Turks immediately' was clearly now on the path of doing so eventually. Indeed, it would be a short time only before such a break was made.[36]

When the break came officially, therefore, in June of 1916 – with Hussein dramatically firing the first shot himself – it did so by sparking a month-long battle in Mecca between the initially outgunned Arabs and the determined, though small (just some 1,500 men) Turkish garrison.[37] Finally, however, on 9 July with the assistance of both Egyptian troops and of British artillery, Mecca was taken by Hussein's Hashemite fighters. Their victory in Islam's holiest city was celebrated throughout the Arab world as it came after the Turks had desecrated Mecca by spraying artillery fire widely and indiscriminately. By that time Clayton had sent in already some of his Arab Bureau men, notably Lieutenant Colonel Stewart Newcombe and Major Herbert Garland, in order to help direct Arab affairs on the ground. Soon to follow, in October, would be another of Clayton's chosen men, Captain T. E. Lawrence. These British operatives, together with a number of others, would prove to be at the centre of the Arab Revolt as it unfolded over the next two years.

For almost a full year until Allenby's arrival in Cairo at the end of June 1917, both the Hijaz territory and the composition of the Arab Revolt – overwhelmingly comprised of the Bedouin, at this stage – grew into a small though important fighting theatre in Britain's coordinated effort to usurp the Ottoman Empire's position as suzerain in the Middle East. By the time of Hussein's actions at Mecca, his success there had been matched already by swifter Hashemite rebel victories in Jiddah, Rabegh and Yanbo. To these early successes, would be added others, notably at Umm Lajj, a Red Sea port taken by Hussein's ally, Sharif Nasr bin Ali, in mid-August. Ali was the brother of the Emir of Medina, and in winning and joining forces with the Hashemites, the revolt in the desert put itself on a considerably broader footing. The two leading Arab desert families now were united, which meant that their respective Sunni and Shi'a faiths were equally conjoined, at least in politico-military terms. Pan-Arab nationalism, a movement that might possibly include Syria too, was not (yet) in evidence, however, the Ottomans' highly oppressive regime in Damascus had seen to that. But in the almost endless expanse of the Hijazi desert the Bedouin now were in open revolt against the Turks, and the British were committed to assisting them in what would become a protracted two-year exercise in overthrowing their despised imperial masters. The revolt, as an enthusiastic T. E. Lawrence explained to his mother in a letter written on 1 July, 'has taken a year and a half to do, but now is going very well. … I hope the movement increases, as it promises to do. … This revolt, if it succeeds will be the biggest thing in the Near East since 1550.'[38]

For Lawrence, as well as for the other Arab Bureau men on the spot by the autumn of 1916, the next twenty-four months would prove to be an extraordinary exercise in guerrilla warfare and in the harnessing and deployment in battle of both Arab regular and irregular troops. Lawrence, of course, would emerge later during the 1920s as the singular British figure in the dramatic history of the Arab Revolt, a position he has continued to hold in the public imagination all the way down to today. But at the beginning in 1916, he was just one of a small cadre of British operatives in the service of both the nascent nationalism of the Arab rebels and their princely leadership, and the strategic interests of the British imperial state.

For Lawrence, his time in the Middle East had begun seven years earlier in the summer of 1909 while an undergraduate at Oxford. Fired by a lively historical imagination suffused with a childhood and youth of biblical knowledge and Crusader history, he had made a 1,100-mile solo walking journey through Syria and Palestine during which he examined and sketched the remains of a number of Crusader castles. Though having been dissuaded from making this journey by no less a regional authority than the legendary desert traveller, Charles Doughty

– 'In July and August the heat is very severe. ... The distances to be traversed are very great. You would have nothing to draw upon but the slight margin of strength which you bring with you from Europe' – Lawrence persevered nonetheless and made a great success of the trip.[39] Doughty had no way of knowing, of course, that for the short – just 5' 5" – and wiry Lawrence, the greater the physical demands, the greater the likelihood of completion. He had proven his hardiness already during an extensive cycling trip in France taken the summer before, and so he approached this latest challenge with both confidence and gusto.

   A year later in 1910, having earned by then a first-class degree in Modern History at Jesus College, Lawrence had joined an archaeological dig in Syria at the behest of its director, D. G. Hogarth, the Keeper of Oxford's Ashmolean Museum and an early Lawrence champion. He returned therefore to the Middle East for what would turn out to be an almost unbroken nine-year span. The dig, established on behalf of the British Museum, was located at the ruins of the ancient 4000-year-old Hittite city of Carchemish on the River Euphrates in Syria, and within view of the new 800-mile-long Hijaz Railway under construction just then by the Ottomans in order to link Damascus with Medina. Once completed, the railway would perform double duty as the means by which to transport pilgrims to the Arabian Islamic holy places, as well as to provide a ready means for the deployment of Ottoman troops. From the moment of his arrival at Carchemish, Lawrence took to both the work and the environment exceedingly well. He learnt Arabic rapidly, made friends with the other archaeologists and met fellow travellers such as the intrepid Gertrude Bell, whose serial peregrinations in Syria and elsewhere had made her an authority on the region and whose expertise would be employed by the British government for a generation, especially as it related to Mesopotamia (soon to be renamed Iraq). Lawrence first met Bell at Carchemish in April of 1911. He impressed her readily, even though she was somewhat condescending in her comment that he was 'an interesting boy, he will make a traveller'.[40] For his part, Lawrence was a bit prickly about Bell's evident professional superiority at that time, remarking in a letter home that 'she was really too captious at first'; but 'we parted with mutual expressions of esteem'. Still, Lawrence showed himself to have a cruel streak in remarking in the same letter that Bell was 'not beautiful, (except with a veil on, perhaps)'.[41]

   At this stage Lawrence found more success in making friends with the local Arabs, however, especially with the one he called 'Dahoum' (Selim Ahmed), first mentioned by him as being simply a 'donkey boy'. Nevertheless, he was 'interesting', could 'read a few words' and 'altogether has more intelligence than the rank & file'. Dahoum, of course, would go on to become Lawrence's great protégé and companion (before dying of typhus at just 19-years-of age in 1916), and to whom it is thought Lawrence dedicated – 'To S.A.' – the history of his role in the Arab Revolt, *Seven Pillars of Wisdom*.[42] Under the directorship of Hogarth's successor, Leonard Wooley, beginning in 1912, Lawrence confirmed himself as both a highly skilled archaeologist and a proficient map-maker. This latter skill became clear especially owing to Lawrence's subsequent participation in a military survey of the Sinai Peninsula. Mandated by Kitchener during his time as British agent and consul general of Egypt in 1913, and with a view to what might transpire in the region should war with the Ottomans erupt, the survey was carried out under the auspices of the Palestine Exploration Fund (for whom Kitchener had once done similar work in Palestine when he was a young subaltern). Lawrence's task, as he put it bluntly later, was 'to give archaeological colour to a political job'.[43] Accordingly, early in 1914 Wooley, Lawrence, Dahoum and Stewart Newcombe, at that time still of the Royal Engineers, had embarked on a surreptitious survey of the Sinai that would shortly be published under the title *The Wilderness of Zin*.

A few months later, back in London and hard at work writing up the survey for publication when war broke out in August of 1914, Lawrence was enrolled swiftly in the geographical division of British Military Intelligence. Holding no military rank as a civilian, Lawrence's status was then changed subsequently in October to that of second lieutenant on the Special List – that is, to an officer without an attachment to a regiment, which indeed is what Lawrence would remain for the balance of the war. In December, after a few months of doing 'nothing very exciting', as he complained to a friend about his time at the War Office where British Military Intelligence was based, Lawrence was transferred from London to Cairo in order to join the barely formed Intelligence division of Egypt's War Office. 'Today', he wrote wryly to the same friend from Cairo on Christmas Eve 1914, 'we got the Office, and we all have the Intelligence: it is only a simple process of combining the two.'[44] Such was done quickly, with Newcombe put in place as director, and with Lawrence – as his words would suggest – installed as something less than a typical spit and polish military officer.

Beginning in the New Year 1915, therefore, Lawrence and the other members of the Cairo War Office's small band of intelligence officers had started to look ever more closely at the prevailing geopolitics of the Middle East. To them, the possibilities of using an Arab Revolt against the Ottoman Turks in order to achieve Britain's strategic purposes in the region, while at the same time delivering to the Arabs some form of independence, would grow to become an inevitability. The 'year and a half' that Lawrence referred to earlier in a letter home to his mother thus had become the proving ground for the Intelligence Department's campaign to help spark the revolt. Once having found its feet Cairo Military Intelligence became a beehive of activity, staffed by a number of young officers from military, diplomatic and political backgrounds. Along with Newcombe as director, who was thirty-four years old, had been in Egypt since 1901 following service in the South African War and was known well by Lawrence because of their survey of Sinai together, there was Leonard Wooley, seconded from the dig at Carchemish. In addition, there were two young British members of Parliament, the aristocratic Conservative, Aubrey Herbert and George Lloyd, also a Tory and destined for a long imperial career, including appointment as British high commissioner for Egypt. The Intelligence Department may not have been Cairo's version of Lord Alfred Milner's tutelary South African 'Kindergarten', but the elixir of youthful men on the spot was certainly being drunk in earnest by these five officials. The 'best job going in Egypt' is how Lawrence described what he was doing during the early months of 1915, a feeling that he would maintain – despite occasional protestations to the contrary: 'BORED', as he complained loudly in June – throughout that year and until the Arab Revolt was declared officially in mid-1916.[45]

Of course, much of the work done by Lawrence and the others was a dutiful gathering of information, reading and writing reports, and studying maps, a veritable recipe for daily susurration. Prosaic, it may have been, but these tasks nevertheless were suffused with the heightened atmosphere of wartime and the evident aspirations within the Intelligence Department for the Arabs to rise in rebellion against their Ottoman masters as soon as possible. Broader questions of strategy were entertained from time to time too, of course, and the frequent presence of men such as Clayton, the spy chief to whom Newcombe reported; Sir Reginald Wingate, governor general of the Sudan and Sirdar (commander-in-chief) of the Egyptian Army; and Major General Sir John Maxwell, general officer commanding of the army in Egypt meant that the Cairo Intelligence Department evolved into the nexus of British strategizing during the early part of the war in the Middle East.

Throughout this period Lawrence worked closely with Newcombe and Wooley especially; indeed, we 'had breakfast, lunch, and dinner together daily at the Continental Hotel for nine months', as Newcombe recalled later.[46] Their sense of comradeship was deep therefore, giving an added impetus to and inspiration for their actions to come later in the field. Herbert and Lloyd, on the other hand, both Old Etonians and therefore to the blunt-spoken career engineer Newcombe fundamentally insufferable, did not last long in Cairo and upon their departure were not missed. Lawrence, conversely, although eccentric was hard-working and produced excellent results. Despite obvious high intelligence – of which his first-class degree from Oxford was ample evidence – Lawrence was well liked by his less intellectual peers in Cairo. His eccentricities or, as he called them, his 'little wanton problems of conduct', such as a carefree attitude regarding military dress and deportment, and his age – he was just twenty-six years old for most of 1915 and looked even younger – belied the fact that Lawrence was a seasoned and skilled Middle East hand. Above all, it was this fact that was recognized by his colleagues.[47]

As the months went by the antebellum tension built in Cairo. This was especially true once McMahon's correspondence with Sharif Hussein had commenced in July of 1915. In the meantime, Lawrence's extensive knowledge of Syria was tapped, especially by Clayton, for whom he wrote a long report. In it, Lawrence concluded that 'the only imposed government that will find, in Moslem Syria, any really prepared groundwork or large body of adherents is a Sunni one, speaking Arabic, and pretending to revive the Abbasides or Auyubides'.[48] In other words, Lawrence believed that in the interior of Syria, along the spine of cities he regarded as being authentically Syrian – Damascus, Homs, Hamah and Aleppo (Beirut, on the Mediterranean coast, was thought to be too cosmopolitan to count and therefore was deliberately excluded) – a restoration of a Saladin-style medieval caliphate was the right way forward. Indeed, just such a view had been suggested first by Kitchener during the previous year, but now Lawrence gave to it fulsome expression. Clayton accepted Lawrence's view, in large part because it lent credence to his pre-existing position that France, if possible and with the exception of Beirut, should be excluded from Syria's post-Ottoman future.

Shortly after Lawrence had penned his Syrian report and discussed it with Clayton, he received word of a much different sort. The second youngest of his four brothers, Frank, had been killed on the Western Front on 9 May. Strangely, however, Lawrence's reaction to his brother's death was curiously bloodless, writing to his parents in the following month that 'to die for one's country is a sort of privilege ... I think that at this time it is one's duty to show no signs that would distress others: and to appear bereaved is surely under this condemnation'.[49] Not yet had Wilfred Owen's or Vera Brittain's later view of the awful waste of war seeped into Lawrence's own way of thinking. However, in October when another of his brothers, Will, just a year younger than himself and a pilot with the Royal Flying Corps, was shot down over France and declared missing (his assumed death would be confirmed the following May), Lawrence wrote of feeling 'low' and lamenting that 'they were both younger than I am, and it doesn't seem right, somehow, that I should go on living peacefully in Cairo'.[50]

That autumn and winter and continuing into the spring of 1916 Lawrence's job, in keeping with the heightened atmosphere of the war, had intensified too. Beginning in April he had taken on much of the work required to produce a daily Military Intelligence Bulletin for Egyptian government officials – 'my only joy', he called it. He interviewed prisoners, many of whom were Arabs formerly under Turkish command, supported the new practice of taking aerial photographs in order to sharpen military map-making, and met the inimitable Mark Sykes while on his tour of the Middle East, taken, it may be recalled, at the behest of Kitchener. Lawrence was exceptionally busy with his own work at this point, and therefore Sykes did not make much of an impression on him. Later, however, Lawrence would deride him as being comprised of 'a bundle of prejudices, intuitions, half sciences ... by choice he was a caricaturist rather than an artist, even in statesmanship'.[51] In part, however, and ironically as far as Lawrence was concerned, it was through Sykes's insistent agency that by the beginning of 1916 British policy regarding Hussein and the Arabs had come more sharply into focus. 'There is going to be rather a busy winter in the Levant,' Lawrence had written home in October, and his forecast was correct.[52] Indeed, in that same month Kitchener and Grey, the foreign secretary, had agreed that Sir Henry McMahon should give direct assurances to Hussein about what he could expect territorially in exchange for Arab support in fighting the Ottomans. The exact territorial extent of the promise to the Arabs would have to remain fluid, however, a function of the Anglo-French relationship he implied, but McMahon was as clear as he believed his diplomatic remit allowed him to be. Lawrence was a key part of the background discussions to this end, even if he characterized his job blithely to a friend by writing that 'we do nothing here except sit & think out harassing schemes of Arabian policy'. Given the necessarily sensitive and secretive nature of his intelligence work Lawrence of course gave away nothing of the content of such discussions in his correspondence with family and friends, even making light of the interminableness of his life at the department. 'I am going to be in Cairo till I die,' he joked in February 1916. 'Yesterday I was looking over samples of pyramids at an undertaker's with a view to choosing my style. I like the stepped ones best.'[53]

Despite Lawrence's insouciance which, when exhibited to his less indulgent military peers, was viewed as irritating or even insubordinate, the early months of 1916 proved to be the anteroom of the Arab Revolt. In London throughout January and February, and unbeknownst to Lawrence and the other members of the Cairo Intelligence Department, Sykes and his French counterpart, Picot, had moved closer to an Anglo-French agreement (with nominal Russian participation) about dividing the post-war Middle East into European spheres of influence.[54] They concluded their secret negotiations in March by signing what they called the 'Asia Minor Agreement', afterwards known as the Sykes–Picot Agreement, which was then duly signed and ratified by Sir Edward Grey on 16 May, thereby establishing a working plan for the aftermath of the assumed downfall of the Ottoman Empire and the concomitant move towards nationalism and independence by the Arabs. The provisions of the agreement gave to France northern Mesopotamia, Syria, Lebanon and south-eastern Turkey, while the British were awarded southern Mesopotamia, Transjordan and much of Palestine. 'I should like to draw a line from the "e" in Acre to the last "k" in Kirkuk', as Sykes had phrased it pithily to Asquith in a special meeting at 10 Downing Street on 16 December attended also by Lloyd George and Kitchener. If so, Asquith had replied, 'we must have a political deal. We must come to terms with the French, which means we must come to terms diplomatically.'[55] A few months later such a deal indeed had come to pass with the Sykes–Picot Agreement. Upon leaving No. 10 that morning Sykes believed himself to have 'carried the day', as he wrote to Clayton.[56] Now, with the Russians pacified too by their diplomatic gaining of the Dardanelles, as well as Constantinople, as a fillip to the larger Anglo-French settlement, Sykes might well have thought all was as it should be in the Middle East. Altogether, however, the agreement had worked to undercut the idea of Arab independence. Eventually, as we shall see, it would serve to make a mockery both of McMahon's careful assurances to Hussein and of the Arab Bureau's more robust view of what the fall of the Ottomans might mean for the Middle East's Arab peoples.

In Cairo, meanwhile, the McMahon-Hussein correspondence had continued apace throughout the concurrent Sykes–Picot negotiations in London. But not until the end of April, however, would McMahon be informed of what the proposed Anglo-French agreement contained. In the event, both he and Grey determined that Hussein and the Arabs would not be told of its existence.[57] And there matters would stand as meanwhile, a thousand miles to the southeast of Cairo in Mecca, Sharif Hussein now found himself on the verge of firing the rifle shot that would signal the formal start of the Arab Revolt.

For Lawrence, during the winter and spring of 1916, came an additional assignment in Mesopotamia. Here, the 6th Division of the Indian Expeditionary Force (IEF), commanded by Major General Charles Townshend, had succumbed to besiegement at Kut al Amara, a strategically important town well inside Turkish-held territory. Townshend's predicament, which had begun in December of 1915, had become a full-blown disaster by March. Reinforcements had been called up and the first-of-their-kind aerial food drops by the new Royal Flying Corps had been undertaken, but nothing would suffice to relieve Townshend's beleaguered force. Faced with a staggering 30,000 of his troops killed or wounded, and thousands more likely to become prisoners of war, in London Kitchener decided to intervene directly by offering up to L1-million (L2-million was later requested, but not approved) in ransom money to the Turks. Gertrude Bell, by then on site in Mesopotamia, was acting as the personal envoy of the Indian Viceroy, Lord Hardinge. She was there having been asked by Hardinge in her capacity as a Middle East expert to evaluate the work of the Arab Bureau, especially as it related to Arab national feeling in Mesopotamia and whether or not it was being stoked in ways that the government of India, under whose formal control Mesopotamia lay, could not condone.

A short time earlier, in the autumn of 1915, Bell had spent two months in Cairo during which she had become acquainted with the new practice of aerial photography for use in map-making undertaken by the Intelligence Department with the participation of Lawrence as liaison, as noted earlier. Once having moved on to Mesopotamia Bell suggested, therefore, that someone from Cairo should come out to Basra in order to provide expertise for carrying out aerial reconnaissance in the embattled country. Lawrence was the obvious choice – 'one of the best of our very able intelligence staff here' – wrote McMahon to Sir Percy Cox, at that time chief political officer to the IEF, and Lawrence duly departed for Basra on 20 March.[58] Bell was equally pleased that he was on his way, but would remain wary that in addition to the technical expertise about aerial photography that Lawrence would bring, he was also part of an Arab Bureau scheme to rouse Arab nationalist feeling in Mesopotamia.

Lawrence arrived in Basra on 5 April, expecting to spend only 'ten days or a fortnight' in Mesopotamia.[59] He was welcomed warmly by Bell – 'this week has been greatly enlivened by the appearance of Mr. Lawrence. … We have had great talks and made vast schemes for the government of the universe' – she wrote home expansively.[60] As it turned out, Lawrence was to spend almost six weeks in the country and have a rather depressing and even dangerous time of it while there. In addition to taking the temperature of local Arab national feeling (about which he did not inform Bell), Lawrence would soon be asked also to be one of the conduits for Kitchener's plan to ransom, or indeed 'bribe', the Turks as they lay siege to Kut in order to allow at least the IEF's wounded safe passage out of the embattled town. Bell's offhanded remark about 'schemes' was closer to the mark than even she knew for upon arriving in Basra Lawrence had spoken immediately to Sir Percy Cox of Cairo's desire to see the Mesopotamian Arabs rise up in the same way that those in the Hijaz were poised to do. On this point, as Lawrence informed Clayton, Cox – who thought Mesopotamia's future lay in coming out from under the sub-imperial control of the government of India – 'does not know how Cairene he is'.[61] But while Cox 'favours the hoisting at Bagdad [*sic*] of the British flag and the Arab flag together', Lawrence continued, his view of the ransom proposal recently made by the War Office in London was dim.[62] Regardless, on 9 April Lawrence left Basra en route to Kut in order to participate along with a handful of others – including his erstwhile Cairo colleague, Aubrey Herbert, who had been transferred to Mesopotamia – in the execution of Kitchener's plan, should the final attempt at the garrison's relief fail. On 29 April, after both the relief operation and the negotiations with the Turkish commander indeed had failed, which included the offer of L1-million, General Townshend duly surrendered Kut to the enemy. For the British, the Siege of Kut would be one of the darkest chapters in all of the First World War. Although the Asquith government attempted to limit its negative impact on the British public, the numbers of men (mainly Indian) lost or captured at Kut would speak for themselves, as we shall see shortly.

For Lawrence, the Mesopotamian experience was ultimately dispiriting. Still, having been blindfolded and taken to the Turkish commander's headquarters just outside Kut in order to parley had appealed to his innate sense of adventure and had had its memorable moments, including 'a most excellent dinner in Turkish style', he wrote (too lightly, given the circumstances) to his mother.[63] He wrote these words without, of course, having any knowledge of the horrors to come. Once the British offer had been rejected, the diplomatic failure at Kut led to a forced-march of the remainder of the IEF's men overland to Turkey. During the march many of them were forced to walk barefoot and some 70 per cent of the 12,000 men who were on that grisly passage died from hunger and exposure.[64] As for General Townshend himself, after bidding a stentorian 'good-bye and good luck to all' in his last communication to the troops, he was taken to Constantinople there to languish as a prisoner of war until October of 1918.[65] And what of the intrepid Lawrence? In the aftermath of the diplomatic failure he had returned immediately to Basra where he spent a few days debriefing his superiors on events, as well as acknowledging the surprising though welcome news that Gertrude Bell would be staying on in Mesopotamia permanently as the Arab Bureau's correspondent. He then boarded ship on 11 May for the return journey to Cairo, arriving there on 26 May.

Upon Lawrence's return to Cairo at the end of May the atmosphere within the Arab Bureau was as anticipatory of action in the desert as it had ever been. An Arab Revolt in the Hijaz under Hussein's direction now appeared imminent. The Turks, who were anticipating an Arab rising also, had brought into the region an additional 3,500 troops. In the meantime, Lawrence plunged into writing and issuing the first *Arab Bulletin*, a supplement to the *Military Intelligence Bulletin* that had been a staple of his work for the preceding year, and was designed to keep all members of the Bureau abreast of the latest developments in the Hijaz. On the same day that the first issue of the *Arab Bulletin* came out, 6 June, a pivotal meeting took place in Jiddah between a small Cairo delegation headed by Ronald Storrs, Clayton's oriental secretary and Prince Zeid, the fourth-born and youngest son of Hussein. The British had brought along L10,000 in gold for Hussein – he proceeded to ask for even more – and were surprised to learn that the Hashemites had taken up arms already at Medina, with additional attacks elsewhere to follow soon. Four days later, as we have seen, Hussein would begin the Arab Revolt formally in Mecca. But it really had started as of 5 June, the same day that its godfather, Kitchener, lost his life in the North Sea while en route to attend secret diplomatic meetings in Russia. His ship, the destroyer HMS *Hampshire*, was torpedoed by a German U-boat, sinking in minutes, with almost all hands on board drowned.[66]

As the Arab Revolt commenced, quickly it became all-consuming for Lawrence who at that point remained attached officially to the Cairo Intelligence Department, as well as unofficially to the Arab Bureau. Early Arab victories over the Turks were highly inspiring and desert operations fast became the province of the Bureau as it marshalled supplies in Cairo and then sent them to Arabia. But internecine competition in Cairo and elsewhere among the various persons and parties involved meant also that coordinated British support of the revolt was lacking initially. To some extent, this situation was unavoidable as High Commissioner McMahon in Cairo, General Murray with the EEF in Sinai and General Wingate in Khartoum all had an obvious stake in the success of the revolt. None of them were too sure of the military viability of the Arabs however, especially Wingate, who disparaged Hussein's army initially as being little more than 'a rabble and run on Dervish lines'.[67] But the locus of British engagement for the time being would need to remain Cairo Military Intelligence along with the Arab Bureau, from where Lawrence, with his natural martial instincts aroused and his hopes for the future kindled, boasted to his mother on 1 July that 'it is so good to have helped a bit in making a new nation – and I hate the Turks so much that to see their own people turning on them is very grateful'.[68]

Lawrence would spend the summer of 1916 in Cairo tracking the Revolt's progress, producing the *Arab Bulletin*, and in an almost whimsical nation-building exercise, designing and producing postage stamps for use in Hussein's prospective new Arab state! Meanwhile, British naval power had now begun to be deployed on the Red Sea in order to bombard Turkish-held ports. British aircraft were employed also, as were – commencing that autumn – British operatives on the ground. In October, in an effort to understand more fully the military capabilities of the Sharifian forces, as well as its command structure, Lawrence was chosen to accompany Storrs to Jiddah where, joined by Colonel Cyril Wilson, the British resident, they met with Prince Abdullah. In addition, during this trip the British wished to determine which of Sharif Hussein's four sons was the ideal commander among them, and hence the one with whom they should cultivate close relations. Travelling from Cairo with 'little Lawrence my supercerebral companion', as Storrs termed him, they arrived in Jiddah on 16 October.[69] Located on the coast of the Red Sea about 50 miles directly west of Mecca, Jiddah was both a furnace of dry heat and an assault on the senses, but once past 'the oppressive alley of the food market' and through the 'squadrons of flies, [which] danced up and down like particles of dust in sun-shafts', as Lawrence wrote later, they took refuge at the British Consulate, the site of the meeting to come.[70]

The two-day encounter with Abdullah was dominated initially by Storrs and Wilson, both senior to Lawrence. Gradually however, it was the younger man, equipped with a nuanced understanding of Arabic and a deep well of knowledge about Ottoman troop movements, who impressed greatly the Hashemite prince. 'Is this man God', Abdullah exclaimed to Storrs in amazement, 'to know everything?'[71] Emboldened by the positive impact he was having on Abdullah, but not taken with the man himself as a potential military leader, Lawrence was permitted readily by Storrs to request that he travel first north and then inland in order to meet both of Abdullah's older brothers, Ali and Faisal, and determine which of them might be the right partner to help direct the Arab Revolt. Even though he had been passed over, Abdullah pleaded over the telephone with his sceptical father to allow Lawrence safe passage in Hijazi territory since no British officer had ever before been allowed to proceed beyond the coast. At length, Hussein agreed. Before commencing the journey Lawrence and Storrs dined with the head of the just three-week-old French Military Mission in Jiddah, Colonel Edouard Bremond. During their meal, and much to Lawrence's annoyance, Bremond proceeded to pour cold water on the infant Arab Revolt in the Hijaz, expressing a desire that it not spread to Syria and upset the plans that France had to control the country in the future. It is probable that both Lawrence and Storrs knew something of the Sykes–Picot Agreement at this point, although they did not speak of it to Bremond. Certainly however, in Bremond's view, the desire of France to fill the political vacuum in Syria that would be left by the forced departure of the Ottomans had been made clear to his British counterparts.

More determined than ever, therefore, to aid in the success of the Arab Revolt and, inter alia, deal a blow to French plans for the region, on the next day 19 October, Lawrence and Storrs sailed the short distance north to the port of Rabegh where they met with Prince Ali.[72] But disappointingly Lawrence was just as unimpressed by Ali as a potential partner as he had been with Abdullah. Ali, as Lawrence described him, was 'without force of character' and consequently not the right man to forge an effective Anglo-Arab alliance.[73] Much depended, therefore, on his anticipated meeting with Prince Faisal, Hussein's last remaining son (Zeid, the youngest, was just eighteen years old). In order to meet him, however, Lawrence would need to undertake a gruelling 100-mile journey inland by camel. On the morning of 21 October therefore, and in the company of a handful of Arab guides, Lawrence duly set off for Faisal's camp at Wadi Safra. At thirty years of age, Faisal was only a little older than Lawrence himself. Like his British visitor too he was vital, warlike and wise, and in him, as Lawrence would write later, 'I felt at first glance that this was the man I had come to Arabia to seek'.[74] After some hard camel-riding – 'the novelty of this change was severe' – he wrote understatedly to mark the contrast of this form of diplomacy to that which had kept him 'in a little overcrowded office' in Cairo for the last two years, Lawrence arrived at Faisal's sprawling encampment in the majestic Wadi Safra a few days later. Once there he stayed for a week, observing the impressive Faisal with his tribesmen and camp followers, but gaining from him the sense, despite his evident hospitality, that he harboured a degree of suspicion about British motives. 'Though I know the British do not want it [the Hijaz]', he mused to Lawrence, 'yet what can I say, when they took the Sudan, also not wanting it? They hunger for desolate lands.'[75]

Despite Faisal's suspicions about the motives of the great European power that had sent Lawrence, he was highly impressed nonetheless with the young Englishman who seemed to understand intuitively that in order for the Arab

Revolt to succeed it would have to depend upon a force of tribal irregulars, the antithesis of a modern professional army, British or otherwise. In what was an almost medieval-like arrangement, for the equivalent of L2 per month and with food supplied for their wives and children, Faisal could keep anywhere from a few hundred to over 10,000 men in the field. But there were no guarantees that they would participate or, if so, for how long. Therefore, the tact and forbearance that Faisal needed to demonstrate when negotiating for men with their tribal shaikhs were both of the highest order and immensely time consuming.[76] Thus when it came time for Lawrence to return to Cairo, he did so having seen first-hand the nature of the force upon which the revolt depended and also the overwhelmingly guerrilla style of warfare that would likely have to be employed in order to defeat the conventionally deployed Turkish Army. Mulling over all that he had seen and heard during his week with Faisal, Lawrence set out overland to Jiddah via Yanbo and was back in Cairo by mid-November.

Lawrence's advice and skills now began to be met with ready approbation, especially by Clayton. He was made a regular member of the Arab Bureau, which had the effect of taking him away from general military intelligence. To this end, for example, Lawrence made plain his belief that the British should discontinue thinking, as they had been, that Rabegh be used as a landing point for a conventional invasion force. If they were to arrive there in large numbers, he stated firmly, it doubtless would be seen as portending an occupation, in which case the Arab tribesmen would simply say, 'we are betrayed, and scatter to their tents'. Better, advised Lawrence, to 'stiffen the tribal army' through the increased provision of weapons and materiel, and have them fight in the way to which they were accustomed.[77] Accordingly, after having convinced Clayton of this approach, who in turn found agreement with Generals Murray and Wingate, Lawrence was sent back quickly to Yanbo. He departed therefore on 25 November in an uncertain role but with a heavy responsibility: forge a close working relationship with Faisal in order to maximize the likelihood of the Arab Revolt's success. Swiftly, over the preceding weeks, Lawrence's status had changed significantly. He had gone from being a junior deskman at Cairo Military Intelligence, to that of being a prominent voice within the Arab Bureau, to the key – as yet unofficial – British liaison in the Hijaz and Faisal's chief military adviser.

Accordingly, in early December 1916 Lawrence set himself up in Yanbo, in a tumbledown house on the waterfront, and then went immediately to join Faisal at Nahkl Mubarak, located about 50 miles away directly inland. Since Lawrence's first visit, Faisal had moved his camp from Wadi Safra to Nakhl Mubarak because the Turks, under their commander Fakhri Pasha, had left Medina with a view to marching southwards about 200 miles and taking Mecca. Faisal planned to interdict this move. At that moment Faisal's army consisted of a considerable force of about 5,000 men, but six days later on 9 December they would falter badly when Fakhri attacked and scattered them, forcing Faisal to fall back on Yanbo and putting the continued execution of the revolt itself in grave peril. For a few weeks at the end of the year, therefore, it appeared that the Turks, having wrested back the fighting initiative, would be able to continue in this way to victory. If successful in retaking Mecca, it was conceivable that they could end the Arab Revolt altogether back where it had started a mere six months earlier.

But such a course of action was not to be. In the south Ali got his army on the move, which, while no direct threat to Fakhri, caused the Ottoman commander to revise his plans temporarily. In the meantime, Faisal's men recouped and began to press the attack in their usual guerrilla style, while the British employed their preponderant naval and air power to bombard and attack Fahkri's camp. Hence by the New Year 1917 the tide had turned once again in favour of Faisal's Northern Army, as it was being called, and thereby of the Arab Revolt itself. Chastened but unbowed, on 18 January Fakhri had little choice therefore but to direct his army to fall back on its existing stronghold of Medina. For the Arab Revolt the Turkish retreat came as a kind of victory, suggesting a Turkish loss of initiative and its ready assumption by the Arabs instead. Lawrence, having fallen into despair over the course of events just weeks earlier, turned jubilant now, writing to Stewart Newcombe in mid-January that 'this show is splendid: you cannot imagine greater fun for us, greater vexation and fury for the Turks. We win hands down if we keep the Arabs simple ... to add to them heavy luxuries will only wreck their show, and guerilla does it.'[78]

Over the next few months culminating in July with the reverberating victory at Aqaba these words would define the way in which Lawrence, along with a number of key colleagues, would both work with and advise the Arabs as to how best to fight and defeat the Turks. Immediately after Aqaba, as we shall see, Lawrence would meet Allenby in Cairo, the latter having just taken over command of the EEF from General Murray. Both, it may be argued, just then were at the height of their respective powers, which, when combined, would ultimately win the war against the Ottoman Empire in the Middle East.

In January 1917, however, Lawrence was about to plant himself firmly in the Hijaz, and in so doing accept fully the necessity of guerrilla or, as he also termed it, the 'Eastern' way of war.[79] Initially, like other British officers, he had believed Arab troops to be of 'inferior quality' as conventional forces. But Lawrence came to understand more quickly than his peers that within their 'real sphere of guerilla warfare' the Arabs were confident, skilled and lethal.[80] Thus it was up to the British, Lawrence maintained, to assist in deploying them in such an advantageous fashion. This task would fall to a coterie of British operatives, with whom Lawrence would work closely, eventually emerging at their head. Men such as Herbert Garland, Kinahan Cornwallis, William Boyle, Frederick Peake, Pierce Joyce, Alan Dawnay and of course the indispensable Stewart Newcombe were essential to the ultimate success of Faisal's Northern Army, although they were not the only ones. Lawrence liked and respected Garland immediately, for example, as did the Arabs. He was 'an expert on explosives and machinery' and taught Lawrence about demolition, a skill that once learnt he would employ to devastating effect.[81] Lawrence's liking for Faisal, as noted earlier, had been immediate also and was ongoing. Faisal 'is an absolute ripper', he wrote enthusiastically to Newcombe, and 'we are on the best of terms', he followed up to his mother.

Altogether, Lawrence adapted very quickly to the challenges of desert warfare and as such was part of the planning for the next major Arab operation, an advance on the Red Sea port of Wajh, located about 220 miles north of Yanbo. In a meeting with Faisal on 16 January the decision was made to attack the port city, disrupt the Turkish lines of communication and then concentrate on a significant offensive against the Hijaz Railway, which lay about 150 miles to the east. To that end, in a combined operation, Faisal marched a force of about 10,000 troops north from Umm Lajj, while a British troopship from India, the *Hardinge*, put in a little north of Wajh, disgorging about 550 Arab fighters, who advanced on the town under cover of the ship's fire. All went mostly according to plan. The Turkish garrison was quickly, if messily and with much looting, overwhelmed and the town was in the hands of the Arabs by the end of the month.

Once having achieved the goal of taking Wajh, Faisal's advance stalled for the moment, however, and with it the role of the British Military Mission. Having moved north successfully, Faisal's army had forced the Turks to fall back on the Hijaz Railway, their only line of communication with Medina. In order to protect the line properly, a large number of Turkish troops would be required to spread themselves thinly across hundreds of miles of desert. Medina itself might be impregnable for the time being, but the approaches to it had become vulnerable, putting in peril the Turks' ability to keep the city supplied with food and military ordnance. In response to the Turks' apparent predicament, the British position became one of waiting until the optimal moment to attack Medina. As Major Charles Vickery, an artillery officer who worked with Lawrence, believed, success would come at Medina with 'all armies work[ing] on some concerted plan'.[82] However, not everyone thought that this approach was the right one. Indeed, while no one among the British hierarchy of command needed convincing now that the Arabs fought best when deployed as irregulars, the belief persisted that it was only a matter of time until proper training at the hands of British professionals would change them into a conventional and disciplined force capable of the sort of 'concerted' action that was suggested earlier.

For his part, however, Lawrence was never among that group – exemplified by Vickery – who thought that conventional battlefield deployment was the main form of fighting that the Arab Revolt should take. In the immediate aftermath of the fall of Wajh, Lawrence's job had appeared complete. He was preparing, therefore, albeit unwillingly, to return to Egypt. Indeed, by 31 January 1917 he was back in Cairo apprising his mother in general terms that 'things in Arabia are very pleasant' and that 'the war in Arabia is going very well'.[83] Despite the sanguinary nature of these words sent home, Lawrence's part in the Revolt's future execution remained unclear. Even though Faisal was keen to have him as official British liaison, in place of Newcombe whose position it had been officially up until then, for the time being Lawrence found himself back behind a desk in Cairo. To this end, earlier on 25 January, just as Lawrence was about to leave Wajh, Faisal had cabled General Wilson in Jiddah, who in turn had notified the Arab Bureau of his request to keep Lawrence in the field as liaison. In the cable Faisal insisted that Lawrence remain in place since 'he has given such very good assistance' and understood best out of all the British how to deploy the Arab irregulars for maximum effectiveness.[84] Given that Clayton's opinion of Lawrence was as high as that of Faisal's, he complied readily with the desert chieftain's request. As for Newcombe, he did not mind being shifted out of the liaison role as it was one that had never suited him in the way that it would Lawrence. Accordingly, Lawrence was sent back directly to Wajh for what would prove to be the most eventful year of the Arab Revolt.

For Lawrence in 1917, his developing view of the revolt, of the Arabs, of the modern national principle, of the Ottoman Empire, of Britain's strategic position in the Middle East altogether was coloured always by a romantic vision of what was occurring in the region and of his own part in it. He dreamed, as he would write later, 'of hustling into form, while I lived, the new Asia which time was inexorably bringing upon us'.[85] Lawrence's return to the Hijaz, therefore, at the beginning of February was an appointment with destiny in his view. It would give him, as again he wrote to his mother, the opportunity to witness the hated Turkish flag 'disappear from Arabia'. In this hope, he continued, 'on the whole you may write me down a reasonable optimist'. Neither he nor anyone else was sure then what in fact constituted 'Arabia', and he could do no better than to describe the Arab Movement simply as 'a curious thing'.[86] But of his role in it, he was sure nonetheless: 'I do not suppose that any Englishman before ever had such a place,' he wrote confidently. Lawrence was sure, also, that in Faisal he had found the right leader with whom to partner. And despite the persistent complaints by some of his British colleagues about the unruly and undependable nature of the Arab irregular forces, he remained convinced that if harnessed properly they indeed were the men who could defeat the Ottoman Turks in the desert.[87] In large measure, Lawrence's singular belief in the ineluctable destiny of the Arab Revolt is what set him apart from his fellow British officers, which of course is exactly what made him the indispensable one among their number in the eyes of Faisal.

In February of 1917, therefore, the Arab Revolt began now its northward trajectory, pushing up towards Palestine and Syria into territories where European geo-strategic questions – especially as they concerned France – would become much more pressing. If nothing else, Lawrence's earlier encounter with the head of the French Military Mission in Jiddah, Edouard Bremond, had shown the extent to which the French were adamant about their position in the region's future. Now that Lawrence had become privy to the parameters of the Sykes–Picot Agreement, he was doubly concerned about both the ultimate reach of the revolt and of its ramifications for Arab self-determination in the face of the predatory nature of Great Power politics. As he would state bluntly in a note to Mark Sykes after meeting him in May of that year in Wajh, 'we thought you had been generous to the Arabs.' As far as Sykes was concerned, however, Lawrence was indecipherably fey, someone whose dreams of 'complete independence' for the Arabs were unrealistic in the extreme, dreams that would mean for them even greater 'poverty and chaos'. Indeed, the realpolitik of the situation was something that Sykes thought he understood much better than the young and unconventional Arab adviser and military operative. 'Let him consider this', he wrote later in disparagement of Lawrence, 'as he hopes for the people he is fighting for.'[88]

Little could Sykes have known of course that by then Lawrence was in the throes of thinking very much indeed – although not in the way that he did – about whether or not British actions in the Hijaz were being undertaken honourably, or if in fact they (and the French) ultimately were playing the Arabs for dupes. All through the months of February, March and April of 1917, therefore, Lawrence fought both an on-field battle against the Turks and their use of the railway as a lifeline to support their hold over Medina and a diplomatic one against the French desire to see the Arab Revolt contained so as not to jeopardize their post-war designs on Syria and beyond. Indeed, this period, which would lead up to and include the daring Lawrence-led Arab victory at Aqaba in July, might be said to stand at the very heart of the Arab Revolt, at least as far as he was concerned.

Even though the spring of that year brought Lawrence into closer contact with the fighting front as it had developed along the railway line, most of the guerrilla and demolition work that comprised it had been undertaken by Herbert Garland and Stewart Newcombe. Beginning in February, they had struck at Tuweira by derailing a Turkish train and demolishing a bridge, and then had continued elsewhere in the same successful manner. In both of these acts, the British-advised Arab-guerrilla warriors had demonstrated a clear capacity for success against Fakhri Pasha's Turks, now stretched almost to breaking point along over 400 miles of exposed railway line. Lawrence would join his colleagues soon enough in these acts of serial mayhem, but before that he was sent by Faisal to Abdullah's encampment at Wadi Ais, over a hundred miles southeast of Wajh, in order, as Lawrence noted in his diary, 'to explain, reconnoitre, and if possible mine the railway or take a station.'[89]

The five-day journey on camelback would be an exhausting one for Lawrence – his first one in command, and at the new rank of captain, to which he had just been raised. For Captain Lawrence, it would be a journey replete with boils, dysentery and malaria. Exacerbating these physical ills, on just the second night into the trek, a dispute broke out within the dozen members of his Arab escort. They were a mixed crew, and two among them, an Ageyl tribesman and a Moroccan, got into a quarrel, which then escalated quickly and led to the former's murder. In order to avoid deadly and divisive reprisals by the murdered man's outraged Ageyl kinsmen, Lawrence was compelled to assume the distasteful role of executioner – 'which would make civilized man shun justice like a plague', he wrote later – and shot the culprit. Accordingly, the execution of 'Hamed the Moor' became an excruciating episode for Lawrence, as he related it later. Sick with fever and with his hands shaking, it had taken him three shots – chest, wrist and finally neck – to kill the culpable but unfortunate Ageyl tribesman. In so doing, however, and despite the act's repugnance to him, Lawrence had entered fully into the bloody nature of the revolt, even though ironically his first direct victim had been an Arab rather than a Turk.[90]

Carrying out this ad hoc death sentence had appalled Lawrence. But as a rebel leader it was a necessary act, which is how he would choose to view it eventually.

Afterwards, still sick and light-headed, Lawrence was lifted into the saddle of his camel and the 'awful night', as he called it, was left behind.[91] An excruciating few days later, but with his mounted escort pacified now, Abdullah's camp at Wadi Ais was reached. Immediately after reporting to him on the journey and delivering a number of letters from Faisal, Lawrence collapsed into his tent where he remained for the next ten days until he had regained his physical health and moral equilibrium.

The bloody baptism of Hamed's execution would act for Lawrence as a kind of entrepôt to a new phase of action in the Arab Revolt. Advising and strategizing would continue of course to be essential features of his Sharifian remit, but on the immediate horizon was a plan for action against the strategic port of Aqaba, located at the top of the arm that runs west from the northern coast of the Red Sea. Lawrence, along with some others, had been thinking about such a plan for weeks. In its initial iteration the town itself was to be the focus of their attack. However, Lawrence began to argue strongly against this idea as being flawed *unless* the track leading from Aqaba along Wadi Itm to the Ma'an Plateau, and hence to the Hijaz Railway, could be won and held also. That is to say, Aqaba should be attacked from its landward side and not, as would have been conventional, by a naval bombardment. Altogether, the proposed Aqaba plan was as risky as it was daring, but agreement between Lawrence and Faisal over its revised execution was reached around the middle of February. Lawrence chose not to inform Cairo of their deliberations, however, lest the thought of Arabs controlling the key port of Aqaba appear too unsettling in diplomatic terms for the British official mind.

In the meantime, Faisal worked to bind together as much inter-tribal support for the Aqaba plan as he could muster. 'His strong point is handling tribes', Lawrence had written home of Faisal, a short time earlier, 'he has the manner that gets on perfectly with tribesmen, and they all love him.'[92] Such was to prove true because men from the various tribes such as the Howeitat, the Billi, the Beni Atiyeh and others began to enlist in anticipation of the coming raid on the unsuspecting port.

By the time Lawrence had returned to Wajh and consulted Faisal about the coming attack on Aqaba, the prospect of Anglo-French collusion over Syria had become an overwhelming preoccupation for both of them. Even though the Aqaba plan remained front of mind, prevarication over its execution prevailed. This state of affairs was partly of Faisal's own making, and partly it was because of the fact that various British operatives, such as Newcombe, did not agree that it should be staged according to Lawrence's revised plan. Still, discussions and planning for the attack on Aqaba continued apace, not necessarily in a coordinated form, but inexorably leading up to concerted action. For Lawrence, his scheme for approaching Aqaba from inland and therefore away from the Turkish guns pointed seaward – his 'useful diversion', as he called it – found an irrepressible tribal champion in the Howeitat leader, Auda abu Tayi. Auda, a fierce-looking Bedouin with a leathery face, a hooked nose, and a withering reputation for death and destruction, would become one of the heroic leaders of the Arab Revolt beginning at Aqaba.[93] If Faisal was the man Lawrence had come to the desert to seek, then

Auda was his equivalent for his plan to take Aqaba. He was the Howeitat's master type, as Lawrence wrote later of him in great admiration.[94]

As plans for the attack on Aqaba coalesced, hundreds of miles to the north of Wajh the EEF under General Murray, as we saw earlier, had launched two attacks in Sinai already, unsuccessfully so in the second instance. Nevertheless, the EEF now was in place to fight that autumn in what would be the 3rd Battle of Gaza under Allenby as its new commander. For Clayton, the Lawrence-Faisal Aqaba plan – once known by him – did indeed seem too risky (as Lawrence had expected) because it meant the possibility of Aqaba remaining under Arab control after the war, an obvious diplomatic complication. On the other hand, the plan appealed to Clayton in that a move north by the Arab Revolt, if successful, would mean support for the EEF in its planned advance through Palestine and into Syria, and therefore the likelihood of a much stronger British post-war bargaining position vis-à-vis the French. In the event, Clayton, in the grip of a classic dilemma, chose to do nothing. Meanwhile, after having been buffeted himself by conflicting thoughts on the matter, on 9 May a resolute Lawrence decided 'to go my own way, with or without orders' [from Clayton], and proceeded to mount his camel and ride out of Wajh on what would be a long and deceptive arc through some 600 miles of desert until arriving at Aqaba two months later on 6 July.[95] In leaving Wajh Lawrence had with him Auda and some other tribal chieftains, a small group of about 45 camel-men, rifles, ammunition, explosives, food, water and 20,000 gold sovereigns to use for recruitment. The Aqaba plan, which had had a long and mostly secret gestation, was now about to come to fruition and alter both Lawrence's life and the course of the Arab Revolt in ways that would become clear beginning in July.

Lawrence's long turning ride to Aqaba would contain just about every element of desert guerrilla warfare about which he – now routinely dressed in Arab clothing – was quickly making himself expert. Initially, the ride was plodding and uncomfortable physically, marred by the return of the detested boils and of high fever. Then, however, the ride became deadly. Swallowed up by the vastness of the Arabian Desert and baked by the relentless scorching sun of the hottest time of the year, the small raiding party seemed infinitesimal in size and even more vulnerable in that dwarfing and harsh environment than it had been when setting out from the relative coastal comforts of Wajh. Lawrence and his Arab comrades rode hard nonetheless, dynamiting a railway bridge, and – in Lawrence's case – diverting briefly northwards into reconnaissance work around Damascus. He also decided to backtrack – in a scene made famous by David Lean in his epic film, *Lawrence of Arabia* – in order to rescue one of his men, Gasim, who had fallen from his camel unnoticed and would have died if not for Lawrence's willingness to turn around and risk his own life in order to save that of his stricken colleague.

During these first weeks of the Aqaba campaign Lawrence also had become vexed increasingly over what he continued to see as the duplicitous nature of Britain's support for the Arab Revolt. His departure from Wajh had come just two days after his acrimonious meeting there with Mark Sykes. He, as well as others in his circle such as Wilson and Newcombe, believed themselves now to be labouring under a cloud of dishonesty when they thought of what was being asked of the

Arabs in fighting the Ottomans. Later, Lawrence would write of having had no choice but to join this 'conspiracy', which had had the effect on him, he lamented, of 'instead of being proud of what we did together, [being] continually and bitterly ashamed'.[96] The guilt Lawrence felt in this regard was intense, prompting him to write a short message to Clayton which, though left unsent, captures well his state of mind in June of 1917: 'I've decided to go off alone to Damascus, hoping to get killed on the way: for all sakes try and clear up this show before it goes further. We are calling them to fight for us on a lie, and I can't stand it.'[97]

Although it seems that Lawrence had reached the nadir of his campaign existence at this point, he managed nonetheless to emerge from its debilitating grip fairly quickly. Vowing, as he put it later, 'to make the Arab Revolt the engine of its own success, as well as handmaid to our Egyptian campaign', he returned hurriedly from Damascus determined to press on with the Aqaba raid which, if victorious, would plant the Northern Arab Army firmly on the road to Syria, the ultimate goal of the Arab Revolt.[98] By the middle of June, therefore, the small force that had set out from Wajh five weeks earlier had swelled in size to around 700, and would continue to grow so that by the time of its final push on Aqaba in early July it numbered some 2,000 men, comprised mostly of Auda's Howeitat.[99]

In approaching Aqaba, the Arabs surprised the Turks – as was Lawrence's expectation – mustering only light resistance initially. Soon, however, the Turks stiffened their presence along the vital road leading from Ma'an to Aqaba with an infusion of some 500 men. This Turkish defensive force needed to be defeated if the Arab raid on Aqaba was to succeed. Battle ensued therefore, warily at first, but then with increasing ferocity when Auda galvanized his men with a mounted charge that broke and scattered the Turks and resulted in a general slaughter. Lawrence, in the vanguard of this charge upon his swift racing camel, accidentally brained it with an errant pistol shot. The dying beast collapsed underneath him in a thunderous heap of blood and dust and Lawrence, as he wrote later, was 'torn completely from the saddle, [and] sailed grandly through the air for a great distance'.[100] Surviving the mishap however, he, Auda and the victorious Arabs found themselves now just days away from reaching Aqaba. Following the track through Wadi Itm on 4 July for the last few miles they could see that the Turks had begun to abandon their smaller posts, falling back on two larger and better-defended ones. Altogether, the Turks were down now to just 300 desperate and hungry men. A parley was attempted by the Arabs, but at first the doggedly resistant Turks refused to engage. Finally, at the third attempt, they offered to surrender after forty-eight hours if no Turkish relief force had come by then. Rebuffed in this way, the Arab forces grew insistent on a battlefield victory. Hungry, unruly and full of enmity for the hated Turk, a final attack by them now seemed likely. In the event, when it came the attack on Aqaba proved to be spectacular and overwhelming. Accordingly, the outgunned and outmanned Turks chose to surrender on the morning of 6 July, and with it Aqaba was duly given up to the Arabs. At the last, in a climactic rush into the now-abandoned strategic port, jubilant Arabs galloped through its dusty streets and Lawrence, in a moment of surpassing joy along with many of his compatriots, 'splashed into the sea'.[101]

On that July morning at the very moment that the Arab victory at Aqaba was being celebrated, the newly arrived General Allenby was barely a week into his command of the EEF. Already, as noted earlier, he had undertaken a thorough tour of the Palestine front during which he had been 'impressed by the soldierly spirit and efficiency of the troops'.[102] But, he wrote to his wife on 9 July from his compartment in the special train used for the occasion, 'the Bedouin are not very friendly to strangers, British or Turk'.[103] Allenby's first impressions of his new command were about to change, however, because he was on the verge of hearing directly from Lawrence that a British-advised Bedouin band of Arab irregulars had just forced the surrender of the key Turkish-held port of Aqaba on the Red Sea. Neither Allenby nor anyone else at EEF Headquarters in Cairo, to which he had returned shortly after his inspection tour of Palestine, was aware yet of the fall of Aqaba to the Arabs. And they would not be made aware of it until the spectacle of an exhausted but victorious Lawrence – attired still in Arab dress – arrived in the Egyptian capital on 10 July. He had left Aqaba almost immediately after its occupation and after a forty-nine-hour camel trek across the desert had arrived at Suez. From there he had cabled a short report to Clayton in Cairo, and then boarded a train to take him the rest of the way to the city. As soon as Lawrence had arrived in Cairo he went to see Clayton at the Arab Bureau. The shock of Lawrence's arrival – both his bedraggled appearance and his detailed news of the victory – astounded Clayton, but the reception given to his own man fresh back from the victorious battlefield was a warm one nonetheless. Clayton had been out of touch with Lawrence since the Aqaba caper had got underway two months earlier, without his knowledge or approval it will be recalled, and now here was the newly minted hero himself dressed in flowing robes and looking like an Arab chieftain riding on the welcome tide of triumph.

Within hours of Lawrence's arrival in Cairo, news of the Arab victory at Aqaba had gone round Allenby's General Headquarters, and Lawrence's role in the attack was understood to have been at its heart. His appearance – 'my Arab get-up' – had become 'publicly exciting', he noted somewhat ruefully later (Figure 5). But it was three days before he could purchase anything else to wear, since the 'moths had corrupted all my former store', he complained.[104] Thus it was as 'Lawrence of Arabia', at least in style of dress, that he met Allenby for the very first time. Already having been told of Allenby's 'excellence', Lawrence was summoned to meet the new commander-in-chief on 12 July. Just a few days earlier, Allenby had written to General William Robertson, the CIGS in London, to say 'that a success here, on a considerable scale, would raise all the Arabs of Syria in our cause'.[105] Now, in the form of Lawrence, he had just such a victory. Lawrence's account of his initial meeting with Allenby is so rich in pithy detail, a characteristic of his authorship of *Seven Pillars of Wisdom*, that it is well worth quoting him at length:

> It was a comic interview, for Allenby was physically large and confident, and
> morally so great that the comprehension of our littleness came slow to him. He
> sat in his chair looking at me – not straight, as his custom was, but sideways,
> puzzled. He was newly from France, where for years he had been a tooth of

Figure 5   T. E. Lawrence in Arabia, 1917. As Allenby would have first known him.

the great machine grinding the enemy. He was full of Western ideas of gun power and weight – the worst training for our war – but, as a cavalryman, was already half persuaded to throw up the new school, in this different world of Asia … yet he was hardly prepared for anything so odd as myself – a little bare-footed silk-skirted man offering to hobble the enemy by his preaching if given stores and arms and a fund of two hundred thousand sovereigns to convince and control his converts. Allenby could not make out how much was genuine performer and how much was charlatan. The problem was working behind his eyes, and I left him unhelped to solve it. He did not ask many questions, nor talk much, but studied the map and listened to my unfolding of Eastern Syria and its inhabitants. At the end he put up his chin and said quite directly: 'Well, I will do for you what I can', and that ended it. I was not sure how far I had caught him; but we learned gradually that he meant exactly what he said; and that what General Allenby could do was enough for his very greediest servant.[106]

According to Lawrence, writing later about the change of command in Egypt, the departure of General Murray and 'Allenby's coming had re-made the English'.[107] This claim was not hyperbolic, as events of the succeeding months would show, and manifestly so when applied to Lawrence himself. Allenby did not comment on his impression of Lawrence at the time although later, as we shall see, he would praise him readily. But Lawrence's recent astonishing achievement at Aqaba was clear to him nonetheless, spurring Allenby's own swift action in response. On 16

July therefore, he cabled General Robertson spelling out Lawrence's proposals 'for Arab co-operation against Syrian railway, which he is confident could be carried out'.[108] Indeed, other members of the War Cabinet, such as General Smuts, were alive already to the strategic possibilities emanating from the victory at Aqaba. As he put it in a note to Robertson, 'this conflagration on the flank might materially assist Allenby's advance, and create great confusion for the Turk'.[109]

Key to Lawrence's proposals made to Allenby during their meeting on 12 July was that Aqaba now should replace Wajh as Faisal's base of operations, the effect of which would be to turn the right flank of Allenby's coming general offensive into an Arab wing. Lawrence had said the same thing to Clayton. Indeed, as he recounted later, he told Clayton that 'Aqaba had been taken on my plan by my effort. The cost of it had fallen on my brains and nerves. There was much more I felt inclined to do, and capable of doing – if he thought I had earned the right to be my own master'.[110] Clayton agreed readily with Lawrence, and with the promise of both money and supplies, he returned emboldened to Aqaba. There is no doubt given what they had heard of Aqaba that both Clayton and Allenby thought Lawrence to be exactly the right man to undertake a railway war against the Turks. Indeed, Allenby had begun already to make just such a case persuasively to Robertson: 'I consider that the advantage offered by the Arabs' co-operation in lines proposed by Lawrence are of such importance that every effort should be made to reap full benefit therefrom.' Such benefit, continued Allenby, forecasting the coming comprehensive push by the EEF into Palestine, 'may cause a collapse of the Turkish campaigns in Syria and the Hedjaz [*sic*] and produce far reaching political as well as military results'.[111] Here, encapsulated was the Palestine campaign in prospect, which, as we shall see, would culminate swiftly in the capture of Jerusalem just a few months later in December.

In their July meeting Lawrence had advised Allenby that in order to maximize the participation of the Arab irregulars before they melted away and returned to their homes for the camel grazing season the railway campaign should begin by no later than mid-September. As long as the promised money and supplies came through – the former of which had to be, 'in gold', paper was no good, Allenby requested of the War Office in late-July – then the next phase of the Arab Revolt could commence in earnest.[112] And so it did. But almost at that very moment, when Allenby had just begun to anticipate close command of the campaign, he was forced to absorb a stunning blow emotionally. Just four days after his War Office request he was informed on 30 July that his son, Michael, now nineteen years old and, as we have seen earlier, a lieutenant in the Royal Horse Artillery and a youthful winner of the Military Cross, had suffered a fatal head wound the day before while fighting near Nieuport in Flanders (Figure 6). He had died five hours later without regaining consciousness.[113] Upon receiving the telegram containing this devastating news, Allenby finished immediately a letter to Mabel begun a couple of days earlier while on yet another tour of the Palestine front, in which he had told her lightly that 'most of the people ... look like Biblical characters. Face, dress, everything like pictures from the Bible. Keen, handsome faces; picturesque, Arab dress.' He proceeded now to complete the letter in agony over the loss of

Figure 6 Allenby's only son, Michael, as an eighteen-year-old lieutenant with the Royal Horse Artillery. He was killed in Belgium in July of 1917: 'Michael is always in my thoughts, and every thought of him brings a happy memory.'

their son. 'I wish I could be with you', he lamented, 'but I know how brave you are; and you will be strong to bear this awful blow. You and Michael fill my thoughts, and I feel very near to you both. Every remembrance of him is a joy.'[114] The letter goes on at some length and is a heartbroken father's paean to a dead son, a loss of course shared by countless other parents in the war. For Allenby, the death of his only child was a psychic wound that would remain ever-present in its pain for the rest of his life.[115]

By the end of August, meanwhile, Aqaba had duly replaced Wajh as the new base for the Arab Revolt. During the summer Lawrence had travelled back and forth between Arabia and Cairo in anticipation of the coming campaign, keeping Allenby up to date on his various activities: 'this morning I saw Captain Lawrence', Allenby cabled to Robertson on 8 August, 'just back from Akaba. He reports well on the situation there, and has schemes for further aggression against the Hedjaz railway within the next week or so. He has hopes of keeping the Arabs at this work of harassing the Turkish communications till I am ready to move'.[116] Earlier, in July, having met with Faisal and then, for the first time, Sharif Hussein, Lawrence had felt keenly the weight of the British 'having made him [Hussein] a ruling power', as he wrote to his mother. 'We will have to help him and his sons. … I do hope we play them fair'.[117] Hussein, although not having met Allenby, had heard of the death of his son and sent him a message of condolence on 18 August, which was the same day that 800 Arab troops arrived in Aqaba; within a week, another 800 had joined them.[118]

A full-scale Arab Revolt now was at hand and on 7 September Lawrence set out for the Ma'an plateau with the key Mudawwara station, manned by the Turks, as his main target. Later in the war, in August 1918, Mudawwara would be attacked successfully, almost putting a capstone on the desert war. For now, however, this initial expedition, although amounting to not much more than a pinprick, marked the commencement of the autumn campaign. For the next three months the Arab forces, acting under the command of Faisal but with the close advice and decisive action of Lawrence, would buttress Allenby's broader front to the North. Turkish casualties piled up, at a rate far exceeding that of the Arabs. 'This killing and killing of Turks is horrible', Lawrence wrote to a friend at the time, [but] 'you have done hundreds in the same way before and must do hundreds more if you can'.[119] Despite complaining in the same letter that 'I'm not going to last out this game much longer; nerves going and temper wearing thin', the autumn campaign would see the railway war intensify, with all of Lawrence's guerrilla instincts and accumulated expertise coming to the fore.[120] The weapons, explosives and vehicles used – the Lewis Light Machine Gun, the Vickers Gun and the Screw Gun; the Short Magazine Lee-Enfield rifle, known as 'Old Smelly'; the 'Tulip Mine', designed and named by Lawrence and Herbert Garland because upon detonation it went up like a flower; the Rolls-Royce Armoured Car; as well as other forms of equipment and ordnance, including the BEC2 airplane – all of them would be employed with devastating effect against the Turks and the Hijaz Railway throughout this period. Lawrence's idea of isolating the Turks rather than mounting an all-out assault on their Medina stronghold would prove to be a stroke of military genius, and it marked him out as a guerrilla thinker and leader of rare brilliance.[121]

Well, it was therefore that by 3 October Allenby could write to Mabel and say that the 'Arab rebellion is spreading'.[122] Indeed, it was beginning to gallop by this point, in line with Allenby's prediction, made to Robertson back in July, that 'Lawrence's activities among the Arabs promise great things'.[123] Three months later on 17 October, just two weeks before he would command the 3rd Battle of Gaza, Allenby informed Robertson again that, 'Lawrence is doing good work on the Hedjaz [*sic*] railway'. He went on to add, in light of increasing diplomatic pressure from the French for an on-the-ground presence of their own, that 'the fact is that only Lawrence can deal with the Arabs effectively'.[124] Certainly, in military terms, Allenby would never doubt that his estimation of Lawrence in this regard was true and it would prevail for the next year until Damascus ultimately had been won.

In the meantime, with the Arab Revolt continuing apace although without scoring any major victories yet since Aqaba, Allenby's big push on Gaza was about to commence. Faisal, for one, awaited its outcome with great anticipation. 'Heroic leader and dispenser of victory', he wrote to Allenby, 'May God keep him.'[125] To that end, throughout the early autumn Allenby had been in constant communication with General Robertson about a much-needed infusion of both troops and artillery from the fighting front in France. Given Robertson's prevailing view of the relative unimportance of the Palestine campaign to British strategic policy in the war, he was somewhat reluctant to give Allenby everything for which he asked. Indeed, Robertson insisted that he could not supply Allenby with what he needed for the big offensive until at least November, which would delay Allenby's planned attack by two to three months.[126] Nevertheless, Robertson's slowness to act did not mean refusal, and in supplying Allenby ultimately with much of what he needed he would defer properly to the wishes of the prime minister. After all, such is what had been promised to Allenby by Lloyd George back in June, and he 'is most anxious you should have all you want', wrote Robertson.[127] Later, he reported that 'I have done my best' to reinforce and equip the EEF, and in response Allenby thanked him and informed his superior that he had settled firmly on a plan to 'strike rapidly at Beer Sheba, while holding the enemy's right by an attack on Gaza'.[128] Earlier, General Murray had identified Beer Sheba (today's Be'er Sheva) as 'the Turks' vulnerable point', and Allenby, who agreed with his predecessor's assessment, 'now stood poised to exploit it.'[129]

After months of planning, preparation and 'impressing on my commanders the importance of swift movement', Allenby gave the order for an intense and continuous bombardment of the entrenched coastal fortress of Gaza to begin on 27 October.[130] The Turks, having researched the fighting style of the new British commander-in-chief, assumed that the attack on Gaza would proceed in the way that it did.[131] But the sheer scale of the attack's ferocity was breathtaking nonetheless. At Allenby's command, the sky over Sinai lit up instantly, and with it below came a cacophonous thunder produced by over 200 heavy guns that would go on for hours.[132] The 3rd Battle of Gaza, the largest battle ever fought in the Middle East until that time, had begun and it would last for almost two weeks before a general British advance was made on 7 November, which secured the town in light of the almost complete withdrawal from it by the Ottomans.[133] The preceding days had seen a terrific fight between some 80,000 British, Anzac and Indian troops and almost 50,000 Turks, known collectively as the *Yilderim* ('lightning') Army Group under their German commander, General Friedrich Kress von Kressenstein. Until the Ottomans' Gaza to Beer Sheba fortified line was breached it had stretched across some 60 miles of sand, scrub and hill, serrated by a series of fieldworks built about a mile apart and equipped with artillery and machine guns. This line barred the way into Palestine, and if Allenby's strategic objective of pushing the offensive all the way to Syria was to be achieved it had to be broken through first and Gaza won.

Four days into the attack, on 31 October or 'Z-Day', at the Beer Sheba end of the line in the unforgiving Negev desert, the EEF's Desert Mounted Corps made a stirring victory against the Turks. Comprised of the Australian Mounted Division, the Anzac Mounted Division, the Yeomanry Mounted Division and the Imperial Camel Corps, and under the command of Lieutenant General Harry Chauvel, an Australian, the DMC scored a singular triumph. After having misled the Turks into thinking that no attack was coming at Beer Sheba through the daring spy-craft of the EEF's chief intelligence officer, Colonel Richard Meinertzhagen – the so-called lost haversack ruse of bloodstained false orders falling into enemy hands – the DMC attacked after an undetected overnight waterless march.[134] The gamble was great, but in the form of a mounted bayonet charge by the Australian 4th and 12th Light Horse Regiments, victory was achieved in spectacular fashion by their galloping 'under the guns' and taking the ancient town, reputed to be where Abraham and Isaac had lived and containing the vital wells dug originally by them.[135] As a cavalryman, and therefore in fulfilment of his demand for 'swift movement', Allenby was especially pleased with events at Beer Sheba, although initially he understated the victory's importance in a letter to Mabel on 1 November by calling it a 'smart little battle'. Still, in the Anzacs having made a '25 mile night march, to turn the Turks' flank … all went well. I can't tell you the half of it.'[136]

Once Allenby and the EEF had secured victory all along the Gaza to Beer Sheba line over the next week – 'Von K. was deceived' – he wrote exultantly to Robertson, the drive north to Jerusalem could commence, and with it the fulfilment of Lloyd George's charge to Allenby that he present the Holy City as a gift to the British people by Christmas.[137] Steadily, therefore, with the battle 'in full swing', over the next month the Turks were pushed back by the steady pounding of Allenby's troops and guns.[138] As a number of congratulatory messages over the Battle of Beer Sheba were received by Allenby – 'your success delights me', wrote the former British commander-in-chief Lord French; 'you have done splendidly', added Robertson; you have 'my unbounded admiration', praised Wingate – he continued to drive the EEF hard towards the Holy City.[139] The Bull 'was loose', and a great victory was in the offing. 'We've had a successful day'; 'the Turks have taken an awful hammering'; 'I hear that some parts of the battlefield are carpeted with dead Turks'; 'the flying men are having the time of their lives'; such were a few of Allenby's many messages both to Robertson and to his wife during these days of victory and elation. Accordingly, by 21 November, with 'my battle go[ing] on pretty well', he wrote to Mabel, Allenby had moved his headquarters north of Gaza and into the Judean Hills.[140] 'We are fighting our way up' to Jerusalem, he continued grandly to her, 'by the road taken by Richard Coeur de Lion; and we have reached about the point at which he turned back.'[141]

But there would be no turning back by Allenby of course. In early December, therefore, he had come to within striking distance of Jerusalem and was in correspondence constantly with Robertson about the form that its anticipated British occupation should take. The fighting over the previous few weeks, although successful, had been hard and a trio of final battles would be required in order to take the city. Allenby had seen enough of Ottoman resistance and fortitude to retain a healthy respect for the enemy.[142] He was not surprised, therefore, that they continued to fight strongly, especially now in the extraordinarily rocky and steep terrain around Jerusalem. The Ottomans won the first of these battles, while the British took the second. On 8 December, the third and final battle for Jerusalem took place with the 60th (London) Division overwhelming the city's Ottoman defenders, although many of them were able to escape in retreat and would soon enough therefore be ready to renew the fight. But as of the next day, Jerusalem had

Gen. Allenby leaving after the reading of the Proclamation.

Figure 7 Allenby outside the Jaffa Gate leaving the Old City of Jerusalem after delivering his irenic Proclamation to its residents, 11 December 1917.

been surrendered by the Ottomans and belonged to Allenby and the EEF. Later, he would write that the Palestine campaign owed its success to 'thorough preparation ... deception, and concentration of strength', and that as commander you need to 'trust your luck'.[143] The moment of victory was satisfyingly historic, 'a great feat', as Allenby called it, even though the city's formal act of surrender by its Arab mayor was both confused and anticlimactic.[144]

Two days later on 11 December, Allenby arrived at Jerusalem's Jaffa Gate on horseback, dismounted and strode through it to the ancient city's Citadel where he read aloud the Proclamation of martial law (which was translated into French, Hebrew, Arabic, Russian, Greek and Italian, and guaranteed religious liberty to all) that made the British occupation of Jerusalem official (Figure 7).[145] The memory of Kaiser Wilhelm II having come through the same gate almost twenty years before – indeed, having demanded that the gate be widened in order to accommodate his entourage – was expunged now by the magnanimous figure of the victorious British commander-in-chief as pedestrian. Walking in train behind Allenby was an excited Lawrence, having just come in haste from the desert and greatly pleased to have been included in the impressive procession. Still, Allenby's success at Jerusalem, which had been achieved without any direct Arab assistance, meant that the chief cause for which Lawrence had been fighting was diminished somewhat by comparison. To Robertson, just three days earlier, Allenby had written that even though the Arab situation continued to be promising, with the Hijaz Railway harried constantly and Medina isolated, since Aqaba 'I confess I am so far somewhat disappointed at their contribution'.[146] At this point, Lawrence might well have agreed. Even though he would write later that Allenby's entry into Jerusalem was the 'supreme moment of the war', it was undertaken with a keen sense of strategic frustration and personal inadequacy brought on by the knowledge that the British moment of victory at Jerusalem now required a similar Arab one at Damascus for which 'the ceremony of the Jaffa Gate gave me a new determination'. The New Year 1918 would provide Lawrence, of course, with just such an opportunity.[147]

Chapter 5

DAMASCUS GAINED AND VICTORY WON, 1918

For the first few days after Jerusalem's fall the weather was 'bright and fine', Allenby wrote to Mabel, and so the sun was high overhead when he strode through the Jaffa Gate into the old city at 12 noon on 11 December 1917.[1] Walking into Jerusalem in advance of reading out the official proclamation of its occupancy was suggested by the British government in an attempt to play down the idea of Allenby having 'conquered' Jerusalem. Prominent in this way of thinking was the inimitable image of Kaiser Wilhelm having entered the city in 1898 on a state visit to Palestine while sitting astride a white charger, conjuring intentionally images of Frederick Barbarossa and German participation in the Crusades. In the event, Allenby's victory was presented in the press as the culmination of a modern Crusade anyhow, nowhere more evocatively than in *Punch* magazine.[2] Moreover, from around Britain and across the empire people wrote him to express, as one enamoured woman from Toronto put it, that 'your victory is a wonderful gift to humanity'.[3] Allenby himself, however, did not spend too much time thinking about the fall of Jerusalem in this grandiose way – notwithstanding his reference to Richard the Lionheart made earlier – and was pleased to contrast his modest entry into the city with that of the despised Kaiser a generation earlier. To this end also, in reference to the entry that Christ had made into Jerusalem on Palm Sunday, he noted to Mabel, 'It was said then, that a better man than he [the Kaiser] had walked into the city.'[4]

On the steps of Jerusalem's Citadel, surrounded by British officers, diplomats, religious worthies and thousands of residents of the city, Allenby then read out the official Proclamation, guaranteeing to its hearers under British military rule their safety and livelihoods. As well, respect for all of Jerusalem's holy places, Muslim, Christian and Jewish, was to be maintained assiduously.[5] The tour through the city that followed, however, and despite Allenby's protestations to the contrary, saw him met as a liberator. 'Great enthusiasm' was shown, he remarked, and joyful women reached spontaneously for his outstretched hand in order to kiss it.[6] Lloyd George, naturally, was extremely pleased by Allenby's victorious achievement, with the War Cabinet cabling immediately to him its congratulations 'on the capture of Jerusalem which is an event of historic and world-wide significance'.[7] For having done so, Allenby would be awarded the Knight Grand Cross of the Most Distinguished Order of Saint Michael and Saint George (GCMG). 'I am getting', he wrote home happily, 'gradually, a chest full of ribbons.'[8]

Altogether, the first few days following the city's fall were carnival-like, with much celebrating and broad endorsement of the EEF's presumed mission of driving out the Ottomans altogether from Arab lands. Still, a few discordant notes could be heard from some Arabs who wondered what the victory might mean for them given the newly enhanced status of the Jews, a reality made that much sharper by the triumphalist 'Crusader' coverage. Meanwhile, the French – Francois Georges-Picot had been among those who had marched in Allenby's procession – were uneasy about the robust presence in Palestine of the British military. Picot had queried Allenby directly about the possibility of establishing French civil authority in Palestine, now that the Ottomans had gone. But Allenby had rejected this idea firmly, as Lawrence recounted later admiringly, with his 'chin coming forward (in the way we loved).'[9] Jews, however, both in Jerusalem and elsewhere, were ecstatic with the victory. To them, Allenby's taking of Jerusalem meant that the Balfour Declaration, which had promised British government support for a Jewish national homeland in Palestine and upon which the ink was barely dry since it had been published only on 2 November, was evidently coming to pass, and soon. An additional complication in the Holy Land was the impact that Russia's recently commenced Bolshevik Revolution was having on international affairs. In an intentionally provocative move, the country's new leadership had chosen to reveal the contents of the Sykes–Picot Agreement at the end of November in a highly publicized attempt to denounce the use of secret treaties and embarrass the Allies from whose fighting ranks Lenin had pledged to remove his country.

For the moment T. E. Lawrence was caught up in Jerusalem's heady atmosphere too, which would continue into the New Year. And it would be here in Jerusalem, at the end of February that the American publicist Lowell Thomas first met him. Having seen an obviously European young man in Arab dress walking in the street accompanied by a group of Bedouin, Thomas later asked Ronald Storrs, appointed recently as the British military governor of Jerusalem, for the unknown person's identity. No sooner had Thomas asked the question, than Storrs opened the door to a room adjoining his office and, pointing to a young man seated there reading a book, said: 'I want you to meet Colonel Lawrence, the Uncrowned King of Arabia.'[10] Lawrence may well have been flattered by Storrs's comment for he considered the oriental secretary to be a star, 'the first of us', as he wrote later, 'the most brilliant Englishman in the Near East'.[11] For his part, Thomas had found the man (and the cause) that he had been seeking in coming to the Middle East a month earlier at the behest of US president Woodrow Wilson in order to build support by Americans for the war through the use of inspirational propaganda. Equally, Lawrence was pleased to have been given an outlet by which to publicize the Arab Revolt.[12]

But in December of 1917 that first meeting with Thomas was still two months in the future and Lawrence, despite the celebratory atmosphere in Jerusalem, remained much in the slough of despond. His low state of mind owed itself partly to the challenge of ensuring that the Arab Revolt did not become subsumed by the success of the much larger EEF campaign. But in considerably greater part it was because Lawrence continued to suffer the after-effects of a recent attack during which he had been beaten severely and assaulted. This searing event had occurred on 20–21 November while Lawrence had been held captive briefly by the Turks in the garrison town of Deraa in Syria during a reconnaissance mission.[13]

The Deraa spying episode and its violent outcome – a mission engaged in by Lawrence when he was in the throes of continuing to believe that both he and the British were acting fraudulently in leading the Arab Revolt – would turn out to be no less than the hinge upon which would hang the rest of his life. Much has been written about this event, beginning reluctantly by Lawrence himself and then by a number of others. Controversially, some commentators and historians have chosen to doubt its veracity altogether, such as the late Palestinian-American cultural and literary critic Edward Said.[14] Such doubts have been shown to be without foundation, however, and in Said's case served mainly to buttress his own anti-'Orientalist' ideology. Lawrence would include the violent episode of his capture at the hands of the Turks in *Seven Pillars of Wisdom*, at the end of which he laments 'how in Deraa that night the citadel of my integrity was lost'.[15] Fulsomely, in 1924, he wrote to his close friend and correspondent, Charlotte Shaw: 'About that night. I shouldn't tell you, because decent men don't talk about such things. … For fear of being hurt, or rather to earn five minutes respite from a pain which drove me mad, I gave away the only possession we are born into the world with – our bodily integrity.'[16] Having come to regard this event as 'an unforgiveable matter, an irrecoverable position', its psychological impact on Lawrence cannot be overstated and the decisions about how he would live the rest of his life, as we shall see, would be marked decisively by the long shadow cast by that dark night in Deraa.

In Jerusalem, however, in December, such troubles could be left behind, for the moment at least. The immediate victory celebrations over, both Allenby and Lawrence – 'Jerusalem cheered all of us mightily,' the latter wrote to a friend – hoped to return directly to the business at hand – that is, of continuing to pursue at speed the campaign against the Ottoman Turks as it moved towards its highly anticipated climax.[17] However, the swiftness and success of the action of the preceding weeks were not to be matched during the months that came immediately after the fall of Jerusalem, at least not for Allenby. Although he was pleased with the 'good performance by my troops', which had completed the 'isolation of Jerusalem' and gained him 'elbow room' around the city, as reported to Captain C. W. Battine, the trusted war correspondent of the *Daily Telegraph*, Allenby had recognized also that no offensive move against the retreating Turks could come before at least mid-February in order that sufficient supplies and more men might be brought into theatre.[18] The latter point especially would be a significant challenge because of the size of the Allied manpower increases projected to be required in order to confront the enormous German offensive to come that spring in France. Moreover, Allenby's instructions from London as to the ultimate scope of the Palestine campaign remained unclear, although 'I hope' – as the commander-in-chief of the Imperial General Staff, General Robertson, would write to him on 2 January 1918 – 'for a decision before long'.[19] Meanwhile, for his part Lawrence was to return to the field immediately, which meant reporting to Allenby in order to receive instructions about where to go and what to do.

In order to win the rest of Palestine and then Syria, Allenby had centred his strategic plan on Jericho, about which he informed Lawrence during their meeting at his General Headquarters on 12 December. In the meantime, however, before he could move on Jericho, Allenby told Lawrence to direct the Arab forces to focus their energies on occupying the region around the southern end of the Dead Sea in order to make it impossible for the Turks to regroup and attack his troops from the rear. Second, and as a corollary, Allenby told him that the Arabs were to put an end to Ottoman boat traffic on the Dead Sea itself in order to interdict their supply network. Lawrence agreed, and then suggested to Allenby that during March the Arabs should go one better and fight to gain control of the whole area between the Dead Sea and the Hijaz Railway, a region dominated geographically by the Mountains of Moab. If done well, Lawrence pointed out persuasively, then the EEF could be supplied by rail from Palestine, and the Arab forces would be able to move up to the north end of the Dead Sea and therefore be poised for a general advance on Syria that might come, if approved by London, sometime later in 1918.[20] The latter point, of course, was of vital importance to both Lawrence and Faisal. The Arab Army of regulars, regardless of the great disparity in its current size of 2,000 troops versus Allenby's 95,000, must, they believed, be found in Syria at the end of the campaign working in concert with the EEF if Arab nationalist aspirations were to be recognized properly. Accordingly, the Sharifian forces' commander, the ex-Ottoman officer Jafar Pasha al-Askari, liaised closely with Lieutenant Colonel Pierce Joyce, the head of the British Military Mission at Aqaba in order to try and coordinate anticipated operations. Meanwhile, Arab regular forces would be supplemented by Bedouin tribesmen. The Bedouin, as was their wont, would come and go depending on the season and on the ready provision of payment. But, above all, they could be counted upon to remain loyal to the charismatic Lawrence himself. Together therefore it was hoped by Faisal and Lawrence that Allenby's troops and the Sharifian Army would end up on track for a parallel arrival at Damascus, if not the possibility of the Arabs arriving there first.

A couple of days after his meeting with Allenby in December, Lawrence went back to Cairo for a brief stay followed by a return to Aqaba. It seems that the shock and misery of the recent Deraa experience had been compartmentalized psychologically by Lawrence, at least for the time being, and buoyed by both the Jerusalem celebrations and his positive meeting with Allenby he was keen to re-enter the fray. 'The situation out here is full of surprise turns', he wrote to his parents on 14 December, 'and my finger is one of those helping to mix the pie. An odd life, but it pleases me, on the whole.'[21] The previous six months had worked to make Lawrence acutely aware that his role in the British Middle East campaign had become much more significant than he might have imagined earlier, the realization of which had prompted him to inform a friend that 'after being a sort of a king-maker one will not be allowed to go digging quietly again. Nuisance.'[22] Accordingly, Lawrence back in Aqaba on Christmas Day was poised for renewed action under Allenby's command. Lawrence's increasingly prominent position in the Arab Revolt – 'rumour gradually magnified my importance', he wrote self-deprecatingly later – meant that he was now a wanted man by the Turks.[23] In response therefore, after forming a personal bodyguard of about ninety mostly Ageyl tribesmen: 'cut-throats; but they cut throats only to my order', he commented grimly, Lawrence set out north on 10 January 1918 for Aba al-Lissan, and then onwards to Tafila.[24] The next few months would see Lawrence on the move constantly, pushing man and camel as hard as he could, endeavouring to make a success of what would be the third and final phase of the war in the desert. His Ageyl bodyguard, 'dressed like a bed of tulips, in every colour but white; for that was my constant wear', Lawrence made it his mission to fulfil that which had been assigned to him by Allenby and in the process position the Sharifian forces for maximum impact at the point of the anticipated complete allied victory, whenever that might be.[25]

As the Arab Revolt percolated in the unforgiving country to the south, Allenby, to the north at his newly established General Headquarters at Bir Salem on the Jaffa to Jerusalem road, worked steadily to consolidate and ready the EEF's position for what he envisioned to be a major offensive against that which remained of Ottoman resistance.[26] Doing so was no easy task, however, because their resistance proved to be fierce and dogged and would, ultimately, keep the EEF in the field until October of 1918. Nevertheless, by the end of December and compliments of a brace of battles, Allenby had pushed forward north of Jerusalem and had established a frontline extending from Jaffa on the Mediterranean coast, to Jericho near the Jordan River, which was targeted to be its eastern nexus-point. Meanwhile, however, the ongoing struggle in London over the strategic direction of the war meant that Allenby had to continue to navigate the shoals of political horse-trading, which had the effect of slowing him down in the field. Greater clarity was brought to this question on 21 January when the Supreme War Council – an inter-allied body established by Lloyd George in November that went some distance in transcending the War Cabinet's divisions – submitted for consideration by the government a document called Joint Note 12. In unmistakable terms this document recommended strongly that the Allies should prioritize 'the annihilation of the Turkish Armies and the collapse of Turkish resistance'.[27] This recommendation fits perfectly with the prime minister's expansive strategic view; indeed, he had already despatched General J. C. Smuts, one of the War Council's members, to Egypt whose tour – including spending time with Allenby – saw him endorse the primacy of the campaign in Palestine, as well as its enlargement to include Syria, possibly as early as that May. In the event, Smuts's report, issued on 1 March, put an official imprimatur on what had taken place already. It signalled also Lloyd George's triumph over Robertson, who had resigned by then as CIGS, in favour of Sir Henry Wilson, and it opened up the unfettered completion of the EEF's campaign in Palestine and Syria. Of course, the irony of the situation became clear in that by the end of March the Germans had launched their long-anticipated Michael Offensive on the Western Front, which spearheaded their even larger Spring Offensive in what would prove to be a final push to win the war before American soldiers could enter the line in great numbers. Such was the need for additional Allied troops to withstand the German onslaught that thousands of Allenby's regulars were duly transferred to France, proving Robertson right after all. Nevertheless, Lloyd George – who remained committed wholly to liberating the Holy Land – was able to prevail in the moment, which had cost Robertson his job. 'I am today handing over my duties to General Wilson', he wrote to Allenby on 18 February, 'and wish to thank you sincerely for the cordial and efficient manner in which you have co-operated with me and assisted me. Good luck and God speed.'[28]

Robertson was right in citing cordiality as the mark of his relations with Allenby. Their correspondence had never been less than respectful. But in Wilson, Allenby had gained a chief whose views on the campaign in the Middle East accorded exactly with those of his own. The military disaster in Mesopotamia, centred on Kut as we saw earlier, was cited by Smuts and agreed by Wilson as a sobering reason for transferring two infantry divisions and a cavalry brigade to Palestine, which, together with a division of Indian troops from France, would bring Allenby's troop strength up to what he believed was the required level in order to achieve victory. In addition, a Canadian construction battalion was to be sent, with the promise of a second one to come in due course.[29] Altogether, the question of sufficient troop numbers had been a constant preoccupation for Allenby, and now, happily, it had been answered.[30]

As the politics of the Palestine campaign continued apace in the run-up to renewed action, out in the field Lawrence girded himself for an attack on the Ottoman stronghold of Tafila, located about a hundred miles south of Amman. For the first time working together with the young Prince Zeid, their actions beginning on 25 January proved initially to be a rousing success: 'Zeid beside me clapped his hands with joy at the beautiful order of our plan unrolling in the frosty redness of the setting sun', as Lawrence recalled the scene later. Important too, the operation fulfilled Allenby's first instruction of the Arabs moving to occupy the region south of the Dead Sea that he had made in December.[31] At Tafila, the Turks suffered hundreds of dead and wounded, while Arab casualties remained relatively light and many enemy guns were captured.

However, the winter weather at Tafila was consistently snowy and cold and together with Zeid's immature actions later, as we shall see, the initial stirring victory would prove impossible to maintain. But that disappointment still lay some weeks away. Elsewhere, a few days later at Mezra, located on the east side of the Dead Sea, a second key success was had by another Lawrence-inspired Arab force. Here, the Ottomans' naval base was destroyed making it impossible for them to re-supply their garrisons along the eastern shore. All told, therefore, by the end of January the Arab Revolt had succeeded in doing exactly what it had been charged to do by Allenby during his mid-December meeting with Lawrence in Jerusalem.

However, as noted earlier, the success at Tafila would not stand and as a result the revolt began to stall. The frigid conditions were to blame in part, but so too was the young Zeid's immaturity in choosing to distribute payment wildly to the Bedouin. Directly after the battle Lawrence had chosen immediately to go south to Guweira in order to retrieve L30,000 in gold sovereigns, the amount he thought was necessary to keep the Northern Army in the fight through until March.[32] By the time he got back to Tafila with the money, however, the strategic initiative had been lost under Zeid's jejeune leadership. From the emotional high of consecutive victories over the Ottomans near the end of January, therefore, Lawrence plunged quickly now into despair, especially when he learnt that in addition to losing control of the men, Zeid had made matters worse by distributing in a profligate manner all the gold sovereigns that he had just delivered. Accordingly, with their pockets full, the temporarily sated chieftains and tribesmen had begun to melt away. Future operations thus looked imperilled, not to mention holding the ground that had just been won; indeed, two weeks later such is exactly what happened when the Ottomans re-took Tafila from the Arabs. By this time Lawrence was on the verge of quitting over Zeid's behaviour and the insubordination and immaturity that it had demonstrated. Distressing to Lawrence also, however, was the fact that he had acted unwisely in leaving Zeid in charge during his absence in order to retrieve the gold. Altogether, Lawrence had faltered under the pressure of the moment and in response decided to flee to Allenby's headquarters. Feeling both angry and embarrassed about what had happened at Tafila, he had determined to leave 'my further employment in his hands'.[33]

In the aftermath of the debacle at Tafila, and in departing for Allenby's GHQ at Bir Salem on 19 February, Lawrence had had his mission 'closed down' by Pierce Joyce, and his fiercely devoted Ageyl bodyguard dispersed. 'My will had gone,' Lawrence would recall later. However, it was about to be restored because the defeatism inherent in Lawrence's attitude – if only briefly – was the exact opposite of what the revivified Allenby was feeling now that London had approved his expansive plan of attack.[34] On 25 January when Lawrence was at Tafila and during which time General Robertson remained as CIGS, Allenby had written to him to say that 'I hope to be able to push across the Jordan, and throw a big raid past Salt, against the Hedjaz Railway. If I could destroy 10 or 15 miles of rail and some bridges; and get in touch with the Arabs under Feisal – even temporarily – the effect would be great'.[35] Robertson's messages to Allenby – at least as far as providing additional men was concerned – had always been discouraging. Given that 'there is only one way to win this war and that is by beating the Germans', as he had written to him in November, for example, then it was of a piece that he would write another such note in early February saying that 'I see no prospect whatever of sending you more divisions than you now have'.[36] But now, later that month, with Robertson about to be replaced by Wilson as CIGS and the contents of the Smuts-sponsored Joint Note 12 prevailing, the time at last was right for the full 'Allenby Effect' to be unleashed.

For Lawrence, Allenby unbound in the Middle East, as it were, 'to repair the stalemate of the West', proved an immediate tonic.[37] Shortly after Lawrence arrived at GHQ, Allenby had laid out his plans, which included – much like Lawrence had suggested in December, 'the Jordan scheme seen from the British angle' – the Arabs acting to immobilize the Hijaz Railway and thereby shore up the 'eastern flank'. In so doing, the Arabs would 'relieve him [Allenby] of its burden'. If such could be achieved, with Lawrence back in close association with Faisal and no longer anywhere near the untrustworthy and immature Zeid, then Allenby would be able to 'take at least Damascus; and, if possible, Aleppo, as soon as he could. Turkey was to be put out of the war once and for all'.

Such grand and appealing plans meant that it was a revivified Lawrence who departed GHQ at the end of February, diving back into the war 'completely', notwithstanding persistent doubts about his 'mantle of fraud'.[38] After conferring with Faisal at Aqaba, who was equally enthusiastic about Allenby's plan along with the fact that it meant a further provision of gold, as well as hundreds of camels, Lawrence dashed away quickly to confer with the Arab Bureau at Cairo. From there Lawrence penned a breathless letter to his mother to say that 'this year promises to be more of a run about than last year even!' Alas, there would be no possibility for Lawrence of an earlier proposed trip back home to England, but when he did make it eventually, he promised that it would be as 'a colonel of sorts' and as the holder of 'a D.S.O.'.[39] Altogether, Lawrence was emerging from his winter funk into a prospective spring of renewed campaigning, with the crowning achievement of taking Damascus – spoken of with Faisal at their very first meeting back in October 1916 – as a goal shared now also by Allenby.[40]

By the end of February, therefore, Allenby had begun to put his strategic plan into action, thanks mainly to the work of one of his commanders, General John Shea, a veteran of the South African War who had gone to France in 1914 as a British staff officer, and then later to Palestine as general officer commanding of the battle-hardened 60th (London) Infantry Division. Allenby's long-held first goal of gaining Jericho was achieved on 20–21 February when the Londoners, supported by Anzac troops, drove the Turks out of its ancient rocky and gorge-cut terrain and back across the Jordan River. It was a victory that placed an exclamation point on their earlier success at Jerusalem. Two weeks later, in fiercer action that would last the better part of four days, British troops advanced over to the east side of the Jordan, which put them on the road to strike directly at Amman and the Hijaz Railway. These 'Transjordan Raids', as we shall see, would occupy Allenby from March until May. Their early success, however, would be extremely difficult to maintain.[41]

Taking Jericho was significant for Allenby because it inaugurated his move into Jordan, although at the moment of his success there, 'what my next step will be, I can't yet say', he reported.[42] In adopting this conservative line, however, as he did in writing to C. W. Battine on 22 February, Allenby maintained a certain necessary confidentiality over his plans. By then, contrary to the words used in his letter to Battine, in fact he did have a fairly clear idea of what his next moves would entail: a concerted push across to Amman in an attempt to take out the Hijaz Railway and, with Arab assistance, a shoring up of his vulnerable right flank. Indeed, just a day later he wrote to Robertson, on the verge of losing his position as CIGS, to say that, 'soon, I hope to cross the river, and get to the Hedjaz railway; joining hands with the Arabs, and really breaking the line. The Arabs, led by Lawrence, have been doing pretty well.'[43] A couple of weeks later on 11 March, Allenby wrote once again to Battine informing him that 'I am at the present moment pressing the Turk a bit', although 'he is fighting well again; cheered, no doubt, by the Russian peace'.[44] A mere ten days after that, on 21 March – the same day that the Germans launched their ferocious Spring Offensive on the Western Front – the first of the Transjordan Raids took place and Allenby's larger plan got underway.[45]

Late on the evening of 21 March a small group of men from the 60th Infantry Division, the Londoners, led the way across the Jordan River at Ghoraniyeh – also known as Joshua's Crossing – by attempting to swim into position in order to establish pontoon bridges. These efforts proved unsuccessful, however, owing to the Jordan having become swollen by heavy rains, and by the steady rifle- and artillery-fire of the Turks who occupied entrenched positions along the heights east of the river. Consequently, a second crossing point, Makhadet Hijla, considered traditionally to have been the site of Christ's baptism by St John, was then attempted successfully. Overnight at Makhadet a bridgehead was established by Anzac engineers. By around eight o'clock on the morning of 22 March, therefore, British and Anzac troops from the Desert Mounted Division were able to begin moving across the newly constructed floating bridge. Lacking the element of surprise, however, together with stiff Turkish resistance and a surfeit of mud caused by the spring rains, meant that progress for the British and Anzac troops was incremental and slow. But by the evening of 22 March a secure bridgehead had been achieved at Makhadet, although a similar success at Ghoraniyeh continued to remain elusive. Nevertheless, by the next day, a bridgehead had been achieved there also and the construction of a pontoon crossing was duly underway. Altogether, by the evening of 23 March, five crossings of the Jordan (at this point in its over 200-mile course to the Dead Sea, it lies some 1,200 feet below sea level) had been constructed and the move northeast from Ghoraniyeh towards the small city of El Salt, located about 15 miles away and at an elevation of about 2,500 feet above sea level, was in prospect.

Throughout this intense period the ongoing complication of the massive German assault in France, with its concomitant requirement for a great number of additional British and Imperial troops, meant that Allenby operated under the constant threat of manpower and materiel shortages. For some historians, his actions in pushing relentlessly across the Jordan have been seen therefore in retrospect as ill-advised, if not irresponsible, because of what he knew to be a shortage of men.[46] But one of Allenby's foundational beliefs, which undergirded his ultimate assault on Amman, was the presence and deployment of the Arab Regulars, as well as the Lawrence-directed Arab flying columns, both of which could be harnessed for success if duly inspired and properly led. Allenby's belief in this regard was not over-sanguine; indeed, he understood the liability inherent in placing too much reliance on the flanking power of the Arabs: 'they cannot run alone', he had advised Robertson in February, they 'must have British leaders whom they know and trust.'[47] In Lawrence, of course, they had just such a leader, although even he was not able always – as we have seen – to effect the desired field outcome of those Arabs under his command.

On 21 March, General Wilson, who had assumed the post of CIGS following the resignation of Robertson, began a frequent correspondence with Allenby about events in both Palestine and France. They would get on exceedingly well together. Letters for Charles Battine of the *Daily Telegraph* would continue also. 'Affairs here', Allenby wrote understatedly to Battine on 26 March, 'interesting on the spot, are insignificant beside the struggle of giants in Europe'. That may have been so from Allenby's over-humble perspective. But for the British and Anzac troops involved in the coming assault on Amman, the potential toppling of the Ottoman Empire, which taking the city would constitute a clear step in achieving, was hardly 'insignificant'. Notwithstanding the fact that Allenby continued to write of the offensive east of the Jordan in similar terms, telling Battine on 1 April, for example, that 'my little sideshow dwindles now into a very insignificant affair', events on the ground belied his modest words.[48]

One likely explanation for Allenby's limited sense of what he was going to be able to achieve in Palestine and Syria was a War Office telegram that had been sent to him on 27 March in which he was ordered to 'adopt a policy of active defence in Palestine as soon as the operations you are now undertaking are completed'.[49] The clear implication of this directive was that the grander plan for a comprehensive victory over the Ottomans was being put on hold unless and until the current crisis in France had passed. Accordingly, the telegram went on to ask Allenby pointedly, 'what heavy artillery can you spare?' Releasing artillery for use in France, however, would become the least of Allenby's worries. Much more problematic was the release of troops, which would escalate to the point that eventually 24 battalions – some 60,000 men – would be sent from the Palestine theatre to France. In the event, only some of their number would be replaced with the arrival of mainly Indian infantry from the British Army in India. Still, despite the contents of the War Office telegram, Allenby managed to deploy his remaining men in such a manner as to leave unaffected existing strategic operations.

Accordingly, for Allenby's British and Anzac troops, once having established themselves on the east bank of the Jordan their next objective remained El Salt. The advance on the town, which had been garrisoned well by the Turks but now was being abandoned by them in favour of a fall back on Amman, began on the morning of 24 March. In order to do so, various approach roads were used by the British and Anzacs, while overhead aerial reconnaissance was undertaken together with a small number of bombing runs. This coordinated attack would prove to be too much for the Turks to withstand. Hence by the early evening of 25 March El Salt had been duly occupied by the Allies and the final push to Amman, which lay almost 20 miles to the southeast and another thousand feet up in altitude, was anticipated.

However, the passage to Amman would present serious difficulties for Allenby's troops. The landscape around the city was extremely hilly and rocky, with bogs in places, and the roads and tracks used to traverse the unforgiving landscape made for very slow progress. Messy early-spring weather complicated the situation further, with rain turning to sleet and creating a never-ending morass of mud. Two small and swift-mounted parties of New Zealanders were sent ahead of the general advance in order to blow up sections of the Hijaz Railway running both to the north and south of Amman. But of these two operations the southern demolition attack only was successful. Nonetheless, its execution announced clearly the impending arrival of the British Imperial forces, which, under General Shea, would strike on 27 March, inaugurating a four-day pitched battle in and around Amman.

In defence of the city, the Ottomans were commanded by Enver Pasha and supported by a large contingent of German troops under General Otto Liman von Sanders, who famously had commanded the victorious Ottoman 5th Army at Gallipoli. In anticipating the arrival of the enemy, the Ottomans had had ample time to prepare. Consequently, Amman and its approaches were well garrisoned. Altogether, Enver and Liman had some 20,000 troops at their disposal, many of whom had been brought in recently along the undamaged railway to the north of Amman, and they were supported by about 30 field guns. After some fierce initial fighting on 27 and 28 March, in which British forces suffered over a thousand casualties, the Ottomans first, and then the Germans, counter-attacked on 29 March in territory east of El Salt. They then proceeded to do the same within Amman itself over the following two days.

Meanwhile, a brigade of New Zealand Mounted Rifles had entered Amman on 30 March. They attempted to gain control of the city's railway station and link it to the targeted destruction of the railway viaduct and tunnel north of the city. But the combined strength of the Ottoman-German forces was too strong and therefore later that day the order was given for the Kiwis to retreat from Amman. On the previous day, Allenby had reported to the War Office that, east of the Jordan River, 'there is no material change in the situation' and that '5 miles of railway track south of Amman Station have now been destroyed'.[50] But while these were obvious achievements, they were modest in nature and did not fulfil the principle objective of the raid, which had been to destroy the ability of the Ottomans to use the railway line running into and out of Amman. At best, therefore, at this stage the attack across the Jordan and on Amman itself constituted a very limited achievement. Indeed, as Allenby informed Battine on 1 April, the attack was limited to having 'raided the Hedjaz railway'. He added, with more hope than evidence, that the raid had resulted in 'much damage'.[51]

In the attack's aftermath the forced retreat from Amman through El Salt and back to the Jordan River belied the somewhat rosy hue Allenby had put on the raid. By 2 April, the withdrawal across the Jordan – punctuated by rearguard fighting – was complete, however, leaving intact the two bridgeheads at Ghoraniyeh and Makhadet Hijla. A few days later, Allenby informed the War Office that he had undertaken the building of a permanent bridge at Ghoraniyeh, which, in due course, would be named after him. Today, a hundred years and a number of iterations later, the Allenby Bridge remains one of the main links between Israel and Jordan.[52] Allenby also informed London that he believed the raid to have demonstrated clearly to the Ottomans that at any time 'we can cross Jordan and threaten Amman'. Further, and this is where Allenby sought to connect overtly the impact of the raid with the wider implications for the Arab Revolt, his actions would 'compel [the] Turks to maintain around El Salt larger forces than hitherto', the impact of which will ease the pressure on 'Feisal's operations about Maan'.[53] Altogether therefore, and despite not having achieved the breakthrough for which he had planned, the raid across the Jordan had offered a small success to Allenby within what was otherwise an undeniable rebuttal, if not defeat. For the first time in almost a year, since, as we saw earlier, the Second Battle of Gaza in April of

1917, the EEF had been over-matched in the field. The extended celebration that had been set off by the taking of Jerusalem therefore had now properly come to an end along the ancient banks of the River Jordan. And with the Germans' Spring Offensive ongoing in France, and the War Office therefore putting at least a temporary hold on the expansion of Allenby's Middle East operations, it was no longer clear what might come next. And that, as we shall turn to now, was as true for Lawrence, at work nearby in the Mountains of Moab, as it was for Allenby.

The allied setback at Amman had forced the Arab Northern Army – under the direction of Faisal, Jafar and Lawrence – to focus its efforts eastwards in an attempt to sever the railway line at Ma'an. At the very moment that Allenby's attack on Amman had been turned back, an unknowing Lawrence had written to his mother from Aqaba that 'after four years of this sort of thing I am becoming dried up. ... This is a job too big for me.'[54] He was weary of both the fighting and the responsibility of command: 'It will be a great comfort', he wrote in the same letter, 'when one can lie down & sleep without having to think about things; and speak without having one's every word reported in half a hundred camps.' Still, Lawrence was determined nonetheless to ensure that the Sharifian forces were regarded as occupying an important position in the anticipated success of Allenby's long-term (if delayed) goal of taking Damascus, and not merely as an adjunctive force.[55] Ma'an was well garrisoned by the Ottomans as they considered it to be a key way station on the way southwards to Arabia. Understanding the city's strategic significance therefore, the Arab Northern Army decided to storm it beginning on 13 April, after having launched successful raids by flying column a few days earlier in order to cut the railway line to the north and south.

The direct attack on Ma'an had begun by the time Lawrence arrived there from the north, after having endured a harrowing episode in which he had to shoot one of his servants, Uthman (named Farraj in *Seven Pillars of Wisdom*), who had been fatally wounded, in order to save him from falling into the hands of the Turks who were known to torture their prisoners with little mercy (as Lawrence of course could attest personally). Carrying out the task was a horrible experience for Lawrence, in the event acting as a suitably bloody antecedent to the Battle of Ma'an to come.[56]

The attack at Ma'an marked one of the few times that the Arab Army had fought an entrenched Ottoman force, which thus far had been avoided in favour of guerrilla style, hit and run attacks. In so doing however, a stalemate was achieved, an outcome that proved better than expected. Indeed, as Lawrence wrote later: 'the general conduct showed us that, given fair technical equipment, the Arabs were good enough for anything, with no need of British stiffening, however weighty the affair. This changed our course of mind for the future, and made us much more free to plan: so the failure was not wholly unredeemed.'[57] If anything, Lawrence understated the resolve and battlefield execution of the Sharifian Army over what would be five days of intense fighting at Ma'an. The Ottomans there numbered some 4,000, giving them at least a thousand more men than what the Arabs could muster. But at battle's end, the city – although remaining in Ottoman hands – had been isolated and cut off from the rest of the Hijaz Railway line to the south –

leaving the Turks, as Neil Faulkner notes rightly, 'east of the Jordan more tied to static garrison duty than ever before.'[58]

After sorting out an anarchic and potentially bloody contretemps over looting between the Arab Army's Egyptians and its Bedouins at one of the stations south of Ma'an, which had been taken from the Ottomans, Lawrence remained there for a few days. His supervision was required in the demolition of what would turn out to be about 60 miles of railway track running south from Ma'an to Mudawwara, the largest Turkish station along that stretch of the line. Before the job was completed successfully, however, Lawrence saw to it that further demolition raids began to the north of Ma'an in order to prevent the Turks from reinforcing their beleaguered garrison from above the city. Allenby's earlier limited destruction of the line directly south of Amman meant that the Turks would have been able very soon to send men and equipment to Ma'an, which these operations were designed to prevent, or at least to stall.[59] After having put these plans in motion, Lawrence then departed immediately for Aba al-Lissan, which was followed by a flying visit to Cairo. By 2 May, 'travelling at red hot speed', as he wrote home, he was back at Allenby's Bir Salem headquarters, where he discovered that a Second Transjordan Raid had got underway a couple of days earlier and would last for a few more days still.[60]

During the few weeks that had elapsed between the retreat across the Jordan from the disappointing first raid on Amman and the launching of the second one on 30 April, Allenby had considered whether or not renewing the Transjordan plan was wise. In supporting the Arab Northern Army at Ma'an by drawing Ottoman and German forces away from the point of attack, Allenby had authorized a couple of actions at the heavily fortified Ottoman garrison of Shunet Nimrin. Lieutenant General Harry Chauvel, the Australian commander who had led the Desert Mounted Corps to such a stirring victory at Beer Sheba a few months earlier, had considerably more trouble effecting a similar outcome at Shunet Nimrin, however. Both he and General Shea, in command of the 60th (London) Infantry Division, were not confident about their ability to dislodge the well-entrenched Ottoman troops at Shunet Nimrin, who numbered about 5,000 in total. Exacerbating this challenging state of affairs was the arrival of some envoys from the Bedouin Beni Sakhr tribe who had come independently to Beer Sheba to tell Allenby of their readiness to offer assistance. At that moment, however, and unbeknownst to Allenby, their making good on the offer was simply not possible. But based on their firm assurance that they had 7,000 tribesmen poised in position not far from Ghoraniyeh to assist in assaulting the Turks, Allenby acted quickly and ill-advisedly, advancing by two weeks the provisional timetable that he had established to re-take El Salt. For Allenby, this offensive was to be more than simply a renewed raid, however. Instead, he saw it as leading to a complete overthrow of the Ottoman and German forces east of the Jordan River.

Once having arrived at Allenby's GHQ, Lawrence's reaction to this startling news – especially that concerning the Beni Sakhr's putative undertaking, about which he had not been consulted – was one of alarm. By then, however, the new raid across the Jordan was already underway and nothing could be done to halt it.

A few days earlier, Allenby had written to General Wilson in London, informing him that 'here, I have had some local fights. ... The Arabs are doing well, East of the Jordan; and I have been helping them by forcing the Turks to keep a big force of all arms opposite my bridgehead in the Jordan. ... Generally, things are going well here.'[61] Allenby had been buoyed by the news of recent Arab success at Ma'an, making him more sanguine than he should have been about what might be achieved closer to Amman. Clearly, Lawrence knew the nuances of how and where and when irregular Arab troops would choose to fight, and with what strength, and in their proposed deployment as part of the Second Transjordan Raid they would prove useless, as he likely would have predicted if he had been asked. As we shall see, the Beni Sakhr's abdication of its promised role, combined with the enduring strength of the enemy, would make the tactical situation along the Jordan extraordinarily difficult for Allenby during the early days of May.

In commencing battle early on the morning of 30 April under the command of General Chauvel, the combined British, Anzac and Indian forces began operations at Shunet Nimrin, located at the foot of the sharp rise leading into the Mountains of Moab.[62] The atmosphere that day was especially febrile, with the Ottomans and Germans determinedly well entrenched. A protracted artillery firefight ensued, the result of which were heavy casualties for the Allies combined with very little dislodgement of the enemy.[63] Meanwhile, Anzac cavalry and mounted troops were deployed in order to assist in achieving a parallel breakthrough that had El Salt as its goal. Indeed, around eight o'clock that morning the Australian Light Horsemen would prove critical in retaking the town. But under the command of Liman, the Germans and Ottomans counter-attacked successfully over the following two days at El Salt, while at Shunet Nimrin, the Londoners were unable to push its defenders out of position. All told therefore, by 1 May the success of the Second Transjordan Raid looked doubtful. Moreover, bringing up supplies of ammunition, field dressings, water and food had become increasingly difficult for the Allies. Thus Allenby faced a bad situation, one made worse by the fact that the promised support of the Beni Sakhr tribesmen had not materialized. Therefore, on the afternoon of 3 May Allenby flew to meet Chauvel at his field headquarters, which was located a little west of the recently constructed bridge at Ghoraniyeh. There he was told bluntly what he understood already to be the situation: El Salt had been re-taken and was being held by the Ottomans, and capturing Shunet Nimrin was proving to be impossible. Chastened by the disappointing battlefield reality of the previous four days, Allenby could instruct Chauvel only to issue the order to withdraw. By that evening, consequently, and for the second time within about four weeks, Allenby's men would have to retreat across the Jordan River having failed once again to achieve their tactical objectives.

This unwelcome retreat took two days, but at least the new bridge at Ghoraniyeh, and the bridgehead at Makhadet Hijla, had been made secure. Operational casualties were significant, however. The Londoners bore the brunt of them, having suffered over 1,100 of the almost 1,700 casualties that would be counted. But, if there was a glimmer of hope to be had from the disappointing operation, the Ottomans and Germans themselves had been weakened by having suffered a similar number of casualties, in addition to which almost a thousand of their number had been taken prisoner. Allenby had hoped for much better of course in launching the Second Transjordan Raid, as it came to be called even though, as we know, its intention was much larger than what the term 'raid' implies, but it had not been a total loss.

Still, there was no denying that the raid had been a tactical failure, just as the first one had been. And some, like General Chauvel, were quick to brand it as such. But what the two Transjordan Raids had offered in tactical failure, they made up for in strategic success. Their impact on Liman and on the Ottoman and German high command was to convince them that Amman would continue to be Allenby's ultimate strategic objective, and that therefore he would attempt to strike at it again. Consequently, the Ottoman left flank remained in place and to it flowed heavy reinforcements. Indeed, the whole of the Ottoman 4th Army became employed in securing the Jordan Valley, which meant that its right flank running over to the Mediterranean Sea was relatively weak by comparison. Accordingly, this vulnerability was one that Allenby, as we shall see, would exploit fully not very far in the future. Such thinking accounts, therefore, for why as early as 5 May Allenby could write to Clive Wigram, the king's assistant private secretary, and one of his many old army colleagues, in order to say that 'my own projects have been modified'. Accordingly, Allenby was prepared to wait and 'to watch for opportunity for striking a blow, or to help the Arabs'.[64] Similarly, his view that the Second Transjordan Raid had helped pin down the enemy even if its ultimate goals had not been realized, made it possible for him now to counter Chauvel's criticism of it by coming back at him furiously with the comment: 'Failure be damned! It's been a great success.'[65] Heading into the blazing hot summer season in Palestine, such then was Allenby's determined state of mind.

If Allenby was determined to re-ignite the momentum of the EEF despite the tactical failure of the Transjordan Raids, which he needed to do, Lawrence meanwhile, was equally committed to ensuring that the Beni Sakhr debacle did not sideline the perceived trustworthiness and the effectiveness of the Sharifian Army. Throughout May Allenby adopted the posture of pause, in large measure because the transfer of thousands of his troops to France now was ongoing in earnest and the arrival in Palestine of scores of lightly trained and untested Indian troops who required intensive acclimation before they would be ready to fight. As a result, no action was anticipated until the end of the summer. Indeed, in a letter to Allenby written on 29 May Wilson told him that because of the pressing situation in France where the Germans continued to attack desperately as part of their Spring Offensive not very much help was going to be forthcoming to the so-called outer theatres of the war for at least a year. Therefore, Wilson continued, 'as regards Palestine all we can do during the summer is to help you all we can with railway construction.'[66] In the circumstances that limited promise would simply have to suffice, and Allenby resigned himself to the prevailing situation, his mood lightening enough to tell Wilson sardonically later that as for the summer 'I am now campaigning against mosquitos'.[67]

Shortly after conferring with Allenby at Bir Salem at the beginning of May Lawrence had gone back south to meet Faisal in order to relay the bad news of the Second Transjordan Raid, including the failure of the Beni Sakhr to make good on their promise of support. Lawrence then proceeded to elicit his own promise from Faisal to 'admonish' them, but both men remained more greatly concerned that Allenby had gone ahead with the raid based on the Beni Sakhr's commitment of support without first having consulted either one of them. 'Did the British mistrust him?' was how Lawrence recalled later Faisal's fear in this regard.[68] He need not have worried, however. Allenby believed time to be of the essence when he had peremptorily moved up the schedule for attacking across the Jordan, and his trust in Faisal remained firm. 'It is absolutely essential to me that he [Faisal] should continue to be active,' he would write to Wilson in early June. 'He is a sensible, well-informed man; and he is fully alive to the limitations imposed on me. I keep in close touch with him, through Lawrence.'[69] Indeed, they did keep in close touch, as events later that summer would demonstrate clearly.

Nevertheless, these were unsettling times for Faisal. The EEF had faltered at Amman, as well as in the Jordan Valley; the Allies were being pushed to their limit along the Western Front, especially near St. Quentin; and emboldened by their own successful resistance locally, as well as by the German advance in France, the Turks had made a provocative offer to Faisal that he throw over the British and rejoin the ranks of the Ottomans in exchange for a firm promise of Arab independence in the future.[70] He rejected this blandishment, however, writing to his father, Sharif Hussein, that it was little more than a Turkish 'ruse and deception'.[71] But the offer had been unsettling nonetheless and it left Faisal ever more dependent on the ability of his own army in combination with the EEF to ultimately win the day against the Ottomans. Lawrence, meanwhile, was equally unsettled by the fact that Faisal had seen fit to entertain such an offer from the Ottomans, describing it much later as evidence that the Hashemite prince might have been 'selling us'.[72]

In order to help keep the Sharifian Army in the field, and to reassure Faisal of both his own trustworthiness and of the fidelity of the British, Lawrence earlier had convinced Allenby to release 2,000 riding camels from the Imperial Camel Corps Brigade, whose men were being converted into conventional cavalry because of the continuing need for reinforcements. 'What are you going to do with their camels?' Lawrence asked Allenby pointedly in a meeting to determine the ICCB's future. He answered that he was going to pass them over to the quartermaster general for dispersal as divisional transport. Lawrence was sure that with the infusion of such a great number of ships of the desert he could create a strike force of Arab troops that could be used to re-take Deraa, control the railway line and then be poised for deployment on Allenby's right flank whenever he was ready to move on Damascus. After hearing Lawrence say with great confidence that with such an infusion of camels he could 'put a thousand men into Deraa any day you please', Allenby looked across the table and said bluntly to the quartermaster: 'Q, you lose.' Lawrence had got his wish from the commander-in-chief in what he described later was 'a regal gift; the gift of unlimited mobility. The Arabs could now win their war when and where they liked.'[73] Directly afterwards, an immensely pleased

Lawrence dashed off south to Faisal's encampment at Wahida near Aqaba and in relating the news of Allenby's gift of 2,000 camels his 'eagerness' had returned; indeed, 'he was like a boy released from school that day,' his colleague Lieutenant Colonel Pierce Joyce recalled later.[74]

Alas, for Lawrence, the joy of his reaction to the camel caper would not be matched by their planned deployment. Allenby of course would have been only too happy to see a couple of thousand armed camel-riding Arabs enter Deraa. But as Colonel Alan Dawnay, chief of the Hijaz Operational Staff and appointed liaison to Lawrence just a few months earlier, remarked, Allenby still saw it as probably being too big of 'a gamble' to carry off successfully.[75] And a gamble is exactly what it would have been had it proceeded. But even to attempt it Lawrence needed to enlist 2,000 Hijazi regulars, and this task could not be achieved owing to the refusal of Sharif Hussein – despite the pleading of both Lawrence and Faisal – to release them in order to push the Arab Revolt's centre of gravity in a northerly direction and away from its roots in the Hijaz.[76] By the summer of 1918 internecine feuding within the Hashemite royal family had become chronic. Hussein believed Faisal had usurped his authority and thereby put himself into the best position to lead a unified Arab state in the future, should such an eventuality transpire. For Hussein, Mecca was a long way from Damascus, especially in symbolic terms. Complicating the picture further was his Arab rival, Ibn Saud, leader of the Wahhabists, who had his own designs on post-Ottoman Arabia. For Ibn Saud, paying obeisance to either Hussein or Faisal, regardless of their leading role in the war against the Turks, was not part of his plan whatsoever.[77]

Hussein's intransigence on this point, as Lawrence understood it, was keenly disappointing. But ultimately the camel scheme would not matter very much because by the end of May, as we shall see, Lawrence had gone north once again to Ma'an and soon was leading a cadre of British officers and Arab irregulars in a summer of repeatedly successful attacks on the Hijaz Railway. Moreover, by the end of June, Allenby had decided that September would be the month to begin his planned big offensive against the Ottomans, with Damascus and ultimately Aleppo as its targets. This decision had the strategic effect of lessening the value of a strike by the Arabs against Deraa, although in the end they would do so anyhow.

In clarifying his grand plan Allenby just then had been made aware, as had Faisal, of the release by the Foreign Office of a document written in an uncompromising manner by Sir Henry McMahon as high commissioner in Egypt, which was called 'The Declaration to the Seven'. Earlier, and anonymously, a group of seven members of the newly established Party of Syrian Unity, formed in Damascus to advocate for regional independence, had written a memorandum demanding of the Great Powers a post-war 'guarantee of the ultimate independence of Arabia'. In response, McMahon had undertaken to pledge – in a manner that was seen by some to supersede both the Sykes–Picot Agreement and the Balfour Declaration – that the future government of the Arab provinces of the Ottoman Empire occupied by the Allies 'should be based upon the principle of the consent of the governed'.[78] The declaration was in accordance with the national self-determination aspiration contained in Woodrow Wilson's 'Fourteen Points' – as well as the denunciation of secret treaties – which the US president had outlined in January 1918 in a speech to Congress. In McMahon's hands, the very ones that earlier had engaged in the long correspondence with Hussein which can be seen as having instigated the Arab Revolt, the symbolism was clear and the simplicity and directness of the declaration redounded loudly in both Faisal's camp and Allenby's GHQ.

Still, given the fact that just then Dr Chaim Weizmann, leader of the British Zionist Federation, was on tour in Palestine and had met with Faisal at Aqaba on 4 June left no one – least of all Faisal – under any illusions about what Weizmann and the Zionists envisaged for Palestine's future under the terms of the Balfour Declaration.[79] As Lawrence said prophetically at the time, 'Dr Weizmann hopes for a completely Jewish Palestine in fifty years and a Jewish Palestine, under a British façade, for the moment. … Until the military adventure of the Arabs under Feisal has succeeded or failed, he does not require Jewish help, and it would be unwise on our part to permit it to be offered.'[80] As for Allenby, he regarded Weizmann's visit in much the same way, remarking in a letter to Clive Wigram, that the 'Arabs looked on it with grave anxiety and suspicion', although he noted diplomatically that Weizmann had been 'very tactful' in both his words and bearing.[81]

All that summer, meanwhile, Allenby continued in steady preparation 'to make a move in September', as he wrote to Wilson on 24 July.[82] He toured Palestine and its fighting fronts extensively, as military observer of course, but also because it afforded him the opportunity occasionally to cultivate his interests as a long-time naturalist. To this end, for example, he had written to Charles Battine in June that, 'I went, two days ago, halfway down the Dead Sea, in a motor boat to Engedi, a lovely oasis, with water rushing down from a cleft in the mountainside. … The scenery of the Dead Sea is very fine, though very rough and barren.'[83] Of course, Allenby's preoccupation with the coming offensive during which the EEF and the Arabs together, he wrote, 'have a really good opportunity of inflicting a severe defeat on the Turks', animated his every move.[84] Still, he always found time for moments of relaxation. The successful execution of Arab operations in support of the Allied offensive was vital to Allenby, and he insisted to General Wilson therefore that the prompt payment of the Arabs must be a matter of priority to the British government. Accordingly, he informed Wilson that 'I ought to have at least one month's reserve of gold, always in hand; & I hope that you will see to this'.[85] Again, he wrote to Wilson in mid-August emphasizing the need for regular payment of the Arabs, saying that 'I am counting on Feisal's continued cooperation with me. Naturally, I can't push far North unless the Hedjaz railway ceases to be a menace to my right flank.'[86] Altogether for Allenby, his strategic plan was coming together at last, both his part in effecting its outcome militarily and what it might mean afterwards politically and diplomatically. As he summed up his thinking to Wilson not long before launching the anticipated offensive in September, 'If I can smash this Turkish Army, I can with my present force, hold a good forward line. There I can wait upon events.'[87]

As Allenby readied himself and the EEF that summer for the coming offensive, Lawrence and a number of other British officers were continuing to raid furiously in the desert, marked especially by the Battle of Mudawwara, fought on 8 August.

Planned by Lawrence and Colonel Alan Dawnay, and led by Major Robert 'Robin' Buxton of the Imperial Camel Corps, Mudawwara was an ancient outpost for those on the Hajj route to Mecca. Located about mid-way between Damascus and Medina, from 1906 Mudawwara had become an important though isolated water station on the Hijaz Railway line, and under the leadership of various British officers, it had been attacked four times without success, including, as we saw earlier, once by Lawrence himself. But on 8 August over a span of just three early-morning hours Mudawwara would be wrested decisively from its Ottoman defenders in a set piece of guerrilla operational success, and the Arab Revolt reinvigorated in anticipation of Allenby's major offensive to come.[88]

Beyond its signal operational success, however, the Mudawwara attack was designed also to deceive the Turks into thinking that Faisal's force was stronger than it really was because once Mudawwara had been taken the ICC force was to disappear immediately into the desert and then head northwards over 200 miles to Kissir. Once at Kissir, located a short distance south of Amman, the ICC was to take out an important railway viaduct that had not been destroyed during the Second Transjordan Raid. As General William Bartholomew, Allenby's chief of staff, explained the plan to him, 'I think it would be a good thing to send the Camel Corps and that if they appear just at Mudawara and then in the area north of Maan we add considerably to our chance of fooling the Turk until after other events make it unnecessary to do so any longer.'[89] Allenby concurred readily with the plan. Later, when the outcome at Mudawwara was reported to him – a clear victory involving very few ICC casualties and with 21 Turks killed and 150 taken prisoner – and the victorious force then melting into the endless expanse of desert, he was greatly pleased. Indeed, Lawrence would write later that Allenby had become devoted to employing ruses against the Turks. 'After the Meinertzhagen success', he wrote, 'deceptions, which for the ordinary general were just witty hors d'oeuvres before battle, became for Allenby a main point of strategy.'[90] To Battine, on 22 August, Allenby wrote altogether of the Arabs putting in 'some useful work against the Hedjaz railway & its garrisons'.[91] And with Lawrence similarly satisfied: 'This fine performance settled the isolated fate of the Turkish corps at Medina beyond question', all seemed in readiness now for the autumn offensive.[92]

As it turned out, the Kissir stage of the Mudawwara mission had to be called off owing to heavy Turkish patrols near Amman along with the successful German aerial reconnaissance of Arab movements. But the attack on Mudawwara itself had done plenty to unsettle the Ottomans, and by the end of August Lawrence had his sights set on the original target of Deraa, upon which Allenby too had remained focused, especially if it meant a surgical strike in anticipation of his general advance, now planned firmly to begin on 19 September. As Lawrence put it,

> Allenby's confidence was like a wall …, and [he] wanted us to lead off not more than four nor less than two days before he did. His words to me were that three men and a boy with pistols in front of Deraa on September the sixteenth would fill his conception; would be better than thousands a week before or a week after.[93]

As August drew to a close, Allenby continued to prepare for the EEF's major attack to commence some three weeks later. In order to bring the attack off successfully he was trying to balance a number of concerns, including ensuring shipments of gold in order to pay the Arabs, who 'won't fight without it', as he reiterated to Wilson in London; building up his substantially remade forces; and giving the ongoing strife between Hussein and Faisal enough time to lessen so as to maximize the likelihood of a united Arab front.[94] 'They still can't help each other much, at present,' he had written in frustration to Battine in mid-August.[95] This disjunctive state of affairs among the Hashemite Arabs was one that continued to trouble Lawrence as well, who was not naive about the useful but subordinate position that the Arab forces occupied in Allenby's strategic hierarchy. As written much later by Lawrence, Allenby 'cared nothing for our fighting power, and did not reckon us part of his tactical strength. Our purpose, to him, was moral, psychological, diathetic; to keep the enemy command intent upon the trans-Jordan front.'[96] Still, at the time, before the disappointments to come of the Paris Peace Conference coloured permanently Lawrence's view of the revolt, Arab action indeed was valued highly by Allenby. Soon enough, therefore, Allenby would be gratified to learn that 'my Arab ally, Feisal', as he informed Wilson on 11 September, 'has sent off his people to the North'.[97] Accompanying them was Lawrence, along with a handful of other British officers, en route to Deraa. 'I hope you will have the best of good fortune in your coming attack and that you will get a real good haul of Turks,' Wilson had written to Allenby on 2 September. Just over two weeks later all seemed poised to accomplish that very thing.[98] On 9 September, Allenby issued a force order to his generals that 'the Commander-in-Chief intends to take the offensive' by having 'the Army pivot on its positions in the Jordan Valley'.[99] Nine days later, and just a day before the attack commenced, Allenby cabled Wilson to tell him that 'my preparations are as complete as I can make them, and tomorrow they will be tested. I do not think that the Turks have, so far, any inkling of my plan. Meanwhile, my Arab friends are making hay round Deraa, and have timed their raid very nicely.'[100]

For Lawrence and the Arab Revolt, the weeks leading up to Mudawwara, and then to Deraa, would prove climactic. His spirits were high, although he continued to be marked by dissonance over the duplicitousness he believed himself to represent in the revolt. Regardless of these troubles, however, by this point Lawrence was determined to see the revolt through to the end, whatever its ultimate diplomatic and political outcome. He continued to be enamoured of the Arab way of life and of their cause, unflaggingly so. As he had written to a friend that summer, 'you guessed rightly that the Arab appealed to my imagination.'[101] By then, both Arab and Briton had found that Lawrence was of equally great appeal to their imagination too. Robin Buxton, who had not met Lawrence before undertaking command of the raid on Mudowwara, was notably descriptive in remembering him in his role of military leader. 'He is only a boy to look at,' Buxton wrote later. But

he is known to every Arab in this country for his personal bravery and train wrecking exploits. … His influence is astounding not only on the misbeguided [*sic*] native, but also I think on his brother officers and seniors. Out here he lives entirely with the Arab. … He always travels in spotless white … his presence is very stimulating to us all and one has that feeling that things cannot go wrong while he is there.[102]

By early September Lawrence had moved to Azraq, located some 90 miles southeast of Deraa and the site of a strategic oasis, as well as one of the great ancient desert castles in which he had stayed a year earlier. Faisal and many of his Northern Army regulars arrived on 12 March of the month after having resolved the ongoing and bitter familial negotiations with his father. Altogether, with the 'September scheme' against Deraa – of prime strategic importance because it was the junction where the Hijaz Railway went north to Amman and Damascus, and west to Palestine – the Arab Revolt was positioned now to do something of great significance in the latter stages of the war. 'I could feel the taut power of Arab excitement behind me,' wrote Lawrence later.[103] A thousand men now congregated at the castle, Qasr Azraq, and over the next week they would carry out a series of successful flying attacks on the railways around Deraa, confusing the Ottomans who had assumed that once again Amman was to have been the focus of the enemy's attack. Based on that faulty assumption, another deception carried out against the Turks had succeeded, which meant that when Allenby struck with overwhelming ferocity in the west beginning on schedule at 4.30 on the morning of 19 September, they were caught utterly by surprise. 'The Turks are breaking, everywhere,' Allenby wrote confidently to his wife by that afternoon.[104] Indeed, they were breaking everywhere, and the battle that would be named for the Book of Revelation's last battle, Armageddon, and that would yield Damascus to the Allies, was at long last underway.

In Palestine the Ottomans' line of defence, which now lay under siege by Allenby, stretched for some 70 miles from the Mediterranean coast to the Jordan Valley, and then further still to Amman. Allenby's pushing and probing of it over the previous nine months since taking Jerusalem had begun to expose the line's weaknesses, however. But under the command of General Liman von Sanders, and with the support of various other hardened Ottoman battlefield leaders, notably Mustapha Kemal – who, of course as Kemal Ataturk, would gain power and fame later as Turkey's great post-war leader – the Turks certainly remained capable of putting up a stiff defence. But despite the occasional successful feint that suggested otherwise, the Ottomans were severely understrength, a fact made worse by the debilitating heat, humidity, mosquitoes and disease of the desert. Meanwhile, no less afflicted in this regard than were the Ottomans, Allenby's allied forces nonetheless stood across from them poised and ready for battle.

On the morning of 19 September, therefore, the Yildirim Army Group was highly vulnerable to the kind of terrific attack a later generation would term to be one of 'shock and awe'. In raw numbers that day, Allenby had at his disposal preponderant force. Altogether this meant about 70,000 men, comprised of some 57,000 infantrymen, 12,000 mounted troops and Arab regular and irregular forces of approximately 4,000. Liman, on the other hand, could counter with only about half that number, some 35,000, made up mostly of cavalry, with about 3,000 mounted troops. In addition, Allenby also had a comprehensive supply train of mechanized vehicles with which the Turks could not compete, the infrastructural face of modern industrial war made plain by the years after 1914. Indeed, such was the strength and depth of the Allied juggernaut that was drawn up before him that Liman, according to Faulkner, at that very moment considered making 'a wholesale retreat'.[105] In line with this possible outcome General Archibald Wavell, who was one of Allenby's commanders that day and later would be his first major biographer, had remarked earlier that 'obviously the troops of Liman von Sanders could undertake no serious offensive action; the only question was whether they would "stay put" till the day chosen for the battle'.[106]

By the time that day came in September, Allenby had worked out a battle plan centred on the ancient settlement of Megiddo (also called Armageddon) that would overwhelm the Ottomans and force upon them a swift and comprehensive defeat. Megiddo is a plain upon which sits an age-old fortress that long had stood as a sentinel on the route to Nazareth in the northern interior of Palestine. Throughout recorded history, many invading armies had travelled this route, including Napoleon in 1799. For Allenby in 1918 the plain upon which Megiddo sat (known as the Vale of Esdraelon) was of high strategic importance because it linked the Jordan Valley with the Plain of Sharon, which was about 40 miles to the east and located behind the Ottoman front line. Allenby's intention was to break through the western end of this line on 19 September, following upon the feint carried out by the Arab forces at Deraa on 16 September, as well as a second prefatory operation on 18 September in the Judean Hills under the command of Lieutenant General Philip Chetwode designed to distract the Ottomans. 'If we can keep our intentions and dispositions dark', Allenby had written conspiratorially to Wilson on 21 August, 'I think the Turk is likely to suffer a severe defeat. I propose to use my Cavalry very boldly. ... I promise you nothing; but I have great hopes, if all goes even fairly well.'[107]

Accordingly, with the two preliminary operations having done their job of sowing confusion among the Ottomans, Allenby launched his main attack early on 19 August by unleashing an artillery barrage belched up by the combined propulsive power of almost 400 field guns. From their smoking mouths they poured down a withering and pulverizing carpet of steel onto the Ottomans' entrenched front line at Nahr al-Faliq at the astonishing rate of some 1,000 shells per minute. After 20 minutes of this deafening cacophony – 'our ears could hear nothing and in that place brother could not recognize brother. The very earth was forced to quake,' wrote an utterly dazed Ottoman soldier later – the guns were re-calibrated so as to allow for the British and Indian infantry to advance on the enemy positions.[108] These troops did so under the command of Lieutenant General Sir Edward Bulfin in the style of a creeping barrage, a tactic used first though not very effectively by the British at the Somme in August 1916, but subsequently employed to much greater effect by the Canadians in order to achieve their memorable victory at Vimy Ridge the following year.

Given the overwhelming nature of the main attack – notwithstanding a last-minute Indian deserter's informing the Turks of its precise location – the day turned swiftly into a disaster for the Ottomans. In Nazareth, at his General Headquarters, Liman had been rendered incommunicative owing to the successful bombing by the Royal Air Force – as the Royal Flying Corps and the Royal Naval Air Service had become in April – of the main telephone exchange at Afula early that morning. Consequently, he had no clear idea of what was happening to the Ottoman 7th and 8th Armies. But even if he had had an idea Liman would have been distraught to know that his troops had broken under the ferocity of the British attack and now were in retreat, trying desperately to escape from their ardent pursuers on the ground, while being harassed also from the air. Meanwhile, the Desert Mounted Corps under the redoubtable Australian general, Harry Chauvel, were on the move northwards along the coast towards the rear of the collapsing Ottoman positions. 'My battle is a big one; &, so far, is very successful', Allenby wrote to Mabel on 20 April, 'I think I have taken some 10,000 prisoners & 80 or 90 guns.'[109] He was right, even in his surmise of numbers. The beleaguered and demoralized Ottoman forces were collapsing all-round, with very little sustained resistance and almost no possibility of countering Allenby's calculated onslaught. Indeed, Allenby's battle plan would be praised later for being as 'brilliant in execution as it had been in conception', anticipating the style employed later by the Germans for their enormously successful 'blitzkrieg of 1939'.[110] Accordingly, the pressure exerted on the Turks by the Allies remained unrelenting. The Desert Mounted Corps continued to advance at speed – 'a mission of which all cavalry soldiers have dreamed', as one leading participant recalled the moment – breaking into the Vale of Esdraelon and cutting off the roads and railway lines by which the panicked Turks were trying now to escape.[111] The outcome of the Allies' success at Megiddo forced the Turks to wheel east in what would become a doomed attempt at retreating along the Jordan Valley. Barely twenty-four hours into the battle, victory for the British-led forces thus looked imminent.

Meanwhile, the Arab troops, having succeeded in rendering useless the railway lines around Deraa, had settled into a brief holding pattern. Doing so had come at the explicit order of Allenby. In a clutch of messages sent by airplane to Faisal at Azraq, Allenby had begun by congratulating him 'upon the great achievement of your gallant troops about Deraa, the effect of which has, by throwing the enemy's communications into confusion, had an important bearing upon the success of my own operations. Thanks to our combined efforts, the Turkish army is defeated and is everywhere in full retreat.'[112] As we have seen, though as yet somewhat premature in citing victory, Allenby's confidence in the outcome of the battle was nevertheless justified. But, as a function of that anticipated victory, he had made plain his chief concern about its potential aftermath to Alan Dawnay. In a note to Pierce Joyce at Azraq, Dawnay stated that 'above all he [Allenby] does NOT wish Feisal to dash off, on his own, to Damascus or elsewhere – we shall soon be able to put him there as part of our own operations. ... So use all of your restraining influence, and get Lawrence to do the same, to prevent Feisal from any act of rashness in the north.'[113]

The prospect of making his own move soon against Damascus now was in view and therefore Allenby stood perched on the cusp of having to leave what to him was the entirely comfortable world of military operations for the far less amenable atmosphere of politics and diplomacy. However, before that could happen, there would need to be a few more days of fighting, and to these he was attuned acutely. By the early morning of 21 April the Ottoman 7th and 8th Armies, the former under the command of Kemal, had been pushed out of Nablus entirely and were retreating in a long and straggly line down the Wadi Fara to the Jordan Valley. Of the Yildirim Army Group and the three Ottoman Armies that despite being badly undermanned and lacking in resolve had engaged Allenby's forces two days earlier, there was one only left in the field, the 4th under the command of Jemal Pasha. The retreat of the 7th and 8th Armies, in fact, had turned into a thoroughgoing rout during which RAF planes had dropped nearly 20,000 pounds of bombs and had emptied over 50,000 rounds of machine-gun fire on the beaten and cowering Turks below. As Lawrence described the scene evocatively later,

> the modern motor road, the only way of escape for the Turkish divisions, was scalloped between cliff and precipice in a murderous defile. For four hours our aeroplanes replaced one another in series above the doomed columns. ... When the smoke had cleared it was seen that the organization of the enemy had melted away. They were a dispersed horde of trembling individuals, hiding for their lives in every fold of the vast hills.[114]

The disaster that had befallen the main body of the Ottoman Army, therefore, was almost total. The exception to this state of affairs was the 4th Army. But although not much damaged owing to the southerly position that it had taken up near Ma'an, it was of no use now after having been cut off from the north by the successful demolition work of the Arabs around Deraa. Lawrence of course had been in the middle of these actions, mostly now from the front passenger seat of 'Blue Mist', his reinforced Rolls-Royce tender which, like the other ones in use, had proven to be almost indestructible. His automobile was worth 'rubies' in the desert, as Lawrence enthused: 'Great was Rolls, and great was Royce!'[115] And now, nearing the conclusion of the Arab Revolt, he would enter Damascus triumphantly in Blue Mist in just a little over a week's time.

From 22 to 25 of September the combined British Imperial forces continued to push forward, taking three more key Ottoman strongholds: El Salt, Amman and Samakh. The first two of these were especially gratifying given the earlier failure of the Transjordan Raids to take them permanently. Meanwhile, Allenby was disappointed to have learnt that Liman had barely escaped capture at Nazareth, fleeing just six hours before the 'cavalry had surrounded his house', as he reported to Wilson.[116] But the ongoing allied victories portended that the Turkish Army had been 'practically destroyed', as Allenby informed Mabel. A day later on 22 September he continued writing to his wife that, 'all goes well; prisoners pour in. ... The Turks have lost everything W. of Jordan. Railway, rolling stock, lorries, wagons, horses, camels, etc.'[117]

'Bloody bull's about' is the way that word had travelled among the officers and men whenever Allenby happened to tour the Allied camps and lines, which, given his penchant for spit and polish, was sometimes intended to be understood pejoratively. But in the excitement, fear and adrenaline of war, Allenby's commanding presence and clipped orders were calming and insistent, and he pushed his forces – as Nelson had done his seamen likewise – to 'annihilate' the enemy, so as to make impossible its recapitulation. Hence the battle continued to be waged – even fiercely so at Samakh in the face of exceptionally strong German resistance to the Anzac Light Horsemen – despite the thousands of Ottoman prisoners having been taken and all manner of enemy war materiel retrieved. The eventual capture of Samakh by the Allies however, on 25 September, would signal the end of a furious week of conquest. On that date, and for all practical purposes, Palestine had ceased to be a province – a *vilayet* – of the Ottoman Empire.[118]

On the next day, 26 September, Allenby sent out a special force order to all ranks expressing his thanks and admiration for the 'great deeds of the past week. … Such a complete victory', he stated, 'has seldom been known in all the history of war.'[119] In the celebratory atmosphere of the moment, Allenby might be excused for having resorted to such hyperbole. But in the context of the glacial way in which the war had been fought on the Western Front, Allenby's force order captures well his prevailing state of mind at that moment. By that time too, congratulations on the victory had started to arrive at Allenby's GHQ. 'Well done,' wrote Wilson. 'The whole thing is really a gem.'[120] 'I hail with you the approaching liberation of the whole of Palestine by you,' telegraphed Chaim Weizmann.[121] In even more fulsome terms, King George sent Allenby a telegram saying, 'I am confident that this success which has effected the liberation of Palestine from Turkish rule will rank as a great exploit in the history of the British Empire.'[122] Gratified by words of such high commendation, the enormity of the victory – and what Allenby anticipated now to be its culminating moment at Damascus – was beginning now to become abundantly clear to him. 'The senders' of congratulatory messages, he wrote to Mabel, 'don't yet know the completeness of the victory.'[123] Given the king's effusive praise, one might say that such a realization had begun already to become apparent at Buckingham Palace; still, for Allenby, the final pieces of the victory had yet to be put in place.

To assist in that victory, the Arabs moved now from their base at Umtaiye in order to be nearer to Deraa. In so doing they put themselves in position to both take the town directly and to move on Damascus as swiftly as possible; as swiftly, that is, as they might dare given Allenby's prohibition on unauthorized action in this regard. By 27 September the all but beaten Turks had duly abandoned Deraa and had begun to fall back on Damascus. But in a wanton display of cruelty en route they had engaged in much killing and maiming. One episode in particular, the murder of a number of Syrian men, women, children and babies at the village of Tafas during the Turkish retreat, would spark an equally murderous rampage by the advancing Arabs, a scene that would be rendered chillingly by David Lean many years later in *Lawrence of Arabia*.[124] 'We killed and killed,' Lawrence lamented afterwards, in a kind of frenzy of bloody vengeance and putative national liberation in which he participated readily. All that remained now, it seemed, for any of them, was to travel the last few miles to Damascus in order to make complete the conquest of the Ottomans. For Allenby too, such was the plan. 'I hope that my cavalry will reach [there] tomorrow,' he wrote to Mabel on 29 September. 'Things are going swimmingly.'[125] And so they were.

In anticipation of the imminent taking of Damascus, Allenby had written to Faisal in order rescind his earlier prohibition against the Arabs moving north. 'There is no objection to Your Highness,' he wrote on 25 September, 'entering Damascus as soon as you consider that you can do so with safety.'[126] Allenby had been given permission by the British government to allow the Arabs to administer Damascus once it had been wrested from the Ottomans, although ultimate control of the city would remain in his hands as commander-in-chief. He was both aware of and sympathetic to the symbolic value of the Arabs arriving at Damascus first, and had instructed Harry Chauvel, at the head of the Desert Mounted Corps and in the vanguard of the Allied forces moving north, to 'let the Arabs go first, if possible.'[127] However, Allenby was constrained in his desire to give the Arabs their well earned due of arriving at Damascus ahead of anyone else by the interests of the French as contained in the Sykes–Picot Agreement. Nonetheless, he believed that he would be able 'to safeguard French and Arab interests' by ensuring that both symbolism and realpolitik would work together.[128] Accordingly, he sought and was given authorization by London for the Arab flag to be hoisted over the city of 300,000 residents when he would arrive there in victory.[129] Meanwhile, Faisal, who had entered Deraa on 29 September to scenes of both residual carnage and wild celebration, was preparing to move on to Damascus, as of course also was Lawrence.

On the next day, 30 September, the last day of fighting – save for the final thrust northwards to Aleppo that would come later – concluded with the elimination of the Ottoman 4th Army. At six o'clock on the following morning, the first day of October, the Desert Mounted Corps under the command of Chauvel entered Damascus from which most of the remaining Ottoman troops had fled north. They had done so just a few hours ahead of the arrival of the Anzacs, who in turn were followed by a Bedouin force of about 1,500 men, headed by both Nasir and Auda abu Tayi in a scene of almost unbounded joyous celebration (Figure 8). The wanton killing that had so disgusted Lawrence when he had arrived at Deraa just three days earlier – 'one of the nights in which mankind went crazy,' he would write later in despair, 'when death seemed impossible, however many died to the right or left' – gratifyingly was not to be seen in Damascus.[130] Still, shortly after the Bedouin entered the city they had begun to loot on a wide scale, and their treatment of both Turkish prisoners and of their wounded was abominable.[131] Lawrence, in Arab dress as usual and riding in Blue Mist, arrived at Damascus along with the Bedouin. He was exhausted both physically and mentally, but having lived the previous two years in anticipation of winning this very city, his sense of gratification could not have been greater. Savouring the joyous and semi-anarchic spectacle that signalled victory and potential liberation for the Arabs, Lawrence was 'cheered by name, covered with flowers, kissed indefinitely,' as he recounted later, 'and splashed with attar of roses from the house-tops'.[132]

Audeh Abou Tiyeh, British ally of the desert.

Figure 8 Fierce, proud and a key British ally during the war in the desert, Auda abu Tayi, the Howeitat warrior, was 'the greatest fighting man in northern Arabia', reputed to have killed seventy-five men by his own hand.

Meanwhile, while Damascus erupted in celebration on 1 October, Allenby remained at his GHQ in anticipation of an imminent departure for the Syrian capital city. He informed the War Office that both the Desert Mounted Corps and the Arabs had occupied Damascus earlier that day, and then he wrote to Mabel, who had come out to Cairo from London during the latter part of the campaign, to say that he would be leaving soon travelling via Tiberias and that he expected to be in Damascus on 3 October.[133] Allenby duly set out the next day, passing by 'Hattin – scene of Saladin's great victory over the Crusaders [in 1187]', which, he added matter-of-factly, 'had regained Jerusalem for the Moslems [*sic*] till I came'.[134] During those two intervening days, however, until Allenby got to Damascus, the situation in the city had turned from a joyous, though undisciplined, celebration, to a contest of wills between Faisal's representatives and some of the leading members of the local political opposition. Complicating this deteriorating situation was that both parties claimed to be acting in accordance with the wishes of Sharif Hussein, the self-proclaimed king of the Arabs, who, just the day before, had written a congratulatory note to Allenby telling him that, as their liberator, 'I ask almighty God to enable me to kiss you between your eyes'.[135]

In the meantime, the local Damascene opposition group was led by two Algerian brothers, Abd el-Kader and Muhammad Said, who stood at the head of a large body of their exiled countrymen. As little more than armed and formerly pro-Turkish thugs, however, the two brothers were told that their claim to control the new Arab administration in Damascus was completely illegitimate and without foundation. The brothers disputed this charge vociferously, repeating the canard that they were acting in the name of Hussein which, they insisted, had been demonstrated by the raising of the Sharifian flag over the city. For his part, Lawrence despised both brothers as being nothing more than unprincipled pro-French political opportunists. As well, he believed them to be 'insane' and 'religious fanatics of the worse kind'. He was determined, therefore, that a genuine follower of Faisal and Hussein be put in charge of the embryonic Arab administration.[136] In his view, Shukri el-Ayubi, a leading and respected citizen of Damascus and recently released by the Ottomans from prison, was just such a man. Accordingly, Shukri was brought to the Town Hall – 'its steps and stairs were packed with a swaying mob' – and declared by Lawrence along with Auda to be the city's new temporary Arab military governor.[137] Harry Chauvel, having entered the city first early that morning, had decided to pull back his Anzac horsemen to outside its boundaries in order to leave the day of celebration to the Arabs, agreed with Lawrence's move, pending Allenby's imminent arrival. And there, briefly, matters would stand until both Faisal and Allenby arrived in Damascus within hours of each other on the third day of October.

For the triumphal journey to Damascus, Faisal had taken a train from Deraa, along the way basking in the joy of having played a key role in finally chasing the Ottomans from the country. Equally, however, he was concerned greatly by the formidable problems of trying to form a new Arab government in their place. In order to maximize the importance and occasion of his entry into Damascus, Faisal had decided to mark the occasion by entering the city mounted triumphantly on horseback and therefore his train was halted a short distance from the city. While marshalling there that morning, however, Faisal was informed that Allenby expected him to come as soon as possible to the Hotel Victoria in the centre of Damascus because he was not planning to spend the night in the city and wished to be on his way by three o'clock that afternoon (Figure 9). Accordingly, the victorious entry of Faisal and his retinue, along with hundreds of Arab Northern Army regulars and Bedouin irregulars, would have to wait. In the event, when his parade-like entry did occur that evening after the bilateral meeting with Allenby was over, the celebrations of two days earlier would be largely repeated, although this time they centred on Faisal mounted regally on his bay Arab stallion. Full of

Figure 9 Allenby emerging from the Hotel Victoria in Damascus on 3 October 1918 after a tense and trying meeting with Prince Faisal and T. E. Lawrence.

emotion as he shed tears of joy at the exultation of the Arab people, they pushed close to him, reaching out their hands and kissing his own. 'The flags of the Arab Revolt were everywhere,' Faisal's main biographer recounts. 'For now at least, the city was at his feet.'[138]

Allenby's arrival at Damascus had preceded Faisal's own by a few hours and was done conventionally in an open-top Rolls-Royce and with little fanfare. His entrance into Jerusalem, by contrast, by walking through the Jaffa Gate had been of greater moment, although then as now he continued to eschew the traditional conqueror's trope of sitting astride a horse. That Faisal would choose to do so, however, was understandable to Allenby and he did not see it as being in any way comparable to the Kaiser's unwarranted entry into Jerusalem in 1898 or, for that matter, a similar visit to Damascus that he had made later the same year. The Hotel Victoria, where Allenby had summoned Faisal to meet him, was a much smaller and less grand version of Cairo's Shepheard's Hotel, but traditionally it had been at the heart of Damascene political life. The meeting between Allenby and Faisal, which would be their first ever, was pregnant with both importance and symbolism. A number of others would be present at their encounter, including Lawrence and Chauvel. Lawrence would act as interpreter, but by this point his psychic dissonance had returned in a pronounced way and he had resolved already to quit the deserts of the Middle East and head for home.[139] He did not keep detailed notes of the meeting, writing later mainly of the two principals and how they made 'a strange contrast: Feisal, large-eyed, colourless and worn, like a fine dagger; Allenby, gigantic and red and merry, fit representative of the Power which had thrown a girdle of humour and strong dealing round the world'.[140]

As requested by Allenby, Faisal hurried to the centre of Damascus and at 2.30 that afternoon the two men began what would turn out to be not much more than a half-hour meeting between them. Allenby led off by voicing his immediate approval of what Lawrence had established by way of an Arab civic administration over the previous two days of tumult, and confirmed that the respected Syrian political leader, Ali Riza Rikabi, would take over as military governor from what had proven already to be a too-burdensome task for the over-matched Shukri. But these were mere preliminaries leading up to the heart of the encounter, which was to make clear the scope and content of putative Arab sovereignty over the territory from which the Ottomans had just been expelled so decisively, with the final act of their complete expulsion from the Middle East yet to come.

The only thorough recounting of the historic meeting between Allenby and Faisal on 3 October 1918 is that made by Harry Chauvel, who kept shorthand notes of it. Eventually, eleven years later in 1929, he would turn these notes into a three-page document.[141] Both the passage of time in writing it and the less-than-verbatim notetaking of a thirty-minute meeting held many years earlier may have rendered Chauvel's account not wholly reliable; still, his report remains the only full reprise of the Allenby-Faisal encounter, one that would leave Faisal shaken and disappointed, and confirm Lawrence's departure for England as soon as possible followed by his taking up of the Arab cause at Westminster.

Just prior to meeting with Faisal, Allenby had been given updated instructions by London, which essentially ordered him to implement the provisions of the Sykes–Picot Agreement. The British government considered both the agreement and the Balfour Declaration to be operative, meaning that a form of Arab control under French influence would prevail henceforth in the northern 'A' zone, as configured by Sykes–Picot, while the same kind of arrangement but under British influence would exist in the southern 'B' zone. Palestine – to which the Balfour Declaration applied – would exist outside of the Arab sphere altogether, as would Lebanon. Allenby, in informing Faisal of these conditions, told him also that he would be obliged to accept the presence of a French liaison officer who, for the time being at least, would work with Lawrence. It might well be assumed that little of what transpired between Allenby and Faisal is what the Arab leader wished to hear however, and therefore, according to Chauvel, to all of these provisions 'Feisal objected very strongly'. Meanwhile, Lawrence, who was participating in these brief proceedings with a growing sense of discomfort, then was asked directly by Allenby: 'But did you not tell him that the French were to have the Protectorate over Syria?' Lawrence replied, according to Chauvel, 'No Sir, I know nothing about it.' In responding in this way to Allenby Lawrence clearly was being disingenuous for both he and Faisal were well aware of the Anglo-French agreement which, by then, had been in the public domain for many months. Not only that but, as we have seen, Lawrence had met with Mark Sykes in person at Wajh in the previous year. As a consequence, however, the atmosphere in the meeting room at the hotel turned testy very quickly. But Allenby, not about to be challenged in this regard, told Faisal firmly that 'he must accept the situation as it was and that the whole matter would be settled at the conclusion of the War'. Being under Allenby's command, Faisal could do little other than to obey. Greatly dismayed with what he had been told, however, Faisal then left the hotel resignedly, observed Chauvel, 'with his entourage (less Lawrence) and went out of the City again to take on his triumphal entry'.

At this point in the afternoon's proceedings, a visibly upset Lawrence told Allenby that he would refuse to work with a French liaison officer to advise Faisal, and since he was due for leave he would like to take it now and depart for England immediately. In response, Allenby offered Lawrence a cryptic, 'Yes! I think you had,' and the meeting came to an end frostily. Chauvel's words bristle with evidence of tension between Allenby and Lawrence at the conclusion of this historic meeting, although it is worth noting that in neither man's account of the same event do they even hint at the existence of strife between them, much less offer an elaboration of a rift having occurred.[142] But Lawrence remained determined to go home all the same, which he began to do the very next day by driving in Blue Mist en route first for Egypt, and then later taking ship for England. During his short stopover in Cairo he gave Mabel a special Baluchi carpet, which would become for her a prized possession and about which Allenby would remind Lawrence of its 'romantic' provenance almost ten years later at the time of the publication of *Seven Pillars of Wisdom*.[143] From Cairo, just before departing for London, Lawrence would write elegiacally to the British base commandant at Aqaba: 'The old war is closing, and my use is gone. We were an odd little set, and we have, I expect, changed History in the East. I wonder how the Powers will let the Arabs get on.'[144] Meanwhile, Allenby, as planned, had left Damascus immediately after the meeting and was soon back at his GHQ at Bir

Figure 10 A victorious Allenby greets jubilant Syrians upon entering Aleppo, 27 October 1918.

Salem, writing to Mabel of having met with Faisal, 'a fine, slim sharp featured man' with whom he had had what was described as a 'satisfactory talk'.[145]

For Allenby, the war was effectively over too, although the final pursuit of the remnant Turks who remained in the field meant that an Anglo-Arab force ran them to ground at the key northern Syrian city of Aleppo on 26 October. On that day, the city fell after a spirited fight between 2 evenly matched contingents of about 3,000 men each.[146] Five days later, and less than two weeks before a general armistice would be declared on the Western Front, the Armistice of Mudros was signed by the Ottomans and the British at the eponymously named harbour on the Greek island of Lemnos. What Allenby's EEF and Faisal's Arabs had wrought together on the field of battle across much of the Middle East during the previous year and a half – 'a glorious and memorable achievement', as King George put it in a congratulatory message to Allenby – would be turned over now to the peacemakers at Paris, who would congregate there to begin their deliberations in just a little over two months' time.[147] A supremely militarily victorious Allenby was set fair now to depart the battlefields of the Middle East for its halls of political power, a change, as we shall see, that would come to dominate the next seven years of his life (Figure 10).

Chapter 6

IMPERIAL PROCONSUL IN EGYPT, 1919–21

Allenby's victory over the Ottoman Turks and their German allies in Palestine and Syria in October 1918 was comprehensive. His forces had destroyed their armed presence in the region by inflicting many thousands of casualties and taking prisoner over 71,000 Turco-German soldiers.[1] Stunningly, the Ottomans had been removed as suzerain of a vast domain over which they had ruled for some 400 years. Indeed, in an era replete with world-historical events, the usurpation of the Ottomans' position in the Middle East would prove to be one of the most important and long-standing outcomes of the entire war. While Allenby was aware of the sweeping nature of what had been accomplished under his command, he found little time to ruminate on its long-term implications. The speed of contemporary events was such that it forced him immediately to follow up the fighting with a series of diplomatic actions. As he wrote to Clive Wigram, the king's assistant private secretary, on 5 October, 'things look very different now to what they did 6 months ago; both here and in Europe'.[2] That was certainly true, and for the balance of October Allenby had continued to fight against what was left of Turkish resistance until – as noted in Chapter 5 – ultimate victory was achieved at Aleppo on 26 October, and the Armistice of Mudros signed on 31 October. Symbolically, the signing of the armistice came exactly one year to the day after the stirring victory over the Ottomans at Beer Sheba led by the Desert Mounted Corps had put the whole EEF on the road to victory in Jerusalem. These final military operations in Syria, while necessarily valedictory, were merely, however, the prelude to an intense and constant preoccupation with what the entire campaign portended for the future of politics and government in the Middle East.

Allenby's diplomatic and political career, it might be said, had begun on 3 October 1918 in Damascus where, as we saw earlier, he had made it clear to Sharif Faisal that the Arabs would be receiving only a portion of what they believed to be their full right of conquest in Syria. This position, grounded in the claims of the Sykes–Picot Agreement, as well as in the rhetoric of the Balfour Declaration, meant everything that would transpire subsequent to 3 October was viewed necessarily by both the Allies and the Arabs through a politico-diplomatic lens. For Allenby, this situation perforce made him into something – an imperial administrator, to start – that he would not otherwise have ever thought himself to be. Still, as long as military operations were in progress his command remained supreme, and this meant also a continuing responsibility for civil affairs. As he had informed the War Office on 6 October from Damascus, 'an Arab administration was in being and the Arab flag was flying from Government buildings.'[3] He had expected this development; indeed, he had invited Faisal, as we saw earlier, to put it into effect.

During these early post-bellum days in Damascus the political situation remained relatively quiet. Allenby was on the move constantly, to Acre, to Beirut, back to Damascus, in order to stay in the vanguard of events, as well as to set the terms of debate about the future of the region. In the middle of October, he dined with Faisal in Damascus, as he wrote to Mabel, and had 'an excellent dinner; Arab dishes, but all good'. The conversation was cordial but became pointed in places when it touched upon the declining Arab governing position and the corresponding rise in that of the French. 'He [Faisal] is nervous about the peace settlement,' Allenby continued to Mabel; 'but I tell him he must trust the Entente powers to treat him fairly.' To Allenby, Faisal was an impressive and honourable leader, 'strong in will, & straight in principle'.[4] But the complicated political reality, both European and Arab, mitigated against Faisal achieving all that he wanted and, critically, to that which he believed his people were entitled.

Earlier, during their tense meeting at the Hotel Victoria on 3 October, Allenby had informed Faisal that the Arab forces fighting in Palestine and Syria had been recognized by the British government as holding belligerent status.[5] Such recognition meant that their position in relation to the Allies was a formal one, and therefore it suggested a reserved place for them during the peace negotiations to come in Paris. Certainly, as Allenby told Faisal on more than one occasion, the making of the peace would be the time during which the Arab position would become clarified. But Allenby never laboured under the illusion that Faisal and the Arabs would achieve *all* that they thought was their due. Indeed, while pleased that at Damascus 'civil government is making progress', as he wrote to Mabel, still 'there are many conflicting political interests, which to some extent keep back our reorganization'.[6] A little later on 23 October, Allenby maintained in a report to the CIGS in London, General Sir Henry Wilson, that 'the Arab Government is getting to work satisfactorily'. But shortly thereafter he followed up this report with a message confirming the creation of three new European-supervised Occupied Enemy Territories, at a stroke undercutting the Arab position. Altogether, therefore, the political situation in the conquered Arab lands remained fluid.

The creation of OET North, South and East, as Allenby called them, was an exercise in Indirect Rule, one of the chief markers of British colonial governance as it had developed in a number of places around the world, especially over the preceding generation. Accordingly, as he explained to the War Office, 'as far as possible the Turkish system of government will be continued and the existing machinery utilized'.[7] As a form of imperial collaboration this kind of governing style had long been used by the British in Canada, India, Nigeria, British East Africa and elsewhere, and its usefulness as an interim measure in the Middle East – mutatis mutandis – was one that came naturally to Allenby. The former Turkish administrative areas and their records were to be used, therefore, in order to smooth the way forward for the new regime, one that needed to be scrupulously apolitical, he emphasized. Accordingly, none of the officials tasked with OET administration, stated Allenby, should engage in 'any political propaganda or take part in any political questions'.⁸

The OET's boundaries were exclusive of Mesopotamia and the Hijaz, but otherwise they corresponded closely with the provisions of the Sykes–Picot Agreement, meaning that OET North was French-run and that OET South was British-run. OET East was centred on Damascus and therefore was at the heart of Faisal's new Arab government, at least for the time being. Indeed, altogether, there was little doubt that the provisions of the OET, at least for Allenby, were meant to be temporary, and although their existence would carry with it the prospect of inertia, as governing structures they were not intended to be permanent. Like his British colleagues, in this situation Allenby distrusted the French implicitly, although of course without ever saying so publicly. Allenby could see plainly Faisal's similar distrust of the French in Syria, who 'mean', said the Arab leader prophetically, 'to get hold of the country'.⁹ Naturally, Allenby was called upon to maintain a scrupulous fairness in his own public utterances about the new political arrangements. But in private he wrote and spoke forthrightly about the prevailing situation, especially as it concerned France. For example, Allenby regarded the co-author of the Sykes–Picot Agreement Francois Georges-Picot, who just then was under consideration to become the French governor of OET North, as being nothing more than 'a superficially clever man, but shallow & transparent. I know him well, & he knows me', he wrote to General Wilson, on 9 November.¹⁰ The overriding problem with Picot and the French, as Allenby saw it, was that if they were allowed to achieve all that they wished in the Levant – which would necessarily preclude Arab access to the Mediterranean Sea – there would be 'sudden trouble'. In an especially transparent message to Wilson, Allenby went on at length about his view of the prevailing post-war situation in the Middle East. 'The future', he forecast with prescience, 'when martial law no longer prevails, is not so cloudless. Distrust of the French is not, in any way, abated.' Conversely, Arab faith in the British remained strong, Allenby believed, because of their long relationship with Faisal. Without this faith, however, he emphasized, 'there would be blood, fire & ruin throughout all Arabia. ... If we act up to our declared principles regarding the rights of self-determination of peoples, we shall retain that confidence. If not, there will be chaos.'¹¹

On 11 November, two days after writing these telling words to Wilson, in the Forest of Compiegne the Allies and Germans finally brokered a general armistice, signalling the end of the First World War. After more than four years of almost incalculable death, destruction and dislocation, all appeared to be over at last. 'That closes the war', Allenby wrote simply but in great relief to his mother, Catherine, 'except for the inevitable troubles that will arise during the rearrangement of nations and borders.'¹² Attempting to solve these troubles was to be at the heart of Allenby's rapidly expanding proconsular career, and therefore as he closed out the year 1918, his administrative responsibility for the lands that he had just won for the victorious Allies continued apace.

Allenby's mature, post-war view of the Sykes–Picot Agreement was that as a piece of diplomacy it had come to fit very badly the developing situation on the ground in the Middle East. In taking this view he was joined by a number of others, such as General Reginald Wingate, the British high commissioner for Egypt during the previous two years and the man whom Allenby would succeed, as we shall see, in March of 1919. Wingate wrote to him in November to say that Sykes–Picot would require 'much alteration if not complete scrapping'.[13] Even more earnestly, however, T. E. Lawrence had begun to dispute the agreement worked out between Mark Sykes and Picot three years earlier in 1916. Having departed Cairo on 15 October, Lawrence had reached London on 28 October and once there began immediately to champion the Arab cause.[14] Lawrence was clear in telling the Lloyd George government – specifically the members of its Eastern Committee, which was responsible for British policy in the Middle East – that they could count on Faisal's support for Britain's position in the region, but only for as long as they remained anti-French. 'Our whole attitude to the French is hardening here,' wrote David Hogarth, Lawrence's old archaeology colleague, now back in London. 'TEL has put the wind up everybody and done much good.'[15] Lawrence was keen also – as he had shown first upon meeting Lowell Thomas earlier that year – to use the British press to support the Arab cause. Accordingly, he wrote immediately to Geoffrey Dawson, editor of *The Times*, to say 'that the Arabs came into the war without making a previous treaty with us, and have consistently refused to listen to the temptation of other powers. They have never had a press agent, or tried to make themselves out a case, but fought as hard as they could (I'll swear to that) and suffered hardships.'[16] Indeed, British claims to suzerainty over Palestine and Mesopotamia (which there were focused on Mosul and its oilfields) had drawn no opposition from Faisal. But the quid pro quo for that stance, in Faisal's view, was British support for his own claims to Syria and Lebanon against those made by the French.

As a result, throughout October and November Faisal attempted to enact a policy of capacious Arab administration in the region which, as it pertained to Lebanon specifically, had provoked French resistance and a commensurate move by Allenby to calm both Britain's erstwhile wartime allies and the Arabs. Shukri el-Ayubi, once having been replaced as the short-lived military governor of Damascus, was then inserted into Beirut by Faisal as military governor there. The French objected immediately to this unilateral appointment, arguing that it violated the provisions of the 'A' (Blue) Zone of Sykes–Picot, which had placed Lebanon under French control. For the time being, Allenby agreed reluctantly with the French and pressed Faisal to have Shukri step down. Faisal resisted such pressure, however, but to no avail. Therefore, on 10 October British officers in Beirut were instructed by their commander, General Edward Bulfin, to remove the Arab flag from all public buildings in the city. Unsurprisingly, Faisal could not be appeased over this measure and he reacted strongly to it by sending a tersely worded cable to Allenby protesting that 'I see no need to explain or elaborate to you what disgrace befell the Arab flag in Beirut, the very same standard of the nation that you told me recently was included by His Majesty King George V as part of Britain's allies'.[17]

Alas, Allenby had discovered very quickly that operating in the politico-diplomatic world was thankless, ever-shifting and usually elusive of a decisive outcome which, to him, was almost the complete antithesis of much of his long-time military experience. In response to Faisal's protest over Beirut, Allenby repeated what he had said already, which was that until the peace-making deliberations at Paris had taken place and binding judgements rendered for the future of the region, it was his responsibility to ensure that military rule continued to be enforced effectively in Lebanon and everywhere else that his authority held sway. Still, Allenby recognized both the need for and usefulness of Faisal exercising greater personal authority over his people and territory, which he granted on 21 October by according him full political control – under supervisory British military rule – in areas 'A' and 'B' – as delineated in the Sykes–Picot Agreement.[18] Accordingly, a few weeks later Faisal travelled to newly liberated Aleppo in order to demonstrate that Syria, in his view, had become in effect an independent Arab state. On 6 November Faisal entered the city in triumph therefore, and on 11 November he gave a rousing speech in which he appealed to Arab generosity and patriotic determination in creating Syria as a new post-Ottoman pluralistic state: 'The Arabs were Arabs before Moses, and Jesus and Muhammad …, and anyone who sows discord between Muslim, Christian and Jew is not an Arab. I am an Arab before all else. … I ask my brothers to consider me as a servant of this land.'[19]

Faisal's insistence on an Arab Syria had been emboldened by the Anglo-French Declaration made just two days earlier in which both Britain and France appeared to have superseded the Sykes–Picot Agreement by promising 'the complete and final liberation of the peoples so long oppressed by the Turks and the establishment of national governments and administrations deriving their authority from the initiative and free choice of the native populations'.[20] On the day that Faisal had entered Aleppo, 6 November, Picot had arrived in Beirut where he had insisted that Syria be turned over to the French. Very quickly his expectation in this regard was dashed, however, with the impact of the Declaration of 9 November effectively nullifying the Sykes–Picot Agreement even though its full text had included an undefined 'functional' role for both the British and the French in the future political development of the Arab Middle East. The exact nature of this prospective functional role remained anybody's guess, and of course would have to wait upon the Paris peace negotiations and beyond to be realized fully. However, for Allenby, the Anglo-French Declaration was precisely what he had been looking for in order to ease tensions both in the Arab street and in his diplomatic relationship with Faisal. As he had written to Wilson on 19 October, 'If a statement, by the Governments, French & British, could be published – to the effect – that, after the war, the wishes of the inhabitants could be considered in deciding on the form of Government in conquered territories – it would do much to restore confidence.'[21] In this instance, anyway, Allenby had got exactly that for which he had asked.

Later, on 22 November, after experiencing the heady Arab nationalist atmosphere in Aleppo, Faisal would depart Beirut for France and the impending Paris Peace Conference. Already, the Foreign Office had asked Allenby whether or not the time was right to have the Arabs represent themselves directly at the upcoming conference, to which he had replied with an enthusiastic yes. Concurrently, at Westminster Lawrence continued to argue the Arab case persuasively to the

Eastern Committee. He had cabled Sharif Hussein on 8 November in order to inform him that Allenby would be in touch also to ask about who he wanted to be his chosen representative at Paris. Lawrence told the sharif that the obvious and really only choice to fulfil this role was Faisal. Hussein agreed readily – any lingering suspicion between father and son had dissipated in the aftermath of the taking of Damascus – and therefore he had instructed Faisal to proceed immediately to Paris as his plenipotentiary. Once there, the sharif emphasized, Faisal was to remain closely in line with 'our loyal ally Great Britain' in order to achieve the best possible diplomatic result for the new Arab nation.[22]

Altogether, at least as far as Allenby was concerned, by the end of November, the initial political and diplomatic challenges generated by the Ottomans' defeat had been met. His counsel was being accepted at the highest levels of the British government; he had effected a concordat with Faisal; and he was doing his best to maintain civil relations with the French. To this latter point can be added the person of Mark Sykes, who, like Picot, had arrived in the Middle East in November. In London, a short time before that, the ever-enterprising Sykes had put together a small mission headed by himself and had convinced the Foreign Office of the mission's efficacy in obtaining for Britain 'as satisfactory a settlement of Middle Eastern questions as military and political circumstances will permit'. Thusly charged, he then had set off on 30 October for Palestine via Paris and Rome.[23] Once having arrived in Palestine he reported to Allenby, as Picot had also done, both of whom were present there in the capacity of 'political adviser' to their respective governments. Any and all communications that they would make with their home governments, therefore, were required to go through Allenby as military commander. It seems that Allenby liked both men well enough, writing to Wilson, for example, to say that he was glad Picot had come, 'as now I have someone to whom I can talk plainly'.[24] Allenby had never met Sykes before, but anticipated that he would fall into the same category as Picot. Wilson, however, was not so sanguine about Sykes. 'I hope Mark Sykes behaves himself,' he opined in a letter to Allenby in early December. 'He is a good fellow but cracked and his blessed Sykes–Picot Agreement must be torn up *somehow*.'[25]

In effect, the 'tearing up' of Sykes–Picot had happened already on the day that the general Anglo-French Declaration had been published a month earlier. Still, the exact outcome of the Woodrow Wilson-style aspirations for national self-determination that the Declaration contained were a long way from being fulfilled in the Middle East, if they were to be fulfilled at all. In the meantime, Allenby remained at the centre of affairs, travelling around his temporary military fiefdom in a constant attempt to take its political temperature and control the potential for an anti-European Arab uprising. The likelihood of such an unwelcome event was one that he continued to lay principally at the feet of the French, however, as he explained in a note to General Wilson on 14 December: 'I'm just back from Aleppo, Beirut etc. … Feeling of the Arabs towards French is still bitter, and the French don't do much to soften matters.' All the same, Allenby was pleased to inform Wilson in a soft rebuttal that Sykes 'has been decidedly useful & helpful' and, he added, as a bonus, actually 'gets on well with Picot'.[26]

Adding another layer of complexity to the already tense situation in the Middle East over which Allenby presided was the continuing pressure exerted by Chaim Weizmann and his fellow Zionists for the British to fulfil the promises contained in the Balfour Declaration. Partly out of genuine gratification, and partly as a way to curry Allenby's favour, various groups of both Jews and Arabs in the region had chosen to honour him in a number of ways as their champion. For example, in Jerusalem the Provisional Committee of Palestine Jews had planted a garden called 'Allenby Wood' in order, Allenby was told, 'to ever remember your name with love and gratitude as the redeemer of our Holy Land'.[27] Similarly, a poem published in Damascus in Arabic, and then translated into English, was dedicated to him: 'O Allenby ... thou hast scattered the mobs of Turks from a country where we had made the tyranny of the Turk a worship'.[28] As Allenby recognized readily, however, insistent Zionism was something that clashed strongly – even irreconcilably – with the almost 600,000 Arabs who were resident permanently in Palestine, compared to the vastly smaller Jewish resident population of just 66,000. As he wrote to the War Office in December, 'it must be realized that Arab nation's ambitions count for little in Palestine where [the] non-Jewish population is concerned chiefly with maintenance in Palestine itself of a position which they consider Zionism threatens'.[29] As a statement of crystalline clarity as to the prevailing situation in Palestine, Allenby showed himself to have a nuanced estimation of what lay in store for the peacemakers who would be gathering soon at Paris. However, before any of that could happen, Allenby spent his second Christmas in the Middle East – indeed, the first one anywhere marked by peace on earth since five years earlier in 1913.

After the Christmas and New Year holidays were over, the victorious Allies readied themselves for the Paris Peace Conference, which began on 18 January 1919. Allenby, meanwhile, and by way of sharp contrast, had found himself forced to actually *keep* the peace in the Middle East. First, he did so amid the overzealous celebrations by some of his own troops following the announcement of the armistice on 11 November, and then later, more seriously among a large number of unruly and frustrated soldiers who had not yet been demobilized. Protracted demobilization, the need for some troops to remain on active duty, and attendant indiscipline, occurred regularly in post-armistice Europe, and therefore it should come as no surprise that the same problems afflicted the EEF in the Middle East. Idle Anzac soldiers, and Bedouin irregulars in particular, came to blows on more than one occasion. In the most extreme of these incidents, an Anzac trooper from the Desert Mounted Division was murdered by an Arab thief in the village of Surafend in Palestine. In response, a group of his Anzac mates then launched a vigilante attack, which resulted in widespread violence during which about fifty Arab villagers were killed. Ordered to intervene, Allenby gave the Anzac troops responsible for the killings a vituperative verbal thrashing, during which he chose to call them 'cowards and murderers'. The assembled rankers rejected this characterization, however, as being both grossly unfair and much too harsh. As a result, they refused to name any of their number as being responsible for the massacre and in the end no one was charged. There was even a hint of insubordination in how the Anzacs responded to Allenby's dressing down that pricked his pride, especially since he had held the Anzac Mounted Division in high esteem based on their earlier exploits at Beer Sheba.[30] In the end, the stand-off between Allenby and the Anzacs at Surafend was resolved, but they would remain bitter about the episode for a long time.

The Anzacs, however, certainly were not alone in demonstrating their desire to be done with the war and what, for them, had turned into an interminable police action in the inhospitable desert thousands of miles away from home. In January, it was English troops in Aleppo and Damascus who protested vociferously about the slowness of demobilization, which prompted Allenby shortly thereafter to issue a Special Order of the Day regarding the need for greater discipline by the troops.[31] In a pointed statement, and in words redolent of the age in which he lived, Allenby reminded the EEF that the 'good name' of the British Army depended upon 'the individual conduct of each member of the Force'. Yes, he told them, demobilization was slow, but that was no excuse for giving in to the 'special temptations' of 'Wine and Women'. He implored the men to remember therefore that they would want to return home to their loved ones with their 'physical and moral energies unimpaired'. Finally, he appealed to their sense of soldierly pride by stating that 'the honour of the Egyptian Expeditionary Force is in your hands. I do not fear to leave it there.'

On a much different note around the same time in January, and nursing a grief that would never end, Allenby had remembered his dead son by acknowledging to Mabel that 'this [7 January] is Michael's birthday. He is 21 today.'[32] But his time now was spent overwhelmingly in consideration of the geopolitical future of the Middle East. He had moved his permanent headquarters to the coastal city of Haifa where, he informed Mabel, 'I am comfortably installed'.[33] From here he continued to tour his vast regional command in order to see that the terms of the Mudros armistice were being enforced. Alas, he complained to General Wingate on 15 January, the Turks were being 'dilatory' in fulfilling its terms.[34] In early February, therefore, after a brief trip across the Mediterranean, Allenby spent thirty-six hours in Constantinople during which he demanded and received full compliance with the Mudros armistice, specifically the requirement that all Turkish regiments be disbanded immediately. In what can be seen as a testament to Allenby's commanding manner, Turkish dilatoriness in this regard ended forthwith and the remaining Turkish troops were stood down within days.[35]

Throughout February – punctuated on 16 January by the unexpected death of Sykes, who had contracted Spanish influenza and by the time of his demise had gone to Paris – Allenby continued to navigate the shoals of Anglo-French politics and diplomacy in the Middle East. In particular, he resisted the constant attempts by the French to assert a more pronounced military presence in either Lebanon or Syria.[36] He would not waver in this stance, despite the steady imprecations of Picot that the size of the French military detachment should be increased. As Allenby explained to Wilson, he had refused the Frenchman's overtures on both military – 'I already have sufficient troops … , [and] do not recognize Monsieur Picot as having any right to give an opinion as to the number of troops necessary in my theatre of operations' – and political grounds: 'Should more French troops arrive while the Peace Conference is sitting', he continued, ' it will convey to the inhabitants, who are openly suspicious of French intentions, the impression that the future of Syria has already been decided on.'[37]

There is little doubt that Allenby felt himself now to be in the hothouse of world affairs', a not disagreeable place in which to find himself necessarily, but clearly not his normal Officers' Mess milieu. Certainly, as he wrote to a friend at the beginning of March, 'there is plenty to do and plenty to think about. All nations and would-be nations and all shades of religions and politics are up against each other and trying to get me to commit myself on their side. I am keeping up my end, so far; but there is need to walk warily.'[38] Indeed, in occupying this role Allenby had become for the moment a less exalted version of President Woodrow Wilson, whose luxurious suite at the Hotel du Prince Murat in Paris had been turned into a diplomatic salon for exactly the kind of special pleading referred to by Allenby in his words quoted earlier.

A few days later, on 12 March, and in keeping with his new administrative role, Allenby was asked to come to Paris in order to apprise Wilson and the other leading statesmen of the Peace Conference of the prevailing political situation in the Middle East, who just then were beginning to give over their attention to its close examination. 'Don't you think it would be a good plan to get Allenby to Paris as soon as possible,' Philip Kerr, the future Lord Lothian and David Lloyd George's private secretary, had written to the prime minister on 28 February. 'He can speak with much more authority about Syria, Palestine and Turkish questions generally than anybody else and his advice ought to be invaluable when it comes to military questions involved.'[39] Accordingly, Allenby was duly invited and he arrived in Paris on 19 March.

Once there, and over the next 48 hours, Allenby would live within a whirlwind of high-level diplomatic talks. As Margaret MacMillan has pointed out, 'for six months in 1919, Paris was the capital of the world', and Allenby's welcome there was as the conquering hero of, if not the biggest battlefield of the First World War, certainly one of its most storied.[40] He took up residence at the Hotel Majestic, one of the two main sites occupied by the British delegation at the conference, and 'with a most comfortable suite of rooms & a motor car at my disposal', as Allenby informed Mabel, he then proceeded to bring a dose of realpolitik to the delegates' understanding of the geopolitics of the Middle East.[41] Amused rather than overawed by the popular attention his arrival had generated – 'I have been interviewed & snapshotted, cinematographed and stared at continually' – Allenby addressed the Conference's Council of Four on 20 January.[42] On that day Wilson, Lloyd George, Georges Clemenceau of France and Vittorio Orlando of Italy listened intently to the man who just a few hours earlier had been lionized in the streets of Paris as something none of them had ever been, a victorious military commander. Allenby's reputation, both that of being the uncompromising 'Bull' and also now of having won a signal military victory, thus preceded him. Adding to Allenby's air of authority was his imposing physical heft in standing over six-feet tall and weighing some 200 pounds. As usual for him too, he spoke with a directness and a brevity that typically was not part of the verbal arsenal of those whom he now addressed. Clemenceau, in particular, did not appreciate Allenby's bluntness in explaining why he believed that imposing a French mandate upon Syria would court military disaster. Even less would he have appreciated Allenby's answer to the question, which had been asked earlier and elsewhere by President Wilson, of why it appeared that French interests were being shunted aside in the Middle East in favour of those of both the British and the Arabs. Allenby had expected a question along these lines and answered it simply, as well as colloquially. 'When I was at school, if I saw two boys fighting, the one big and the other small', he recounted phlegmatically, 'I first kicked the big boy, not the small one.'[43] The implication regarding the French position in the Middle East was clear, and coming from a proven warrior like Allenby, it seemed to have the desired effect on most of those who heard it.

The major outcome of the session with Allenby as far as the Council of Four was concerned, however, was for Wilson to suggest that an Inter-Allied Commission of Inquiry be sent to Syria in order to determine the wishes of the people in a manner that was in accord with the Anglo-French Declaration made the previous November. By this time the US president had little regard for whatever was left of Sykes–Picot, which he would mock later as sounding less like a diplomatic agreement and more like a type of tea. Would not a proper commission, however, Wilson queried, based on his cherished and emergent principle of national self-determination, be the right way forward?[44] Unsurprisingly, the French, who had come to be more keenly aware of the depth of Syrian animosity towards them, rejected Wilson's idea flatly. At the same time too, however, Wilson managed to annoy the British by suggesting that such a commission's remit should be expanded to include both Mesopotamia and Palestine. In the end the commission was struck, but owing to Anglo-French reluctance to participate in its formation and deliberations, the Americans would end up being its sole members, as we shall see.

During Allenby's brief and busy stay in Paris dominated by his meeting with the 'swells', as he described the members of the Council of Four to a friend, he had found time also to hold an important luncheon party. Included in it were both Faisal and T. E. Lawrence, the latter of whom had arrived in Paris in early January and had been in constant contact ever since with both the British and the Arab delegations.[45] But by the time that Allenby met with both of them over lunch his attention had been drawn away determinedly from the Arabs by the Foreign Office acting on the direction of Lloyd George.[46] Even though the conference proceedings were otherwise all-encompassing for the prime minister – 'Wilson and Lloyd George struck me as being the leading men, by a long way', remarked Allenby – the political situation in Egypt, which, from a British perspective, had begun to fray noticeably during the waning days of the war, had now turned into an open nationalist rebellion accompanied by widespread acts of public disorder.[47]

In response, the British government had begun to consider employing a firmer hand in Cairo than that which had been demonstrated by General Wingate, who was being blamed for having not done enough to prevent the deteriorating conditions that had spawned such disorderly outbreaks in the first place. Wingate's recall recently to London by the government for consultations over the crisis had been made for precisely this reason. In considering who might replace him in Cairo, the prime minister, without need of prompting, had had his perpetually high view of Allenby confirmed by Lord Curzon, the former viceroy of India who would become foreign secretary that October. Curzon regarded Allenby as 'the most prestigious British official, civil or military, in the Middle East'. Curzon's commendatory view of Allenby however, as we shall see, would change soon enough, but for the moment both he and other leading members of the government were united in seeing Allenby as the right man to tackle the crisis unfolding in Egypt.[48]

On the morning of 20 March, therefore, Allenby was informed that the British government wished to appoint him special high commissioner for Egypt and Sudan. He accepted the appointment without a moment's hesitation, in large part because he believed it would be a temporary one only while Wingate remained in England.[49] 'Now I return to a restless Egypt,' he wrote to Mabel on 21 March, the day of his departure. 'This Egyptian complication is a new one,' he continued, although he thought his presence there would 'have a calming effect; but the unrest has got a deep root, & there will be hard work to do'.[50] Leaving Paris and travelling via Marseilles and Malta, Allenby reached Egypt on 25 March, where he plunged immediately into the new role of Imperial proconsul while at the same time remaining – for the time being, at least – commander-in-chief throughout the conquered Allied territories of the Middle East.

By the time Allenby reached Cairo, where Mabel had been staying for some months while he had been in Palestine and Paris, the urban riots that had reached a climax a little earlier in March had begun to peter out. The Egyptian situation would continue to be volatile, however, and found its 'deep roots', as Allenby had pointed out, in a rising and broadening group of nationalists centred on the charismatic political figure of Saad Zaghlul, and what would soon become his main political instrument, the *Wafd* party. Born in 1859, Zaghlul was a graduate of El-Azhar University in Cairo, Egypt's oldest and most prestigious seat of higher learning. Subsequently, he had qualified in law and embarked upon a career that had gained for him considerable wealth and political status. In 1892, Zaghlul had been appointed to the Egyptian Court of Appeal, and then later he had become minister of education followed by minister of justice in the years prior to the First World War. From 1895, Zaghlul was married to the daughter (Safiya Khanum) of the prominent Egyptian politician and two-time Prime Minister Mustafa Fahmi. Altogether, by the time Allenby arrived in Egypt at the end of March 1919, Zaghlul was the most important nationalist politician in the country, and the one with whom he would have to negotiate in order to manage the ongoing tide of political unrest.[51]

Egyptian political unrest of a modern nationalist style was traceable back to 1882 and the anti-European uprising of that year led by the disaffected army officer Colonel Ahmed Urabi. In response to the uprising, which was seen as a grave threat to Britain's political and financial position in Egypt, the government under William Gladstone had ordered a naval bombardment of Alexandria, followed by the invasion and occupation of the country. The next quarter of a century would be marked by the increasing control of Egyptian and concomitant Sudanese affairs by Britain, a situation that was mediated most clearly by the British agent and consul general from 1883 until 1907, Evelyn Baring, Lord Cromer.[52] By the time of his retirement, modern Egyptian nationalism was a coming force, although both he and his successors (Sir Eldon Gorst, Lord Kitchener and Sir Henry McMahon) had managed to prevent any sort of general breakdown in Egyptian civil society. Not so, however, under the high commissionership (as the position, noted earlier, had begun to be called in 1914 when a British protectorate over Egypt was declared) of General Wingate. Appointed in October 1916, Wingate was vastly experienced in imperial affairs, having been Sirdar of the Egyptian Army and chief administrator of Sudan for the previous seventeen years, since almost right after Kitchener's re-conquest of the country in 1898.[53] He considered himself to be 'close friends' with Allenby, and certainly there is no evidence of personal animus being directed at him, or vice versa, once the new Egyptian appointment had been made.[54]

Still, for Wingate, once having had agreed to receive a Zaghlul-led nationalist deputation on 13 November 1918, two days after the war in Europe had ended, his high commissionership began to unravel. In receiving the deputation, and then in agreeing with its request to go as a *Wafd* – that is, a delegation, to London in order to put its nationalist demands to the British government in advance of the Peace Conference – Wingate had set himself up for a clash with the Foreign Office. He was of the opinion, shared also by Sir Milne Cheetham, acting high commissioner during Wingate's absence, that the hitherto reasonable and incremental nationalist demands for political reform in Egypt should have been accorded a fuller and more sympathetic hearing by the British. If such had happened, they believed, then the increasingly febrile political temperature in Egypt would not have risen to the point of boiling over, as it had done dramatically in March. Instead of ameliorating the growing sense of grievance with some well-placed concessions – such as allowing the Zaghlul-led delegation to proceed to London, as Wingate wrote to Allenby not long after the latter had taken up his new post – the British government had done nothing, and 'then, as I anticipated, the trouble began.'[55] In a candid missive to Allenby written in London, Wingate lamented that

> I only wish the authorities here had sanctioned my return to Egypt for, I think together we could have evolved order out of the present chaos. ... The small and noisy clique of Nationalists have much to answer for; but had the advice of the responsible man on the spot been taken, I think this trouble might have been avoided.[56]

Wingate is too self-exculpatory here, however, in overlooking the fact that in addition to the request for parley made to him by Zaghlul, the nationalist leader had asked also for the much larger concession of the abolishment altogether of Britain's protectorate over Egypt. Still, regardless of what Wingate regarded to have been missed political opportunities, Allenby was charged now with bringing order of a more permanent kind to a highly restive Egypt, a task of unenviable proportions, as we shall see.

The rioting in March prior to Allenby's arrival in Egypt – carried out by Zaghlul's nationalist supporters – had been widespread and highly destructive of both life and property. Triggered by the refusal of Curzon at the Foreign Office to agree to a proposed visit to London, this time made by the Egyptian prime minister Hussein Rushdi, and the subsequent arrest of Zaghlul under Cheetham's orders on 8 March, anti-British rallies intensified immediately. On the same day as his arrest, Zaghlul, Rushdi and two of their colleagues were deported to Malta, which inflamed further the protesters who turned violent by tearing up railway lines, cutting telegraph wires and burning down a number of houses lived in by Europeans. Then, making a bad situation that much worse, at Deirut, south of Cairo, a group of mainly British military officers and government officials travelling by train was attacked by a frenzied mob and with 'women taking [a] leading part in orgy', as Allenby reported ruefully later to the Foreign Office, eight of the group were brutally killed and mutilated.[57] Altogether, at that moment the British living in Cairo and beyond believed themselves to be on the cusp of an Egyptian version of the 1857 Indian Mutiny, as that cataclysmic rebellion in the history of the British Raj was then called. Therefore, it was to a very shaky and still volatile Egypt that Allenby had arrived near the end of March. But, as he wrote with evident hope and relief to his mother a few days later on 31 March, less than a week after moving into the British Residency on the banks of the Nile in central Cairo: 'Riots and violence have abated.'[58] And with the sanguinity typical of the man, he set to work immediately to try to keep the situation that way.

Allenby's attitude in the early days of his special high commissionership would be essentially irenic. In adopting a conciliatory line towards Egyptian nationalists, he belied his 'Bull' stereotype which, as we have seen, was more of a caricature of him anyway than an immutable character trait. In pursuing both public order and political stability, Allenby was immediately of the opinion that concessions to the nationalists must be made if civil breakdown were to be avoided.[59] Despite the late March pause in rioting, the sociopolitical situation in Egypt continued hot into April, with a general strike being the next step threatened by the Wafdists. Allenby's first response to the situation was to seek Foreign Office permission to have the recently incarcerated and exiled Wafdist nationalist leadership released from their Maltese prison and returned to Egypt. At the Foreign Office Curzon was against the idea, however, arguing that such a concession would admit to British weakness at a time when a stiff and uncompromising backbone was needed. In taking this line, which his most recent biographer describes unconvincingly as Curzon being simply 'slow to understand the strength of Egyptian nationalism', it might be said better that the speed at which his understanding moved was glacial.[60] Curzon showed himself to be utterly of the wrong opinion in advising Allenby to clamp down even harder on the nationalists. In response, the new high commissioner – whose disaffection for his erstwhile champion would begin here – did the only sensible thing that he could do, which was to ignore Curzon's ill-considered advice and go above him to the prime minister. Accordingly, a week after first requesting

Foreign Office permission to release the political exiles, Allenby's higher-level intervention yielded the desired result: the Wafdists indeed would be released from prison and allowed to travel to London for an interview with the British government. Consequently, on 7 April the Wafdist exiles learnt of their impending release and four days later they duly boarded ship in Malta and sailed for England. Meanwhile in Egypt, in response to their liberation from jail and as Allenby had hoped, the political temperature began to fall.

Releasing Zaghlul and his accomplices from prison and allowing them to go to London, while the right thing to do in the circumstances was not of course about to solve the Egyptian crisis in one fell stroke. As Allenby wrote to his mother on 9 April, 'we have had some trying days – Cairo seething with excitement. There have been several collisions between the people & the soldiers.'[61] His release of the nationalist leaders, while a safety valve for the immediate maintenance of public order, was not necessarily popular with many of his own countrymen: 'I don't suppose the whole of British opinion will approve of this!' Allenby was unprepared, however, for the unbridled ferocity of the negative reaction to his actions by some British soldiers and politicians, as we shall see. But in the short term his act of clemency towards the Wafdist leadership gave him the opportunity to reconstitute the Egyptian government by putting the former prime minister, Hussein Rushdi, having returned from exile, back into office. Allenby, while surprised at the level of local British animus towards his actions, was not unduly concerned about how his actions might be interpreted at home. He was confident, as he put it, that 'I took the right steps'.

For his part, Wingate continued to be among those who thought that concessions of the sort made by Allenby were the right ones, but only, he stressed, *after* public order had been restored completely and a new and stable government put in place. In a letter to Allenby at the time, he argued that 'to give way now *after* the agitators have been guilty of every sort of breach of law and order, might produce temporary tranquility, but when the extremists know that they can terrorise our Government by lawless methods, they will unhesitatingly resort to them again whenever they cannot get their way'.[62] As valedictory words in seeking how to handle resistance to British Imperial rule as it was found anywhere in the world in the twentieth century, none could be more apt than these. To be sure, Allenby was under no illusions as to the efficacy of the incremental nature of his response to the Egyptian crisis. But, even though he had 'the whole country occupied by my troops now', as he wrote to his mother at the beginning of April, un-sheathing the sword completely through the full-scale imposition of martial law was equally unrealistic in his view given that, to him, the ultimate goal of British rule in Egypt was civil order and constitutional progress.[63]

In the event, however, the softer side of seeking civil order was rejected firmly by thousands of those same British troops in Egypt. Outraged by what they believed to be Allenby's weakness in the face of Wafd-inspired rioting and resistance, as well as by the slowness of their own post-war demobilization, they mutinied severely at al-Qantara on 20 April. From some 400,000 British troops in Egypt at the end of 1918 the number had dropped to around 150,000 in April of the following year.

But despite this significant reduction in their number, among those who remained in uniform frustration reigned supreme. 'They can keep me I suppose', groused one Tommy, 'but I'm damned if they can make me work.'[64]

On the same day as the al-Qantara mutiny, the compromise that Allenby had worked out earlier on 9 April with Rushdi to re-form the Egyptian government came apart when the putative prime minister resigned peremptorily. Allenby had hoped that Rushdi might be able to convince his countrymen 'to bring about cessation of strike ... I am under the impression that Ministry is genuinely endeavouring to arrive at a solution', he had cabled cryptically to the Foreign Office on 13 April.[65] But Rushdi could not achieve this result and his departure as prime minister at the end of April for the second time in a span of a few weeks sparked a renewal of widespread rioting in Egypt. This time, however, in responding to it, Allenby acted more in character for a career military commander than he had done earlier by proceeding to clamp down hard on the thousands of participating rioters and strikers. Baring his teeth in this uncompromising way had the desired effect. On 22 April Allenby issued a proclamation stating that all government workers were required to return to work on pain of their pay being withheld, and those who did not return would be considered as having resigned their post. Allenby stated further that anyone who interfered with those complying with the proclamation would be liable to immediate arrest and prosecution under martial law.[66] Virtually overnight, Allenby's hard-line proclamation had had the desired effect, and by the end of the month a relative quietude had settled over Egypt.

Allenby's first tumultuous month in office thus had come to an end with a reasonable outcome in what would be an ongoing attempt, as Mabel put it hopefully in a letter home, 'to bridge over the gap that there understandably is between us & the Egyptians'.[67] As much as Allenby's time and efforts now were monopolized by the demands of his Egyptian appointment, however, the situation in Palestine and Syria, over which he remained in charge as commander-in-chief, remained equally pressing. The Paris Peace Conference continued apace, as it would until drawing to a close in June. Faisal had remained in Paris during this period, locked in almost daily meetings over the future of Syria and Palestine. Here he argued with all the principal participants over the future of the Middle East, a future that it was hoped would yield for the region peace, stability, fairness and long-term political viability. For Faisal and Syria, however, France remained the great inhibitor for securing what he thought to be both morally just and diplomatically achievable. Equally, French officials, beginning with President Clemenceau, regarded Faisal as the chief stumbling block to ensuring that France's original position as future suzerain of Syria – as made plain by the Sykes–Picot Agreement – was respected.

In April, while Allenby was battling to control the swathe of disorder in Egypt – 'El Azhar, the great Moslem religious college in Cairo', he wrote to his mother, 'is the centre of disaffection now' – an exasperated Faisal was preparing to abandon Paris for Syria, setting 12 April as his target date for departure.[68] At the centre of Faisal's frustration continued to sit the French, especially Clemenceau, who just at that moment, however, was given a measure of sympathy by all conference attendees because he had survived an attempt on his life by an assassin in Paris on 19 February. Once having recovered from his non-life-threatening injuries, however, Clemenceau had rejoined the conference in earnest at the beginning of March. But his intransigence over Syria showed little sign of having weakened, at least not until the end of the month when a small meeting was held in which Lawrence advocated that the French negotiate directly with Faisal in order to reach an accommodation that would preclude the expected findings of President Wilson's Inter-Allied Commission of Inquiry. The French responded positively to Lawrence's intervention, and early in April Picot met with Faisal, followed by a meeting on 13 April between Clemenceau and Faisal themselves, which Faisal delayed his departure from Paris in order to attend. This latter meeting engendered an extensive and, at times, promising correspondence between the two leaders over the next two weeks, until Faisal left eventually for Beirut on 27 April.

In this intense fortnight-long diplomatic encounter between Faisal and Clemenceau lay the political future of Syria. At its heart was the French President's insistence that Syria must come under the mandatory control of France, regardless of whether or not the Syrian people were resistant to such an outcome. Despite high hopes, however, according to Lawrence the Faisal-Clemenceau discussions proved to be an abject failure. 'In a nutshell', he wrote in early May to the Foreign Office after the talks had ended, 'nothing has passed. Clemenceau tried to make a bargain with Feisal, to acknowledge the independence of Syria in return for Feisal's statement that France was the only qualified mandatory. Feisal refused.'[69]

For Allenby the Gordian knot of the Franco-Syrian relationship thus continued to exist and the possibly of cutting through it remained of pressing insistence. On 12 May he experienced that relationship directly upon meeting with Faisal in Damascus. Accompanied by Mabel, Allenby arrived to great acclaim in the city in a kind of reprise of the celebratory scene he had experienced there the previous October. An official dinner was held by Faisal in Allenby's honour, and then the two men met privately to discuss the prevailing political situation, both its Paris-based negotiating component and its ramifications for Syria – indeed for the whole post-Ottoman Middle East. Naturally, the recent riots in Egypt were top of mind for Allenby, and inasmuch as they might be linked to the potential for a Pan-Arab uprising, his concern was acute for the immediate political future of Syria. Pointedly, however, Allenby had arrived in Damascus with the (faulty) understanding that Faisal had come to some sort of agreement with Clemenceau about Syria's future. But he would leave the city a short time later under no illusions in this regard. At the conclusion of his talks with Faisal, and then upon returning to Cairo, Allenby cabled the Foreign Office to say that contrary to Faisal having agreed to accept the acknowledgement of Syrian independence in exchange for the imposition of a French mandate, no such undertaking had been made. 'Faisal states frankly', he wrote, 'that he had never any intention of carrying out this arrangement and that Syria was bitterly opposed to French penetration in any form whatever. He said that Great Britain would be welcome as a Mandatory Power.'[70]

The seeming endless roil of Franco-Syrian inability to come to an agreement over the latter's future continued to disturb Allenby greatly. He may, from time to time, have limned his letters and reports with an optimism unwarranted by the situation, but he was never less than realistic about its intractability. As he wrote to General Wilson on 17 May, 'Feisal is as bitterly anti-French, after his stay in Paris, as he was before he left Syria for Europe. I saw him at Damascus on the 12th last and had long talks with him. He told me, plainly, that he would have no French in Syria.'[71] The tension between the two countries therefore remained undiminished, and because of it Allenby understood that a violent reaction by the Syrian people was a likely outcome. If the British themselves were to evacuate Syria – which was a course of action now being considered by the Lloyd George government – then in Allenby's view the situation would worsen even that much more quickly. Indeed, on 22 May, General Wilson wrote to an anxious Clemenceau and stated plainly that Allenby's supervision of the situation in Syria was his and his alone, as it 'has been all along', and therefore 'under these circumstances I am sure you will agree that no further reinforcement by French troops is advisable and necessary unless asked for by Allenby'.[72] The British were not, and never had been, inclined to take up a mandatory task in Syria, and 'he [Faisal] understands clearly that Great Britain will not accept a mandate for Syria', he reiterated to Clemenceau.[73] But Allenby was of the view, as he wrote to the War Office on 30 May, that unless the Inter-Allied Commission were to proceed to Syria very soon, then 'it is certain that he [Faisal] will raise the Arabs against the French'.[74] Clearly, Allenby's advice on this point was of such an intensity that it was met shortly thereafter with permission for him to 'announce that the Commission … will arrive in the East almost immediately. The American representatives have already started. … His Majesty's Government rely upon you to see that the Commissioners are given every facility in prosecuting their enquiries.'[75]

Allenby's announcement of the impending arrival in the Middle East of the Inter-Allied commissioners had a temporary calming effect on Faisal. Indeed, Faisal's return to Syria early in May had been undertaken in part to prepare the way for what he hoped would be their imminent arrival.[76] The British, but especially the French, continued to delay and obfuscate over their participation in the commission. However, as Ali Allawi observes rightly, the commission's very existence 'was vitally important for Faisal's strategy in pressuring the Allies for an independent Syria and fending off French ambitions for the country'.[77] The American commissioners only therefore, Henry King and Charles Crane, sailed into Jaffa on 10 June, and immediately set to work on what would prove to be an intensive six-week consultation and survey of the political situation in Syria. Named formally as the 'International Commission on Mandatory Turkey', it would be known popularly as the 'King–Crane Commission'. Henry King, a theologian, was the long-serving president of Oberlin College in Ohio and a former colleague of President Wilson's during his time heading Princeton University before moving into politics. King's co-commissioner, Charles Crane, was a wealthy Chicago industrial magnate and self-styled 'Arabist' who had contributed a substantial amount of money to Wilson's two presidential campaigns.

The commissioners' approach to gathering the views, hopes and ideas of Syrians for what they would like to see happen to their country in the aftermath of the Turkish expulsion was a comprehensive one. They received almost 1,900 petitions in addition to conducting scores of interviews and gathering copious amounts of information from a range of sources. From the end of June the commission took up residence in Damascus where the Syrian General Congress, a newly elected nationalist body comprised mainly of Faisal's supporters, insisted strongly that France had no place whatsoever in Syria's future. Equally, the Congress stressed in a provocative manner that the Zionists had no right either to 'the establishment of a Jewish commonwealth in that part of southern Syria which is known as Palestine'.[78] Allenby met with the two commissioners on 30 June and reported to the War Office that 'they are making good progress. I was favourably impressed by their earnest ability and impartiality'.[79] In fact, such was their progress that there was little doubt that if the uncompromising position of the Syrian General Congress prevailed the commission's recommendations would be rejected outright by both France and Britain, creating an enormous problem for both countries, as well as for Allenby as the chief European man on the spot.

A short time before the Inter-Allied Commission had taken up its work, Allenby had passed on to Lord Curzon a telegram from Faisal in which he had asked plainly whether or not the 'League of Nations is prepared to put into force recommendations made by Commission and whether Commission is authorized to recommend the giving of Mandate to any power wanted by the great majority of population'.[80] The answer to Faisal's queries would soon become clear. The commission wrapped up its work in July and then proceeded to relocate in Istanbul where King and Crane wrote their report. On 28 August they submitted it to the US Embassy in Paris. And there, embargoed and untouched, the report would remain on the shelf until being published eventually over three years later in December of 1922. The report's three-year embargo was a keen disappointment to many, but is comprehensible in light of its pro-Syrian conclusions. The chief of these conclusions was that Syrian independence indeed should occur, but only after a limited non-French (i.e. British) mandatory period. Second, the report recommended also that no Jewish homeland should be created in Palestine owing to the fact that the vast majority of Palestine's resident population were Arabs, and that they would object – most likely violently – to the imposition of any such Jewish polity. The fate of the King–Crane Commission's report was like many other government or quasi-government studies in that its findings clashed absolutely with what other stronger political forces wished to see occur. It languished, therefore, unread and unheeded until a new and different configuration of the Middle East had been established firmly. In hindsight, the commission's work offers a tantalizing counterfactual presence in the tangled history of the making of the modern Middle East. But in the summer of 1919 with the commission's work complete, with President Wilson unwilling to insist on the acceptance of its recommendations, and with no avenue to press its findings on either the French or the British, the status quo in the Middle East remained unchanged. Indeed, the only thing that had changed was an even greater heightening in the ongoing animosity between the two European countries most directly involved in the region's future, and the position in that mix too of the United States.[81]

Despite Faisal's call for Syrian independence and Chaim Weizmann's continuing demands for the establishment of a Jewish homeland in Palestine to match the intent of the Balfour Declaration, for Allenby the geopolitical situation in Syria and Palestine would continue to be one overwhelmingly of maintaining military security. In this regard, the situation was like that found in Egypt, which while Allenby had been preoccupied with events in the Levant had settled happily into a less fevered phase. In this way, and with the shelving of the recommendations of the Inter-Allied Commission, he remarked that the 'volcano is extinct', although doing so was a mark of a too-ready optimism over Egyptians affairs in particular, as we shall see.[82]

In the meantime, one of the features of this moment in the midst of what until recently had been an Egyptian maelstrom, as we saw earlier, was the decision by the Lloyd George government to send to Egypt a special commission of inquiry in order to examine closely the circumstances of the intermittent disorders and violence. But just as important as figuring out the political pathology of recent events in Egypt was determining the right constitutional course to take for the country's future. The 'Milner Mission', as this special commission would be known owing to its head, Alfred Lord Milner, the colonial secretary, was slated to begin its task in December. But before it did so Allenby decided to return to England for a holiday, as well as to receive a royal honour – 'I am to be made a Viscount', he wrote to his mother early in August – 'which', he added pithily, 'is a respectable title'.[83] The title came accompanied by a parliamentary grant of L50,000 for having achieved a great military victory, and he was also promoted field marshal.[84] Now, as 'Allenby of Megiddo … the crucial point of last year's campaign', he wrote to Mabel in order to explain the choice of name, his star had risen high.

Arriving at London's Victoria Station on 16 September, therefore, Allenby was met like the triumphant general he had become over the previous two years since he had last been in England. Indeed, in the edition of *Punch* magazine published the next day, he was portrayed unsurprisingly as a Knight Templar having returned lately from Palestine singing, 'Hither I come, Lady-Love, Lady-Love, Welcome me Home.' Britannia's answer? 'I do indeed –with all my Heart.'[85] Allenby, never keen on such saccharine portrayals of his military achievements, would savour them nonetheless during the next three weeks spent in England. Much of this time he spent in Felixstowe at the old family home, visiting his aged mother, as well as various relations and friends (Figure 11). But he found occasion also for other equally satisfying engagements, such as being granted the freedom of the City of London. But not all of Allenby's time was spent in a round of socializing and feting. Early in September he crossed the Channel to France where he met with Lloyd George, the Foreign Secretary Arthur Balfour, and other members of the Cabinet.[86] They had gathered first in Deauville before removing to Fontainebleau, in the midst of 'big talks', as Allenby described what would be the final round of Anglo-French discussions to determine the nature and extent of the countries' joint presence in the Middle East, a presence, as we saw, that would ignore completely the findings and recommendations of the recent King–Crane Commission.[87]

At the top of the agenda was the expected departure of British troops from Syria and Allenby's stepping down from the position of commander-in-chief there, to be replaced by the Frenchman General Henri Gouraud. By this point in the run

Figure 11 Allenby with his devoted mother, Catherine, then eighty-eight years of age, at home in Felixstowe in 1919. Mabel is on the far left.

of affairs, the British and the French had agreed finally that Syria would come under the mandatory control of the latter in exchange for a similar situation to prevail for the British in Palestine and Mesopotamia. The road to this diplomatic outcome had been a long and convoluted one, as we have seen. To affirm it, Lloyd George insisted to Clemenceau on 13 October that 'we are most anxious that the arrangements for the occupation of Syria after the withdrawal of British troops should work smoothly'.[88] The date confirmed for this to take place was 1 November. In the meantime, Allenby returned to London. Faisal, however, having journeyed to France in anticipation of such a decision, remained angry and vexed over what he regarded as Great Power manipulation of Syria's future. Regardless, Lloyd George was keen now to have the Syrian succession plan wrapped up as quickly as possible.[89] Stalling this outcome was a last-minute contretemps, however, in the form of a report published in a French newspaper in which it was stated that the British had recently brought into Beirut a shipment of arms and ammunition intended to be distributed to the Arabs: a parting gift to their erstwhile desert allies, as it were, the implication of course being that such weaponry could be used against the mandatory French. Lloyd George, on the verge of finally completing these interminable negotiations with the French over the Middle East – at least for the time being – was emphatic in soliciting Allenby's solemn word that in fact there was no truth to the report (which there was not) and then in relaying that message to Clemenceau: 'Field-Marshal Allenby contradicts categorically' the imputation that such ordnance had been imported into Beirut.[90] In the event, Clemenceau was mollified, the Anglo-French agreement held and all British troops were duly withdrawn from Syria by the end of November. By that time Allenby had given up his command and was ensconced back in Cairo, as 'High Commissioner', now without qualification, just ahead of the arrival of Milner's Mission.

In December 1919, when Lord Milner arrived in Cairo to undertake his inquiry into the state of political affairs in Egypt he had for some time been a kind of high priest of the British Empire or, as he had described it himself some years earlier in words that were not nearly as stark then as they would appear now, a 'British Race Patriot' (notwithstanding his German birth).[91] Appointed colonial secretary by Lloyd George in 1918, by then he had enjoyed already a long run as both imperial administrator and colonialist ideologue. Starting as director general of accounts in Egypt under Cromer in 1889, his years as British high commissioner for South Africa during the Second Anglo-Boer War, and governor of the Transvaal afterwards, had sharpened Milner's abiding belief in the British Empire as a great and progressive force in the world.[92] At that time, there was no shortage of prominent young men willing to fall in line with Milner's expansive view of the British Empire's global mission, and by early in the twentieth century they had coalesced around him in Cape Town in what had become known as 'Milner's Kindergarten'. Of their number, Philip Kerr (later Lord Lothian), Lionel Curtis, Geoffrey Dawson and John Buchan (later Lord Tweedsmuir) became the best known. As young civil servants in South Africa with Milner as their chief, they had drunk deeply at the well of ideas such as British racial superiority, the key role of the Rhodes Trust and the Rhodes Scholarships in promoting British Imperial idealism, and the importance of Imperial Federation. They would proceed from being under Milner's tutelage to have careers of their own in various forms of British public service and opinion-making. Milner himself would wrap up his Imperial life, as we shall see, with what would turn out to be a three-month mission to Cairo, followed by a considerable amount of negotiation over its recommendations upon his return to London.

A short time before Milner's arrival in Egypt, Allenby had arrived back in Cairo from his celebratory visit home and from there had gone almost directly to Beirut in order to meet and brief General Gouraud on the Frenchman's new command. 'So far, there has been no trouble with the Arabs; but there is still grave danger of it,' Allenby informed his mother on 25 November.[93] Meanwhile, he assured her, 'Egypt is quiet, for the moment. I'm pretty busy, in these days; but the work is interesting & diversified.'[94] Indeed, Allenby was busy, in particular with attempting to consolidate the membership of a new Egyptian government. 'Suitable men are scarce,' he continued to Catherine Allenby.[95] But with Wahba Pasha, a widely respected Coptic Christian at the government's head, it was hoped that the political situation might be kept reasonably quiet in order that the soon-to-arrive Milner would be able to conduct his inquiry free from the distractions of civil unrest. However, Allenby's optimism on this count would not be vindicated, as coterminous with Milner's arrival in December came a renewal of violent protest by the Wafdists. Milner and the seven other members of his mission arrived in

Cairo on 7 December, at which time they were met immediately by vociferous protesters. In fact, Wafdist denunciations of Milner and his colleagues were of such a scale that they were forced to remain inside their hotel for the first few days after their arrival until the insistent protesters could be broken up. In dispersing them, Allenby employed the various powers available to him under martial law, including summary detention, censorship and the banning of newspaper reporting, the imposition of a curfew and the army's brief occupation of El-Azhar University, the location of a large number of agitated students and their sometime radical teachers, the *ulama*. Altogether, in Allenby's darkening view, Egypt appeared to be sliding back into the situation that he had inherited earlier that spring upon first arriving in the country.

Adding to the prevailing tension of the situation in Egypt, late that autumn was a sinister twist. As Wafdist protests continued apace, British Military Intelligence uncovered a plot to assassinate Allenby by a collection of disaffected Egyptian nationalists and residual Ottoman dissenters.[96] The plot came to naught, as would another one with a different genesis many years later in 1934, by which time Allenby was well into his retirement. On this latter occasion, the perpetrators were mainly Indian nationalists, and with Allenby and his wife travelling in Asia under the assumed name of 'Chapman', the plot was foiled.[97] But the seriousness of the political and security situation in Egypt in 1919 was apparent to all, including now for the first time in earnest to Milner. The threat of political assassination thus had given a new and highly unwelcome dimension to the challenging mix of protest, street violence and boycott in nationalist Egypt.

For the balance of the year and with Milner embarking on a first round of conducting interviews and receiving petitions, Allenby reasserted governmental control over Egyptian civil life. The Wafdists remained firm in boycotting the Milner Mission, which had the effect of making it very difficult for Milner to conduct his work. But open violence, at least for the time being, had been curtailed by Allenby's firm hand. His view of the Milner Mission was one of wariness, combined with a desire to get on with his own work of governance separate from whatever might be the findings and eventual recommendations of the commissioners. Well, might Allenby have thought this way, for both Milner and Lord Curzon believed him to be too eager to grant concessions to the Egyptians, a position that they imputed also to Balfour as the former foreign secretary – Curzon having just succeeded him in October – as well as to the prime minister. In direct consequence, as John Darwin points out persuasively, 'the origins of the Milner Mission lay, therefore, in the determination of both Curzon and Milner to subject Allenby's management of Egyptian politics to a closer and more rigorous scrutiny than Balfour or Lloyd George seemed inclined to give it. ... The two old proconsuls had little respect for Wingate's successor at the Residency.'[98] Accordingly, as far as Allenby was concerned, the less time spent with Milner and his colleagues, the better.

Hence, early in January 1920 Allenby left Cairo in order to undertake an extended tour of Sudan, the vast 1 million-square-mile territory to the south linked to Egypt in the form of a 'condominium', and therefore over which he held proconsular authority. The tour began, however, not in Sudan but, rather, at Jiddah in the

Hijaz, where Sharif Hussein remained locked in an increasingly tense contest for control over the rest of Arabia with Ibn Saud and his keenly devoted Wahhabists. Moreover, Allenby had received reports that Hussein had become upset over the fact that the subsidy being paid to him by the British government as their client had recently been made in paper notes rather than in gold sovereigns. This change in what had been the normal wartime practice disturbed the sharif greatly. Indeed, Hussein had become so 'excited' over the issue that he had considered ending his clientage with the British.[99] By the time Allenby met him in January, however, the intensity of the problem had abated (through the reluctant acceptance by Hussein of the monetary efficacy of paper) and the men had a mutually reassuring meeting. From Jiddah and accompanied by Mabel, Allenby then proceeded across the Red Sea to Port Sudan in order to begin his tour of the country. He would not return to Cairo for some five weeks at which time, on 27 February, he met immediately with Milner in order to discuss at length the Commission's findings during his absence.[100]

In temperament these two imperialists were fairly similar, although Allenby's practical experience of the British Empire as a battlefield commander made him suspicious of the philosophical musings in which Milner chose to engage over the arc and purpose of the wider British Imperial project.[101] To Allenby, nationalist-inspired disorder in Egypt was a specific problem to be solved, and not a test case for proving the civilizing mission of the British Empire, as it appeared to be for Milner. Still, they were of a similar age (Milner, born in 1854, was seven years older than Allenby), had served in some of the same key places over the preceding years and were in firm agreement over the necessity of decisive proconsular action as an antidote to meddling in imperial affairs by those who they considered to be Cabinet amateurs. Like all empires in history the strategic demands of the Imperial centre had to be maintained against the centripetal forces at the periphery, they believed.[102] The centrality of Egypt to Britain's world role – its position as the Empire's 'Clapham Junction' – was of course a sine qua non of London's foreign and imperial policy.[103] But the fact that the gifts – as both Allenby and Milner saw them to be – of sound government, fair taxation, military protection and economic development that accompanied the British strategic imperative were not being received in Egypt in a manner that accorded with British self-understanding of the nature and purpose of the Empire, befuddled them both deeply. Of the *fellahin*, the vast peasant or labouring class in Egypt was this fact especially troubling to Allenby. 'For the first time they [the *fellahin*] are against us,' he had written earlier in 1919. 'Previously, the fellahin have been my friends.'[104] In this respect, however, Allenby was less the hardened agent of repression and more the conduit of constitutional progress. But to Milner, as well as to Curzon and decidedly, as we shall see, to Winston Churchill, Allenby's policy of détente represented a form of surrender. Accordingly, therefore, a reciprocal distrust over the direction that Allenby wished to see Egypt go would continue to mark his relationship with all three of these men.

Gradually, as we shall see however, Milner's view would move some distance closer to Allenby's. Nevertheless, upon Milner's departure for England via

Palestine at the end of February 1920, Allenby was left unimpressed by the results of his mission's work. 'I hope it has done good,' he wrote wearily to his mother, but he feared not: 'Nothing very tangible has been achieved.'[105] Milner of course disagreed, and once back in London he set to work writing up his report, which was completed in May. The Cabinet's response to it was negative, however. Milner had listened well to Egyptian voices of dissent over what they believed to have been a wartime and post-war march by the British towards a reversal in their country's status to that of a crown colony. Indeed, Milner had recognized this prevailing perception and his answer to it was to recommend that Egypt become a one-off, a sui generis within the British Empire – that is, not a crown colony or a dominion, or anything else hitherto known to British constitutional forms, but rather that it become a kind of 'satellite' within Britain's orbit.[106] The late Lord Kitchener's idea of creating in Egypt the Middle Eastern equivalent of India, which he had suggested during his time as agent general, may therefore have retained some intrinsic ministerial appeal, at least theoretically.[107] However, the Milner Mission's recommendation that Egypt should become simply an adjunct to the British Imperial state was rejected as being both naive and defeatist by most of the Cabinet, one of whom remarked to Milner cruelly: 'I fear, my Lord, you are getting old.'[108]

Milner's ill-fated recommendations had hinged upon the granting of a form of independence to Egypt – which, in practice, would be dominion-like autonomy including a form of internal self-government – in exchange for a guarantee of British imperial interests backed up by the presence of a permanent imperial garrison. In an attempt to soften the Cabinet's resistance to the report's proposals by first gaining Egyptian agreement, Zaghlul was invited to London and in June earnest discussions with Milner commenced. Regrettably, however, Allenby was not part of these talks. Not due home for a short holiday until August, he remained in Cairo for the early part of the summer. On 3 June he and Mabel hosted an enormous 2,500-person garden party at the residency in honour of the Egyptian King Fuad's birthday. 'I was glad to see so many Egyptians present,' he informed his mother. 'It is a good sign.' Moreover, many of those present had been from El-Azhar University, which met with Allenby's high approval, since, as was noted earlier, he thought 'the Azhar was the centre of much sedition and extremist political activity'. 'But lately', he was pleased to add, 'there has been a decided change, for the better.'[109]

Such positive change, however, did not last. As the summer proceeded, opposition in Egypt to Zaghlul's discussions in London began to grow. Indeed, sporadic protests and violent incidents in Cairo had begun to occur already in May. In August, an agreement by the Cabinet with Zaghlul was reached. Allenby, by then home in England on holiday, liked the result of these talks, but was dismayed to learn that the contents of the agreement had been leaked by Zaghlul and was being understood in Egypt as constituting the starting point for further negotiations, rather than as the basis for a permanent 'alliance' or 'treaty'. Both of these terms were in use in London to describe the apparent Anglo-Egyptian agreement. There the matter would sit uncomfortably for the balance of the summer and into the autumn until the Cabinet itself turned its attention directly to the outcome of the Milner–Zaghlul discussions. Their reaction to the agreement, and what it portended for the future of Egypt within the British Empire, once again was strongly negative. Indeed, the loudest voice in denouncing the agreement belonged to Churchill, by then mid-way through his two-year-long tenure as war secretary and therefore in the cockpit of trying to manage growing colonial nationalism in both Ireland and India. To him, Egypt's demands for an imperial rollback were no different than what Eamon de Valera and Mohandas Gandhi had undertaken in their respective countries, and thus Churchill hit back hard at what he took to be a plan for the unwarranted devolution of British imperial power in Egypt. Likening the British Empire to 'an elastic circle', he argued that the future of Ireland and India, and therefore that of Egypt too, should be worked out 'peacefully and prosperously' within the bounds of what Churchill believed to be the Empire's inherent benignity.[110] Nationalists in all three of these colonies, however, it hardly need be said, recognized neither an elastic circle, nor indeed benignity, in the British Empire of their time.

To the Lloyd George government in 1920, most especially perhaps to Churchill, Egypt, Ireland and India had become an unholy colonial trinity where extreme nationalists were making demands that it was thought would end in constitutional chaos. Speaking for many of his colleagues as CIGS, Sir Henry Wilson's view was that 'if we lose Ireland' – which just then was in the midst of a ferocious insurgency led by de Valera and his military sword arm, Michael Collins – 'we have lost the Empire'.[111] Churchill took up the same theme a short time later in response to Milner's recommendations. 'If we leave out the word "Egypt" … and substitute "Ireland"', he declared flatly to his fellow Cabinet members, 'it would with very small omissions make perfectly good sense, and would constitute a complete acceptance of Mr de Valera's demands'.[112]

Allenby, much closer of course to the tense political situation in Egypt than any of the members of the government, and certainly not a doctrinaire imperialist, was both annoyed and distressed by the intransigence of the Cabinet on this point. Therefore, he was determined to present a different and less strident voice than Zaghlul's in London. Adly Yakan, at the head of a relatively moderate ministry, was seen as being fit for such a purpose in Allenby's view. But when in due course Adly did become prime minister (the following year), it had the effect of sparking the Wafd to protest the usurpation of what it saw as Zaghlul's exclusive role in speaking for Egypt. The denunciations and disruptions therefore that erupted in Egypt in the aftermath of Adly's departure for London in 1921 would have their own decisive impact on how Allenby chose ultimately to cope with Zaghlul. But those events would come later. For the time being, Allenby's summer of waiting on events at Westminster continued apace, broken first by what may have been a mild heart attack – 'I slightly strained my heart and lungs' – while swimming, and then later a meeting with the recently appointed British high commissioner to Palestine, Sir Herbert Samuel.[113]

Ordered by his physician in the aftermath of this incident to undertake a strict regime of bed rest, Allenby's planned visit to Jerusalem in order to welcome

Samuel in person and offer to him some inaugural advice had to be cancelled. 'He will have a difficult and trying work before him,' Allenby opined to his mother on 7 July. 'Curbing the extreme views of his Zionist supporters; & placating the hostility of the Moslems & Christians, who are shocked and angry at the appointment of a Zionist Jew as the first Governor of Palestine. However, he is an honest and considerate man; and I hope all will go well.' Allenby would have much contact with Samuel over the next five years, in what would be their parallel gubernatorial appointments. But Allenby's concerns about his appointment continued, as they did about the attempt to force a Zionist homeland on Palestine, a course of action that he never wavered from believing 'would result in riots and massacre'.[114] He had been insistent in making these points to Lloyd George, stating that 'I think that appointment of a Jew as first Governor will be highly dangerous. ... They [the Arab Muslims] will regard appointment of a Jew ... even if he is a British Jew, as having handed the country over at once to a permanent Zionist Administration.'[115] Although sympathetic to many of the aims of international Zionism, which in the hands of Weizmann were 'bold and progressive', as he wrote to Lloyd George, Allenby nevertheless remained firm in this view, a prescient one, both as it pertained to the immediate future of Mandatory Palestine and to its long-term success as a state.[116] Samuel, for whom, Allenby informed the prime minister, he had the highest personal respect and 'who is [the] best choice that could be made if it is decided that a Jew should be appointed as first Civil Governor', was a seasoned political figure. Indeed, he would go on to serve as the first Jewish Cabinet minister in British history, as well as to lead (what was by then a hopeless job) the Liberal Party during its post-Gladstonian decline, something his considerable political acumen could do nothing ultimately to arrest. But beginning on 1 July 1920, the date that Samuel's controversial appointment in Palestine took effect, he was thrust into post-war Middle Eastern politics that was becoming ever more recriminatory and unpredictable.

Technically, according to international law, Samuel's appointment as British high commissioner to Palestine by the Lloyd George government had been illegal since the Treaty of Sevres, one of the four subsidiary treaties of the Paris Peace Conference, had not yet been signed by the Allies and the representatives of the defunct Ottoman Empire. Be that as it may (the treaty would be signed shortly thereafter, on 10 August), the much greater risk of the appointment of course was the provocative message of triumphal Zionism that it sent to the Arab world. Samuel had long been known to be a strong supporter of Chaim Weizmann, the Zionist Organization and the Balfour Declaration. Allenby's intervention pertaining to the political wisdom of appointing a Jew as governor, as noted earlier, was about the potential for violence in response to such an appointment, as well as its pertinence to Samuel's ethnicity in relation to his nationality. The answer to both of these questions was never less than clear in Allenby's mind, as he could see nothing but disaster resulting from them in a territory whose population was 90 per cent Arab in composition. Nevertheless, Richard Meinertzhagen, Allenby's former political officer in Palestine and a strongly committed Zionist, took exception to his former chief's clear but nuanced position and complained directly to Curzon at the

Foreign Office about what he took to be anti-Semitism on the part of the almost-retired military administration in Palestine. Immediately, Allenby reacted to what he regarded as a calumnious charge by Meinertzhagen: 'I regard his attitude as insufferable,' Allenby complained to a sympathetic Sir Henry Wilson in April. 'I have written to Lord Curzon, stating my disagreement with his [Meinertzhagen's] views; and I have written to the War Office.'[117] Indeed, he had done so stating bluntly to Curzon that 'I am in disagreement with the view of Colonel Meinertzhagen in regard to the military administration in Palestine'.[118] These prompt interventions proved decisive and Meinertzhagen – whose ruse in the run-up to Beer Sheba, it will be recalled, had been an exceptionally effective piece of battlefield deception – would be dismissed, although he would not be sidelined for long.[119] Still, Allenby was disappointed with and 'sorry about this Meinterzhagen affair', he told Wilson. Even though he admitted that the appointment of Samuel was of a 'highly dangerous' nature, Allenby continued to think that ultimately it was the only one that could be made in the circumstances and therefore he was eager to establish a good working relationship with him.[120]

Hence, a few weeks after arriving in Jerusalem in July 1920, Samuel visited the convalescing Allenby in Cairo, still recovering from his heart strain. Their discussions ranged across the leading issues of the day including, of course, Samuel's recent 'good reception in Palestine', as Allenby was surprised though reassured to hear that his guest had received. They also discussed the current state of affairs in Syria, as well as how Faisal might choose to respond over time to the (violent) establishment of the French mandate there, which, with the imprimatur of the recently-held San Remo Conference now upon it, was underway in earnest.[121] Indeed, Faisal was planning to pay a visit to Syria in the days following Samuel's short stay in Cairo. Relieved that the new high commissioner of Palestine appeared to have 'quite the right ideas', as he wrote to his mother, Allenby bade him farewell on 22 July.[122]

The San Remo Conference, which had been held in Italy that April, had brought together the members of the Allied Supreme Council for a week of deliberations over the Mandate System, which had been laid down in Paris the previous year. The conference, attended by Lloyd George and a number of other world leaders, diplomats and ministers, including the prime minister of France, Alexandre Millerand, had focused its attention on the Class 'A' Mandates, that group of former Ottoman colonial territories otherwise called Syria, Mesopotamia and Palestine. The first two of these Mandate territories were recognized by the conference provisionally as constituting states, while Palestine was not accorded (yet) the same status. Just a short time earlier, however, in March, Faisal and the Syrian General Congress had proclaimed the establishment of the Arab Kingdom of Syria, which the French had accepted, but only in anticipation of the soon-to-be confirmation at San Remo of their mandatory control over the country. For the British, a similar situation prevailed in Mesopotamia and Palestine. For Faisal, the confirmation of the French mandate over Syria in April at San Remo subsequently had left him in an extremely tenuous position as the country's King. In response, his aggrieved followers rose up anew against the French, only to be crushed by them at decisive the Battle of Maysalun in June. This comprehensive military defeat would be followed by Faisal's deposition and subsequent departure from Damascus in July, thus ending, as his biographer put it, 'two and a half tumultuous and event-laden years in which Faisal had sought an independent state for the Arabs in Syria'.[123]

For Allenby, the San Remo Conference was an exercise in pitiless realpolitik, the outcome of which – under the Permanent Mandates Commission of the League of Nations established in December 1920 – was to harden borders, a difficult and thankless task.[124] But in so doing, it would make inevitable the continued presence of both the British and the French in the Middle East, as well as to assure the creation of a Jewish homeland in Palestine.[125] As Allenby well knew, both of these outcomes were fraught with the potential for ongoing violence. 'Unsettled and dangerous' the region would remain, reported Major General Sir William Thwaites of the War Office to Allenby in the spring of 1920, owing to the 'willful disregard by the Allies of the wishes of the people of Syria and Palestine, by foisting the French on the former and the Jewish National Home on the latter'.[126] Indeed, in San Remo's aftermath, France's assertion of complete control over Syria duly provoked a desperate Faisal to use Allenby as a conduit by which to inform Lloyd George of his condemnation of General Gouraud's punitive military expedition in the country. An angry Faisal accused the French of conducting nothing less than a war directly against the Syrian people, of which Maysalun was the centrepiece. 'French Artillery and aeroplane explosives', he told Allenby, 'had been used "promiscuously and without pity destroying the villages and tearing to pieces the defenseless inhabitants"'.[127]

But while Faisal continued to implore the British government 'to ask the French to stop these harsh measures', Lloyd George had been more greatly concerned with the recently confirmed mandate Britain herself had assumed in Mesopotamia, which would be known henceforth as the Kingdom of Iraq in reference to its ancient foundational Sumerian city state of Uruk.[128] Here, Gertrude Bell, who had remained in the country in order to become a political officer on the staff of Sir Percy Cox appointed British high commissioner that June, was involved closely in analysing Iraqi society and making recommendations for the form that its mandatory governance should take. Indeed, Bell saw her role in Iraq as extending to that of advising on its eventual independence. Her inveterate Middle Eastern travel and archaeological work, along with her deepening political experience, had yielded a voice with which to be reckoned concerning the future of Iraq, and she wrote a number of memoranda for the British government to that end. In January of 1920, for example, she had written one such memorandum to Edwin Montagu, secretary of state for India and therefore at that time constitutionally responsible for Mesopotamia. In a measured but insistent disquisition, Bell set out what she understood to be both the means to be adopted by the British and the ends to be achieved, in undertaking mandatory responsibility for Iraq. 'We are, I suppose,' she began,

> near the time when we shall be able to set up a civil Government here – a moment
> I daily pray for, for it will cut the bottom out of most of the discontent here. That

is to say, it will do so if the new institutions are conceived on wise and generous lines; otherwise we shall create a permanent state of what is technically called sedition which will lead us, and that before long, into much the same place in which we stand in Egypt or Ireland.[129]

Ultimately, Bell would come to argue for the creation of Arab self-government and administration in Iraq. She was strong, also, in advocating that Sharif Hussein be appointed as the first King of Iraq, which took place duly in August of 1920. Hussein's appointment had come, however, only after a series of San Remo Conference-inspired nationalist disturbances, the like of which her abovementioned words had predicted. Bell would go on, of course, to take a leading role in Iraqi governance for the next half-dozen years. In particular, she would be a keen and important presence, as we shall see, at the Cairo Conference in March of 1921, which was called by Churchill as colonial secretary in order to try and settle permanently Britain's post-war position in the Middle East.

Meanwhile, as much as Palestine, Syria and Iraq would remain always for Allenby key parts of the unfolding political picture in the Middle East, Egypt of course now was his steady preoccupation, and to its insistent demands he never strayed very far or for too long. Shortly after his meeting with Herbert Samuel in July, the Allenbys had departed for their English holiday. Disheartened by the state of the Zaghlul-Milner negotiations in London, he was equally saddened to learn that the French had continued to resort to sustained military deployment in order to enforce their mandate over Syria. Moreover, with the French entering Damascus that month and forcibly dethroning Faisal, Allenby lamented to his mother in yet another of his many missives to her, 'I fear that this will only be the beginning of a lot of trouble. It is very disappointing to me', he concluded, 'but I had not much hope for a peaceful outcome of the quarrel.'[130] Neither, likewise, did there seem to be much hope for a peaceful outcome in Egypt, as he was frustrated to learn upon arriving in London. The Anglo-Egyptian negotiations had dragged on interminably, and the balance of the summer and the early autumn would bring no solution. The negotiations were rancorous, in no small part because of the steady disorders in Egypt, which had taken on a more pronounced anarchical complexion with Allenby out of the country. Making matters worse, the animosity between Zaghlul and Adly Yakan appeared to be terminal.

Complicating the picture even further and exacerbating the existing sociopolitical tensions in Egypt was a persistent rise in the cost of living index. The war had begun the trend, doubling the index in Egypt by its end. However, against most expectations, the post-war period had not seen a decline or even a slowdown in the country's inflationary rate but, rather, a spike brought on by food shortages, the continuing presence of hundreds of thousands of demobilized soldiers whose spending power had lifted prices, and higher wages. The result was that the post-war cost of living index in Egypt was much higher (about 2.5 times) than the pre-war, and no alteration of this trajectory looked to be in sight.[131] Moreover, a downturn in the price of cotton – as was true of a number of other international raw commodities in the years after the war – boded ill for a positive change in Egypt's economic fortunes.[132] As Allenby noted sadly in a letter to his mother written a little later that autumn,

> the chief concern here, now, is the recent sharp fall in the price of cotton. This is world-wide; but it hits Egypt hard, cotton being her main & almost only source of wealth. We are taking what steps we can to guard against possible political trouble, resulting from adverse economic conditions; but the situation is not an easy one to handle by legislation.[133]

At the end of October and before returning to Egypt, in a brief respite from dealing with these pressing problems Allenby journeyed to Cambridge to be conferred the honorary degree of Doctor of Civil Laws, one of his ever-increasing passel of awards. Such awards now numbered nineteen, as he would report happily to his mother later, plus a pastel portrait of him painted by the renowned English artist Eric Kennington, which had been commissioned by Lawrence for his memoir of the Arab Revolt, *Seven Pillars of Wisdom*, and later he would hang in his Clouds Hill cottage. In addition, a group of admiring Zionists had commissioned a bust of Allenby to be erected at Beer Sheba 'in white stone, on a column', where it remains to this day in a rebuilt form in the city's memorial park to him, Allenby Garden.[134] After enjoying these and other lighter moments, however, a few days later Allenby would sit dejectedly in the Cabinet Room at Downing Street while the merits of the Milner Report were debated and, mainly in the trenchant terms employed by Churchill, denounced.[135]

Throughout this challenging period Allenby had remained remarkably optimistic, a testament, it would seem, mainly to his unflappable state of mind. Accordingly, when he and Mabel left to return to Egypt a short time later, Allenby remained confident that the British government would arrive eventually at the right conclusion as to the necessity for Egypt to gain a clear measure of independence by shedding its protectorate status. Upon arriving in Cairo early in December, they found the atmosphere to be charged, but not riotous. 'Politically', Allenby wrote to his mother as soon as they were back at the residency, 'things are quiet'.[136] However, they would not remain so for long. Just then King Fuad had commenced a tour of the country in an attempt to increase his personal popularity by linking his continued reign to the maintenance of governmental stability. 'The extremists', noted Allenby, 'of course, are trying to create opposition to his travelling about'.[137] In this way, therefore, the old year ended. Allenby waited still, and with growing impatience, for 'a decision by His Majesty's Government, as to the future state of Egypt. ... However, we can't expect anything definite just yet'.[138] A week before Christmas the sixth anniversary of the proclamation of the British protectorate in Egypt in 1914 was marked derisively by the Wafd, the result of which was renewed protest against the regime. 'The schools have gone on a 1 day strike', a disappointed Allenby wrote home, 'as is their custom'.

On New Year's Day 1921 in Cairo, while Allenby continued to await a decision by the Lloyd George government on Egyptian reform, in London the prime minister was about to extend an invitation to the chief critic of such prospective reform, Winston Churchill, to become secretary of state for the colonies. Churchill, however, was not sure whether or not to accept the offer, believing that perhaps he was owed something grander, such as chancellor of the exchequer, one of the great offices of state that his father had held (however briefly and without success) in 1886. But Lloyd George was insistent. He wanted Churchill for the Colonial Office. Perhaps the prime minister's insistence simply was in order to remove Churchill from his post as secretary of war, but more likely it was to have him displace Milner, whose work on Egypt had proven interminable and remained yet unresolved. In light of Milner's travails in this regard, it is unsurprising that Churchill wondered whether or not becoming colonial secretary might 'break me'. But he accepted the appointment nonetheless a short time later and was sworn in on 13 February.[139]

For the new colonial secretary Britain's position in the Middle East would take immediate precedence over any other business of state. Churchill entered quickly into its thicket of geo-strategic and political problems, so doing in the first instance by creating a new Middle East Department within the Colonial Office, as well as by recruiting T. E. Lawrence to be its first member. Since returning from the Paris Peace Conference Lawrence had worked hard at writing his history of the Arab Revolt, had wrestled with the demands of fame brought on by Lowell Thomas's portrayal of him as 'Lawrence of Arabia' and had taken up residence in Oxford as a fellow of All Souls College. On 3 January, Lawrence had written to a friend that he had 'long given up politics'.[140] But this situation had changed very quickly following Churchill's request, and given the recent state of affairs in Syria and Faisal's deposition by the French, Lawrence was only too happy to be given the opportunity to have a renewed voice in influencing British policy in the region. 'Winston is a new and very keen mind on the Middle East business', he wrote to Wilfred Scawen Blunt, long a severe critic of the British position in Egypt, '& I hope will take it [his pro-Arab views] the right way. It's a very great chance given me.'[141]

Churchill was very keen indeed, especially over what would be his concerted attempt to try to balance the various British commitments made in the Sykes–Picot Agreement with the McMahon-Hussein correspondence and the Balfour Declaration.[142] In order to do so he believed that a full-scale conference was necessary at which would be gathered 'Everybody Middle East', as Lawrence called its proposed composition to his mother.[143] Cairo was the obvious choice for such an event, and in short order the conference was called at which about forty such people would gather.

Early in the New Year also, while Churchill was deciding whether or not to take up the Colonial Office appointment, Allenby had departed on what was becoming for him an annual tour of Sudan. On 26 January therefore he was in Khartoum, marking 'the 36th ann[iversary] of its fall under Gordon', he wrote home, while also continuing, in a familiar refrain, to anticipate the government's decision 'as to the future status of Egypt'.[144] But it was news of another sort about which Allenby was informed shortly thereafter when he was notified of Churchill's impending conference in Cairo. 'We shall have a lot of visitors next month,' he wrote to his mother. 'Mr Winston Churchill comes out, to confer with officers from Mesopotamia and Palestine. He & others will stay at a hotel in Cairo.'[145]

Churchill and the Colonial Office party, as well as a number of their spouses, and other officials and participants, duly arrived in Cairo on 10 March.[146] The conference began two days later at the opulent Semiramis Hotel in central Cairo – 'very expensive & luxurious: horrible place', wrote Lawrence wryly to his mother, 'makes me Bolshevik' – and for the better part of three weeks worked its way through all the major issues of Britain's position in the Middle East, although for obvious reasons, Egypt did not form a major point of discussion.[147] Allenby attended many of the sessions, as well as hosting the delegates at the residency – 'Churchill & others have been enjoying the garden, which is looking beautiful', he wrote home – and reacquainting himself with Lawrence. 'Have seen Allenby several times, he's very fit', noted Lawrence in advance of Kennington painting the commissioned portrait of his former chief.[148]

As Lawrence had written, 'Everybody Middle East' was there indeed, at least as far as the British were concerned, and the list of such worthies reads like a roll call of early twentieth-century Arabists and other related politicos and militarists: Sir Percy Cox, Gertrude Bell, Herbert Samuel, Major Hubert Young, General Sir Walter Congreve and General Sir Aylmer Haldane. They, along with Churchill, Lawrence, Allenby and others spent many hours in earnest discussion, dividing themselves into two committees, political and military. In this way, within about a week most of the main business had been got through. That is to say, the old 'Sharifian solution', favoured strongly by Lawrence as well as by others, which would see Hussein (and then Faisal) placed on the throne of Mesopotamia (Iraq) and his brother Abdullah on that of Transjordan, was approved. The conference would adhere to the provisions of the Balfour Declaration in Palestine, except for severing from it the territory of Transjordan. In central and eastern Arabia, Ibn Saud would be retained as a paid client of the British in order to make sure that he did not try to challenge any of Hussein, Faisal or Abdullah in their new Arab kingdoms. Saud's 'Wahabism is of the nature of the fanatical Puritanism of the Cromwellians. It is extremely contagious', Allenby warned Wilson presciently.[149] All the better, therefore it was believed, that the British should have it on their side rather than not. In light of the conference's direction, therefore, Lawrence could well claim to his mother that 'we're a happy family: agreed upon everything important: and the trifles are laughed at'. From the perspective of a hundred years on, given the terminal upheaval in the Middle East that this conference helped significantly to create, the insouciance and naivety of Lawrence's casual remarks in his letter home is breathtaking. But of course at the time, in the midst of post-war state-making, few could have been expected to have thought about the future in such terms. One of those few who did, however, was Sir Wyndham Deedes, chief secretary to Herbert Samuel in Jerusalem, who emerged from the conference concerned greatly by the alacrity of the decisions taken, and the potential lack of foresight in attempting to establish so quickly a Jewish homeland – he himself was a Zionist – in the midst of an enormous population of perennially hostile Arabs. 'Have we a policy?' he exclaimed privately. 'Does our Government know where it is going? If you ask Mr Churchill what he thought would be the position in these Arab countries in 20 years' time, could he give you the most shadowy answer? He does not know; he does not think; there is no coordination in what we are doing.'[150]

On the evening of 16 March, Allenby gave a ball at the residency. Indeed, there were a number of grand dinners during these important weeks, including one hosted by Churchill at the Semiramis Hotel, and another by King Fuad at the Abdin Palace.[151] By the time that Allenby hosted his dinner on 16 March the final results of the conference were in view. Four days later, its leading figures, Churchill, Bell and Lawrence, went out to see the Great Sphinx and the pyramid complex at Giza for what would be termed today a 'photo-op'. While there, they maximized the spectacle by choosing to ride camels, which Churchill having never ridden one before had trouble mounting. Nor could he stay aboard the beast successfully once he had gained purchase. 'How the mighty have fallen,' remarked his wife Clementine good-naturedly, who had come along to view the event.[152] Bell and Lawrence, on the other hand, having spent many years in the desert, found camel-riding akin to walking. The photo of the group of them in front of the Sphinx and pyramids of course has since become emblematic of their outsized impact on the Cairo Conference and its singular and still controversial role in bringing about the birth of the modern Middle East.[153]

Once having completed their work in Cairo the Churchills, the Samuels and some others from the conference, including Lawrence, went by special train to Jerusalem.[154] From Jerusalem Lawrence proceeded to meet up with Prince Abdullah across the Jordan River and then spent a week with him in Amman, followed by several days of itinerant travel in Palestine and Transjordan.[155] In approbation of what had been achieved at Cairo, Lawrence would continue in Churchill's employ until the summer of 1922. Allenby, meanwhile, noted in a letter home that by the end of March and the departure of 'Churchill and his political friends, we have been pretty quiet'.[156] But such quietude was about to come to an end abruptly with the arrival back in Egypt from abroad of Saad Zaghlul a short time later on 5 April.

Zaghlul's return home in order mainly to undercut Adly's ministry was met with great excitement by the Wafdists and their supporters. Tens of thousands of Egyptians poured into the streets to greet Zaghlul's train upon its arrival in Cairo from Alexandria where his shipped had docked.[157] The crowds were peaceful, however, so Allenby wisely kept the troops inside their barracks during this exuberant welcome and was happy to report home that even though the reception was 'gigantic and enthusiastic' it had been also 'quite orderly, and not a single mishap occurred'.[158] Nevertheless, Zaghlul's being 'treated as a popular hero' was something to which Allenby could react only with disdain.[159] And well might he have been disdainful of the popular appeal of the Wafd chief, for very soon after Zaghlul's return the 'political excitement' of the early welcome that had been accorded him predictably turned violent.[160] Before the month was up Zaghlul announced that unless his conditions for cooperation with Adly were met – principally the suspension of martial law – he would oppose both Adly's ministry and his ongoing negotiations with the British government. Despite this kind of Wafdist opposition, however, Adly's position remained reasonably strong so Zaghlul had responded to the Egyptian prime minister's unwelcome perseverance by playing the demagogue, which then had yielded the unsurprising effect of inciting public violence.

Throughout these unsettled weeks in Egypt Allenby had bided his time, as he explained to his mother, because 'I want the Egyptians to settle their politics for themselves'.[161] But in May, under Zaghlul's continuing agitation, violent rioting broke out in Alexandria during which about 40 people were killed, both Egyptians and Europeans (mainly Greek and Italian merchants), and over 200 others were wounded. Having no choice now but to step in with force, Allenby reluctantly called out the troops in order to quell the rioters, as well as to administer 'a sharp lesson', as he called it, to the people of Alexandria. By June, through such actions he had wrested control of the city from the rioters, whom he believed had been 'frightened by the results of the last demonstration'.[162] Once again, relative calm prevailed in Egypt, enough at least for the Allenbys to depart for England later that summer, accompanied by Adly, for what would prove to be a final attempt to negotiate political reforms for the country. Just before leaving for home, Allenby was delighted to entertain for lunch at the residency an unexpected guest in the form of 'Colonel Lawrence', who was on his way to the Hijaz as part of his continuing work for the Colonial Office.[163] They spoke of the many issues that continued to absorb their working lives, reminisced briefly about their shared wartime experiences, and then Lawrence departed for Mecca.

Once in London, Allenby found that the negotiations would not yield an agreement, however, and after a few frustrating months he returned to Cairo deeply disappointed at the inability of both parties to resolve the question of Egyptian political reform. Equally lacking in answers was the beleaguered Adly who now, under intense pressure from members of his own government, as well as suffering the effects of the relentless criticism and opprobrium of the Wafdists, buckled under their combined weight and submitted his resignation as prime minister on 2 December.

At that very moment in London Churchill and his co-negotiators were putting the finishing touches on the controversial Anglo-Irish Treaty after an intense series of meetings with Michael Collins and the other members of the Irish delegation. The treaty, signed on 6 December, would create the Irish Free State and of course for many observers represented exactly the kind of concession at gunpoint that should be not have been made by the British. Their number included Allenby, who earlier in July had written to his old soldier-journalist friend, C. W. Battine, to say that the British in Ireland were a bad example for the Egyptians, where they 'see wholesale murder & arson going on and no one being punished for it. It is extraordinary how Governments nowadays object to governing. ... Anyhow, Ireland is a fine mess now'.[164] By December, however, the British in Ireland – in Allenby's view – had decided finally to 'govern' properly, something which was front of mind for him to do also in Egypt. He was angry and fed up with the failure of the constitutional negotiations over Egypt, and equally had reached the end of the line with Zaghlul and the Wafdists. Even though he had not been perturbed greatly by Adly's resignation – after all, such an action in itself had become almost routine in the fluid politics of nationalist Egypt – Allenby was aware that if he did not make a clear move against Zaghlul his own position would probably be understood by Egyptians at large to be one of weakness. Accordingly, on 22 December Allenby issued a gag order against Zaghlul, and then on the following day, in a reprise of one of his first acts as high commissioner the previous year, had him arrested. By Christmas Day, which Allenby spent at the residency monitoring events, the Egyptian nationalist leader was at Suez en route for Aden and an indefinite exile there, and then later in Seychelles.

To Allenby, Zaghlul's arrest and exile had elicited 'a splendid effect here', as he put it in a letter to Sir Henry Wilson a short time later.[165] But the year 1922, the beginning of which passed quietly in Egypt, would contain even more momentous events than those that had closed out the old year. Allenby would push for unilaterally and achieve in Egypt that which would confirm his approach as an activist proconsul. He was determined to enact the political reforms necessary to achieve in Egypt at once both the entrenchment of civil society and the rule of law, while at the same time safeguarding British imperial interests in what had become a rapidly changing political and international environment. Hence beginning in 1922 and during the years that would immediately follow, as we shall see, Allenby would brace himself for the challenge of both bringing to pass and making effective just such reforms.

Chapter 7

RIDING THE WHIRLWIND
EGYPTIAN NATIONALISM, 1922–5

At the beginning of 1922 Allenby was sixty years old, physically strong, mentally vigorous and determined to end Egypt's Protectorate status as a first step in its gradual political independence. To some, the arrest and exile of the Wafd nationalist leader Saad Zaghlul in late December of the year just ended might have appeared, however, to have been motivated by a contrary plan. But to Allenby the only way forward to achieve lasting constitutional reform in Egypt, while at the same maintaining public order, was to do so without Zaghlul's highly disruptive public presence. Sir Henry Wilson, who as CIGS had his eye fixed closely on the restive spots of the British Empire, wrote Allenby to say that 'Valera has made Lloyd George a prisoner. Gandhi has made Reading [the viceroy of India] a prisoner', and the one bright spot is that you have made Zaghloul a prisoner.' He went on to call the recently signed Anglo-Irish Treaty 'infamous', remarking 'what a welter of chaos in Ireland!'[1] But in holding this view of what was taking place in Ireland, Wilson did not elicit from Allenby the sort of agreement that he might have assumed would be offered. Unlike the CIGS, Allenby looked upon the Anglo-Irish Treaty as an inevitable step in the right direction which, in his view, should have taken place already in Egypt. While the resignation recently of Adly Yakan as prime minister had left the country without a head of government, something which Allenby aimed to rectify as soon as possible, Adly's departure also served his purpose in that it made it easier for him to press upon the British government that the time for significant reform in Egypt had arrived in earnest. The completion of the Milner Mission was now almost two years in the past, and Allenby's first order of business in the New Year was to move decisively therefore – and even independently, if necessary – in the direction that its report had recommended.

To that end, in January he began discussions with Adly's close political associate, Abdel Sarwat, about a new moderate government being formed under his leadership. Accordingly, Sarwat would take office as prime minister on 1 March. Over the weeks that intervened, Allenby proceeded to act with both alacrity and determination so that by the time Sarwat had come to power the high commissioner had forced the British government to recognize both the cessation of the Protectorate over Egypt and, concomitantly, the country's independence. As we shall see, Allenby's move in this direction appeared to some observers to have been peremptory or even aggressive, but to him in so doing he had acted merely to bring about what Egypt sorely required at the end of a protracted and still unresolved process of constitutional reform.

During the long period of negotiations with both Zaghlul and Adly the British government had insisted that the Protectorate would be lifted only after the Egyptian leaders had agreed to certain conditions guaranteeing Britain's strategic position in the country. They had refused to meet this condition. Allenby, however, had come to take a different view. Beginning in January he argued instead that the Protectorate should be ended summarily and Egypt's independence granted immediately thereafter. The British strategic position, he contended, in a closely worded twenty-nine-page memorandum that he sent to the foreign secretary, Lord Curzon, on 2 February, would be guaranteed by the presence of the British Army and the Royal Navy in Egypt and the Mediterranean, respectively, as well as by 'the variously penetrating influences of our forty years' moral predominance in the country'.[2] The details of what constituted residual and ancillary British interests beyond those considered to be strategic could be worked out in subsequent negotiations with the Egyptians, Allenby continued, but in any case he had 'laid open', he believed, 'a course which, in my judgement, accords with the general traditions of British policy and British institutions, and is in the true interests of the Empire, while it is consistent with the political development of Egypt which His Majesty's Government have always tried to encourage'.[3] Thus had Allenby made his position clear. Moreover, he then attempted to bring two years of frustrating irresolution to an end by employing a 'unilateral declaration' on the matter of Egypt's independence by asking the British government for an immediate reply to his stated position.

In the event, the government responded immediately, but when it did so Allenby was surprised to read that its reply took the form of a summons for him to return home at once in order to appear in person before the Cabinet. Accordingly, he departed Cairo on the very next day, 3 February, arriving in London a week later. Throughout this seven-day period the British press picked up the story of Allenby's summoning home and *The Times* in particular began to plump now for Allenby's audacious plan for Egyptian political reform. Meanwhile, in the satiric pages of *Punch* on 8 February, a caricatured Allenby was shown to be standing astride the Nile with his feet planted firmly on a snake named 'Disorder'. Beside him stands the figure of Curzon, drawn to look like a snake charmer. The caption reads, Allenby to Curzon: 'Perhaps I'd better keep both my feet down till you've thought of the right tune to charm him with.'[4] Indeed, Allenby felt highly confident about his position during the few days that he stayed in London; so confident, in fact, that he had sought to bolster Curzon's bargaining position within Cabinet by having put a letter of resignation in the hands of the foreign secretary a few weeks earlier: 'situation admits of no delay', Allenby had written to Curzon on 21 January, 'and if my advice is not accepted I shall resign.'[5]

Thus emboldened, Allenby appeared before the prime minister and Cabinet on 15 February to make his case for the immediate independence of Egypt.[6] He explained his position carefully but with force. Lloyd George listened closely, but found it difficult to move off the position that what Allenby was asking for in ending the Protectorate amounted to an enormous concession without any sort of corresponding guarantee from Egypt for the maintenance of core British interests in the country. At this juncture in their discussions one of the Egyptian government officials who had accompanied Allenby to London, Sir Maurice Amos of the judicial branch, interjected to say that the prime minister's description of Allenby's position was not a fair one. Amos's remonstrance sparked considerable debate, and so it went until in a moment of exasperation over what seemed to be the interminable and inconclusive nature of the meeting, Allenby exploded with the words: 'Well, it is no good disputing any longer. I have told you what I think is necessary. You won't have it, and it is none of my business to force you to. I have waited five weeks for a decision, and I can't wait any longer.' Taken aback by this rare but forceful display of why it was that Allenby had acquired his nickname of the Bull, Lloyd George stood up and, placing a pacifying arm on Allenby, said, 'You have waited five weeks, Lord Allenby, wait five more minutes.'[7] At this point, it became clear that Allenby might just win the day, which indeed the prime minister would concede shortly. Curzon, watching on in growing discomfort however, 'well knew how determined Allenby was to have his way'.[8] The foreign secretary had gone back and forth on the issue of Egyptian independence, coming down finally, though tepidly, on Allenby's side and against the doctrinaire imperial position taken by Churchill.[9] Nevertheless, Curzon would complain to Lloyd George shortly after the decisive Cabinet meeting on 15 February had ended that Allenby 'knows he does not cut a heroic figure', and therefore his championing of the Egyptian cause rang false.[10] But by then the foreign secretary had come to recognize that there simply was no use resisting Allenby's demand that the Cabinet move to authorize the abolishment of the Protectorate and with it declare the independence of Egypt. Earlier, Curzon had complained plaintively to Allenby that 'His Majesty's Government have made every effort to meet the views of the Egyptian statesmen and yourself'. But now, in the face of Lloyd George having agreed with Allenby's position, Curzon had little choice but to side with his political chief.[11]

Correspondingly, Allenby could and did claim 'a complete victory' at Cabinet, as he wrote jubilantly to his youngest sister Helen, known as Nell, on 17 February. 'But it's a bit overdue', he continued, '& I must get back [to Egypt], at once, to reap the fruits thereof.'[12] For a moment during these feverish weeks when it had appeared that Allenby might not win the argument and therefore not return to Egypt, it was possible that T. E. Lawrence would be asked to step in as his replacement in Cairo. Just then hard at work in London writing *Seven Pillars of Wisdom* in a small flat not far from where all the action was going on at Downing Street and Westminster, Lawrence told his mother that 'There was a question of me for Egypt, if Allenby came away: but that of course I wouldn't accept. I don't think ever again to govern anything.'[13] In the end, by July, Lawrence was as good as his word. Deeply disillusioned by the way in which the Arabs – especially the Syrians – had been treated at the hands of European politicians, and continuing to suffer psychologically from the impact of his wartime experiences, he walked away from government service forever. 'I very much regret your decision to quit our small group in the Middle East Department of the Colonial Office', Churchill wrote to him mid-month. 'I hope you are not unduly sanguine in your belief that our difficulties are largely surmounted.'[14]

Allenby meanwhile, feeling justifiably triumphant about the way in which the constitutional reform question had gone at Cabinet, left London to return to Egypt on 22 February, arriving in Cairo just as the British government was poised to issue a pronouncement on the country's status that became known quickly as the 'Allenby Declaration'. Published on 28 February, the Allenby Declaration duly abolished the Protectorate, proclaimed Egyptian independence and anticipated the passing of an Act of Indemnity that would apply to all inhabitants of Egypt and thereby supersede martial law. The declaration's promulgation was met with widespread approbation in the country and, in retrospect, serves as a singular moment in modern Egyptian history, marking the move from an overtly colonial past to the first steps towards an independent future. Accordingly, it is no exaggeration to say that because of it Allenby should be seen properly as the key figure in moving Egypt onto a new and progressive constitutional track. The father of modern Egypt is too great a claim to make here for Allenby, certainly too great for the post-colonial tenor of today's world. And the independence that Egypt had won was clearly limited and imperfect, 'an inferior independence', as it has been described.[15] Nevertheless, Allenby's achievement was of a distinctly high order, especially to those who were on the spot when it occurred, such as Sir Walford Selby, first secretary at the British Residency in Cairo from 1919 until 1922, and in that capacity the 'chief negotiator with the Egyptians of that momentous departure of policy in Egypt under Lord Allenby's instructions'. Selby, of whom we will see more shortly, would enjoy a long and successful career in the British Foreign Service (although not without controversy) until retiring in 1940. He was sure in his estimation that the Allenby Declaration, in addition to giving the Egyptians a considerable degree of freedom under the purview of a modern constitution, also 'undoubtedly extricated His Majesty's Government from an impossible situation for which the confusion in London had been in the main degree responsible'.[16] In this dual regard, it might be said that Allenby had pulled off a proconsular conjuring trick of the first magnitude, which was acknowledged widely, including by Serfoulah Youssy, a prominent moderate nationalist member of the government who would serve later as Egyptian minister to Washington. Shortly after the declaration's publication, Youssy wrote to Selby in praise of Allenby's 'statesmanship', adding that 'I sincerely hope that the result we have obtained, which under the circumstances meant the foundation for a sound alliance in days to come, will be carried through & both parties will realize the importance of what Lord Allenby has done'.[17]

In addition to its main features, the Allenby Declaration contained also a number of subsidiary measures. In this regard, security of the communications network of the British Empire was maintained, as was the defence of Egypt against foreign aggression, along with the protection of foreign interests in Egypt, and control of Sudan. All of these provisions were categorized as ancillary or 'reserve subjects'. Accordingly, the old European legal and financial privileges captured by the long-standing policy of the Capitulations were left undisturbed, although as Lanver Mak points out, very soon after the British government abolished the Protectorate the foreign population began to decline, as by 'twos and threes, by tens and then by hundreds, British officials were being sent away'.[18] Consequently, the Allenby Declaration was a clear signal that the road to full independence for Egypt had begun to be travelled and that Egyptians themselves were beginning to control more and more of their national destiny.

In the short term, however, the fact that Egypt had been given any measure of independence at all came as anathema to hard-line imperialists. Among the most pronounced in this regard continued to be Churchill, who is recorded at the moment of the declaration's promulgation as having decried Allenby as 'a man of no principles', who was also a 'weak administrator', and even, in a fillip in which the outraged colonial secretary truly outdid himself, a 'dud' general.[19] Both Churchill and like-minded others saw the Allenby Declaration not as embodying a pronounced measure of constitutional progress for Egypt but, rather, as demonstrating proconsular appeasement symptomatic of British imperial decline, especially so since it had come so close in succession to the Anglo-Irish Treaty.

To Allenby, however, whose arrival back in Cairo at the beginning of March coincided with the inauguration of the new Sarwat ministry, the fact of Parliament's repeal of the 1914 Protectorate did not mean British imperial decline, but rather the continued maintenance of Britain's long-time tutelary position; not, as Darwin observes, 'the prelude to irreversible decline in the strength of Britain's grip in Egypt. Rather, it embodied a stalemate in the struggle for Egyptian independence which persisted.'[20] Darwin may be overcritical here, however, in terming the prevailing Anglo-Egyptian situation a stalemate, for as far as Allenby was concerned the events of February of 1922 represented not a stalemate so much an opportunity for Egypt to take its place gradually in the modern world, even if imperial diehards continued to resist what to them was a weak and ignominious outcome for Britain.

The heightened political atmosphere of January and the subsequent summons to London the following month had prevented temporarily Allenby from taking his annual tour of Sudan. Therefore, shortly after returning to Cairo in March he departed from the British Residency for the south. As noted earlier, the Allenby Declaration had left in place the Anglo-Egyptian condominium over Sudan, and during his six-week tour that would stretch from mid-March until the end of April he made a point of emphasizing the constitutional necessity of its continuing maintenance.[21] Just before Allenby left on his Sudan tour the now semi-independent Egyptian government had begun to take the first steps towards drawing up an Egyptian Constitution. One of these steps, taken on 15 March, was to proclaim in constitutional terms Fuad as king. Even though he had been referred to routinely as king prior to the promulgation of the declaration, his title officially had not been king but, rather, that of sultan. Henceforth as King Fuad I, he inserted himself more firmly into Egyptian politics of the day, either for good or for ill, as we shall see. Symbolically, Fuad's enhanced monarchical position had the good effect of reinforcing the idea that Egyptian governance was both increasingly national and legitimately constitutional. On the other hand, it also politicized the king more overtly, including his constitutional position in relation to that of the exiled Khedive, Abbas Hilmi II, who the British had refused to allow to re-enter Egypt once the Protectorate had been established in 1914. Ever since the former

Khedive had been prohibited from returning to the country, he had lived in Europe on sufferance, proclaiming loudly the injustice of his exiled position, and hoping (with some success) to inspire his remaining followers to dream of his rightful restoration.

In London meanwhile, after a day-long debate on 14 March, Parliament had approved formally the Allenby Declaration, which came just ahead of Fuad's proclamation as king. The high commissioner, in departing for his tour of Sudan immediately thereafter, thus left the new Sarwat government and the king, along with the various nationalist political parties, to begin to reach a multilateral accommodation among themselves in the new world of semi-independent Egyptian politics. For Allenby himself, being in Sudan for a few weeks would provide a keenly required respite from the cut and thrust of metropolitan political life, both as it was practised at Westminster and in Egypt. He returned to Cairo in late April, therefore, refreshed and ready for the job at hand.

Accordingly, a short time later Allenby, whose trust in the king was limited at the best of times, and whom he described as being 'a weak vessel', began to speak directly to him about the need for parliamentary elections in advance of adopting a new national constitution.[22] These discussions would be ongoing, even interminable, and were carried out under the shadow of a deeply troubling problem of growing concern: the rise in Egypt of political murder. Indeed, the list of such 'political outrages', as the government described them, had become a steady feature of Egyptian life over the previous ten years.[23] Of course, elsewhere in the British Empire, such as in Ireland, they had been the stock-in-trade of the recently concluded insurgency and in this way might have been expected to occur also in Egypt. In the context of the Irish Civil War and its aftermath such killings would continue, of course, as Allenby experienced first-hand when his long-time colleague and friend, and recently elected MP, Sir Henry Wilson was killed by Irish Republican Army assassins in London that June. Increasingly, as we shall see, such killings would come also to blight the Egyptian political landscape.

In the meantime, electoral and constitutional discussions continued apace for Allenby, interrupted by a number of other events and proconsular responsibilities. The prince of Wales, the future King Edward VIII, came to Egypt for a two-day visit in June. The decade of the 1920s constituted high times for the prince – one long royal tour, it might be said – as during those years and extending into the early 1930s he would go on sixteen such excursions to the far corners of the then maximally sized British Empire. His brief visit to Egypt in 1922 had been prefaced by a protracted tour of India and the Far East, and like most places he went, and as a mark of the man himself, his visits to far-flung British colonies were accompanied by much frivolity, adultery and sport. His time spent in Egypt was no different, as reported by Allenby to his keenly interested mother. 'The Prince of Wales sailed from Port Said this morning,' he wrote to her on 12 June. 'He enjoyed himself thoroughly; and his visit did a lot of good. ... He told me that his 48 hours here were the best of his whole tour.'[24]

The prince's visit had added a touch of frisson to life at the residency. But for Allenby, of much greater seriousness just then was the ongoing British archaeological work being carried out under the Egyptian Department of Antiquities. In November, such work would yield up the treasures of the ancient King Tutankhamun's tomb at the hands of the Egyptologist Howard Carter. Lord and Lady Carnarvon, occasional guests of the Allenbys at the residency, whose financial backing was essential to Carter's work, were present at the site of the dig in February of 1923 when the boy-king's tomb, in which he had lain in pharaonic splendour for over 3,000 years, was opened officially to widespread international interest and acclaim. Present at the tomb also were the Allenbys in what would be one of the highlights of their time in Egypt, and to which they would return for a final viewing before retiring and leaving the country permanently in 1925.[25]

During this period as well Allenby continued to be in close touch with Sir Herbert Samuel in Jerusalem, a city that in the years following the war had seen an inundation of foreign tourists, especially American Jews, in anticipation of what would become eventually the mass migration of Jews to Palestine from the United States, as well as from many other countries.[26] In September, Allenby himself travelled to Jerusalem, where he had not been for the preceding two years. Reluctant to go even then owing to the ongoing political pressures in Egypt, he was gratified with what he found in Jerusalem once having arrived. Allenby was impressed especially by the political progress that had been made under Samuel as high commissioner, which did much to reassure him after having been concerned greatly, as we saw earlier, that a Jewish governor would be a 'risky experiment' given the majority Arab population of Palestine (Figure 12).[27] For the moment, at least, that particular problem was not in evidence, at least not to the usually perspicacious Allenby.[28]

An international problem of more immediate concern, however, was the surge in post-war Turkish nationalism embodied by the figure of Mustapha Kemal, the hero of the successful Ottoman defence of Gallipoli in 1915. Kemal had emerged from the First World War as a leading Turkish soldier-politician. Beginning in 1920 therefore, he became prime minister of the new Grand National Assembly of Turkey. A few years later in 1923, he would consolidate his executive power by becoming president of the newly declared Turkish Republic. For Kemal, along with many other Turkish nationalists, Turkish independence was a goal that simply must be achieved; after all, they had been fighting the Greco-Turkish War in its name since 1919. However, in order for success to come to pass, the Turks needed to expel the Greeks from the lands that they claimed to be Turkish but during the latter stages of the First World War had been occupied by the Allies in defence of the Greeks. The Greco-Turkish War would climax on 9 September 1922 when the Turks chased the retreating Greeks out of the key city of Smyrna which, until then, the Greeks had been occupying. But it was Constantinople, however, that remained as the focal point of the contested territories left unresolved following Allenby's victory over the Ottomans in the Middle East. Therefore, later that September (while Allenby was visiting Jerusalem), Kemal chose to march his forces against the Anglo-French positions in the Dardanelles that they had garrisoned in order to guarantee the neutral zone specified by the Treaty of Sevres. The treaty's terms had been laid down at Paris but the Turks had refused to ratify them. In

Figure 12 Allenby the imperial proconsul in Jerusalem with former British prime minister and foreign secretary Arthur Balfour (middle) and Sir Herbert Samuel, British high commissioner to Palestine, 1924.

moving against the Dardanelles in this way and in the violation of the Treaty, Kemal almost had sparked a renewal of hostilities between Turkey and Britain. The British Cabinet was divided as to whether or not to take up arms over the provocation, which had become centred on the small port city of Chanak located along the Dardanelles Strait. Allenby, naturally, was alarmed by Turkey's strongly nationalistic action, and the potential nature of its radicalizing effect on Egypt. As he noted understatedly in a letter to his mother, the country 'is somewhat excited over the victories of Mustapha Kemal; chiefly, I think, because they know we shan't like it'.[29]

In the event, a fresh outbreak of war in the Dardanelles was averted mainly because its key advocates, Lloyd George and Churchill, were convinced to relent in the face of both Cabinet and wider government objections. But important too was the categorical refusal by some of the British Dominions to participate in a renewed war so soon after 1918.[30] In particular, as the senior Dominion Canada's firm rejection of the idea of a return to war – put peremptorily to its prime minister, William Lyon Mackenzie King, by Churchill – was a key moment in precluding British (Empire) involvement and preventing the outbreak of hostilities along the Dardanelles. Indeed, for Canada, rejecting Churchill's request for military assistance in 1922 was a clear demonstration of an ever-increasing autonomy over its foreign policy, a position from which henceforth it would never retreat.[31]

To Allenby of course, the crisis over Chanak struck a much different chord than it had done in Canada. Still, challenges from the colonial periphery made against the imperial centre now were an ongoing feature of British Empire affairs, and they certainly bore on his mind as he returned to Cairo and took up again the political struggle of Egyptian constitution-making as it would extend through the latter part of that year and into 1923. But before all else, and on an intensely personal level, Allenby would experience a keenly felt loss at the death of his aged mother in October. Catherine Allenby had lived a long life, outliving her husband by forty-four years. She died in her ninety-second year, after a short final illness. King George sent Allenby his condolences – 'I know how devoted you were to her' – as did a number of friends and colleagues.[32] She had been Allenby's sole parent for much of his youth, a keen supporter of his military and proconsular career and an indefatigable epistolary presence throughout his life, so her death was a hard blow for him to bear. Moreover, her death ended the tangible connection that he had maintained with Felixstowe and the family home, which would be sold off the following year and torn down subsequently. The city's Allenby Park now occupies the site.

The year would end for Allenby on a point of political disappointment also, as Sarwat chose to resign as prime minister in November, a victim of the continuing turmoil over the provisions of the declaration, especially, as we shall see, as they pertained to Sudan. In addition, another point of trouble for Allenby was King Fuad's continuing insistence on inserting himself overtly into party politics, rather than being limited to the ceremonial role expected of him by both Sarwat and the high commissioner, and which was inherent in the practice of constitutional monarchy. Accordingly, Allenby was left once again in the position of trying to navigate his way through the thicket of Egyptian nationalist politics in order to settle on a new governing ministry. He was able to do so successfully, however, by bringing back Mohamed Naseem as prime minister, who had served in that same role just a couple of years earlier. But beyond creating a new ministry, the most pressing political question for Allenby continued to be what to do about Zaghlul. The fiery nationalist leader continued to languish in exile, having been moved recently to Gibraltar from Seychelles on account of his declining health.

The New Year 1923 brought with it further fresh challenges for Allenby. In January, a highly charged meeting of the resident British community in Cairo was held at Shepheard's Hotel, the continuing locus of its social life in the city, over the ongoing spectre of political murder. In their anger and fear at the ongoing nationalist campaign of 'political outrages', many within the British community had chosen to direct their fury at Allenby for not repressing further those Egyptian nationalists responsible for the violence and murder. Indeed, the event that had sparked the impassioned meeting at Shepheard's had taken place less than a week earlier when a professor at Cairo Law School, Dr Newby Robson – 'the son of the Empire which would not leave Egypt except by the sword' – as he was described later by his assassin, was ambushed and shot to death while riding his bicycle home from work.[33] Considering that between the years 1915 and 1924 incidents involving attacks on Europeans (mostly fatal) carried out by cells of violent Egyptian nationalists would number fifty-four, it is little wonder that European Cairenes feared greatly for their safety.[34] The gathering at Shepheard's, from the standpoint of the history of the British abroad, was similar in tone to those held in Calcutta back in 1883 when the Ilbert Bill, introduced in order to place Europeans and Indians on a similar legal footing in Bengal, had sparked persistent outrage and fear among the former group. Eventually, the Gladstone government would pass the bill nonetheless, although in a much-revised form.[35]

Allenby, for his part, was outraged too by these attacks on his countrymen. Martial law remained in place (although not for much longer) and police patrols of the streets were constant. In addition, the government's intelligence activities, designed to infiltrate nationalist cells, were ongoing. As such, there was little more that Allenby could do in the situation. 'We are getting through our troubles', he would write resignedly later to his sister Nell, 'as well as I could expect.'[36]

Politically, one of the issues that continued to percolate and therefore bedevil Allenby also was the way in which the Wafd party, as well as the king, claimed that Sudan should be seen as an indivisible part of Egypt, and therefore the new constitution must recognize this claim officially. Allenby and the British, however, rejected the claim arguing that it violated their right to maintain the Anglo-Egyptian condominium over Sudan as recognized by its inclusion in the declaration's list of reserved subjects. Indeed, in King Fuad's way of thinking, Sudan should have been recognized as coming under his reign as monarch; that is, in addition to being king of Egypt, he also should be 'King of the Sudan', which is how he demanded that he be styled henceforth. The king's persistent obstructionism, as Allenby saw his actions both in this matter and in others to represent, was based essentially on the fact that *any* constitution for Egypt was going to diminish Fuad's autocratic authority in ways that he would reject fundamentally. Allenby made this point clearly to Curzon in April, just weeks after he had been obliged to accept once again the resignation of a prime minister (Nasseem) and engineer his replacement by another (Yehya Ibrahim). 'Your Lordship will remember', Allenby wrote at length to the foreign secretary,

> that the general principle of the establishment of the constitutional Government in Egypt was always unwelcome to King Fuad. ... In conversation with one of his intimates on the subject of the Constitution, the King is reported to have used the following words: 'As in a Bolshevik Government my position would be that of a Lenin and in a Republican Government that of a President of the United States, so in Egypt I must be a King in the full sense of the word.'[37]

The king's attempts to thwart his own prime minister's crafting of an Egyptian constitution throughout the early spring of 1923 – which had been the main reason for Nasseem's resignation and was proving now to be a challenge for his successor Yehya – caused Allenby to undertake directly to advise Fuad about what he believed to be both constitutionally necessary and politically seemly, in bringing to pass in Egypt what had been promised in the declaration of a year earlier. After working persistently to convince the king of the necessity of such a balanced constitution, Allenby's measured advice on the question succeeded in being heard. By the end of April therefore, the Egyptian Constitution had been duly adopted. The country's new constitution would prove to be a sturdy document, as it lasted in much the same form as it had been drafted for most of the next thirty years, until the Egyptian Revolution of 1952 would sweep it away. Even though the 'King, who has little capacity for knowing when to yield', as Allenby reported afterwards to Curzon, 'resisted to the last moment, and then only consented with bad grace', the country had been moved nonetheless into the ranks of those that operated with a parliamentary representative system. Such a system meant of course also the separation of legislative and executive powers, and the responsibility of the Cabinet to Parliament. In the British imperial context of the day, the Egyptian Constitution of 1923 was nothing short of a major achievement, and in limiting the monarch's power to dissolve parliament unilaterally, it had made clear the primacy of the principle that the people ultimately were sovereign. This was constitutional maturation within the accepted gradualist tradition of the British Empire at its best, and Allenby was justified fully in regarding his work in this regard as a supremely progressive step in Egypt's modern political advancement. Moreover, on a practical note as he assured Curzon, 'the public, even those of strongly Zaghulist tendencies, have found little in the text of the Constitution which can be attacked to the benefit of the Zaghulist party'.[38]

For the rest of that spring and into the early summer, Allenby worked towards achieving the concomitant adoption of the Act of Indemnity that would preclude legal proceedings being launched against the Egyptian government for any actions it had carried out during the almost-nine years of martial law that the country had been under since the opening months of the First World War. On 5 July the act was passed and therefore martial law came to an end in Egypt that day through the proclamation made by the Sirdar, Sir Lee Stack. The Egyptian government began fairly quickly now to become national in its composition, as hundreds of Britons, as noted earlier, began to be replaced and were sent home, albeit after having received 'healthy packages of compensation', which was an unwarranted payout in the view of critics.[39] But such payouts, while riling some in the Egyptian press, did not provoke widespread dissent elsewhere. Satisfied therefore that he had done all that he could do in the world of constitution-making for the time being, Allenby departed for England in August and a much-welcomed holiday. He would remain at home until late October, untroubled except for the occasional suggestion by some MPs at Westminster that he had exerted undue pressure on King Fuad in convincing him to accept the Egyptian Constitution. In refuting the MPs' charge he noted to Curzon, however, that it would nonetheless 'render it more difficult in the future for him to take my advice'.[40]

Still, with the fish biting well, and the long English summer to savour, Allenby might be excused for thinking less about Egypt just then and more about enjoying a relaxing break from the hurly-burly of Cairo. Indeed, at that moment the only cloud on the Egyptian horizon for Allenby was the persistently dark one, however, of what to do about the exiled Zaghlul. Well before departing Egypt in August, prior to the termination of martial law which would have made Zaghlul's release automatic in any case, Allenby had decided already to release the nationalist leader and his colleagues from their exile at Gibraltar. In this way, he observed sagely to the Foreign Office, he would gain 'the political advantage that would be lacking if their release were to follow the abolition of martial law'.[41] Accordingly, Zaghlul and his fellow nationalists were duly set free in September. A short while later the newly liberated men landed at Alexandria and were met in the customary manner by a loud and welcoming throng of Egyptians.

By the time Allenby himself got back to Egypt from England in November, Zaghlul had begun to rally his nationalist supporters in advance of the parliamentary elections, the next step in what was adding up to a kind of revolution in Egyptian governance. The elections were to take place early in the New Year, on 12 January 1924. The campaign leading up to the vote proved to be intense and loud, with the Zaghlulists in the nationalist vanguard. Indeed, apart from Zaghlul's Wafd party, there was no other coherent political party in the running, although individual candidates that might be construed as 'moderates' or 'King's men' had put themselves forward also for consideration. Just before the election, thinking it wise to be absent physically from the country for the voting, Allenby departed for Sudan on his annual tour and thus was far to the south of Egypt when it was announced that the Wafdists, unsurprisingly, had won the day on 12 January. The only surprising part of their victory was its sheer size. The new constitution had made provision for a Lower House called the Chamber of Deputies (the Upper House, called the Senate, was to be based partially on an elected franchise and partially on appointment), which was comprised of 214 members. Once the votes of the almost-40,000 electors were tabulated – the composition of the electorate having been determined the previous October – the results showed that 188 of the seats had been won by Zaghlul's Wafdists, with the small balance of twenty-seven seats going to support Yehya Ibrahim, the prime minister. Zaghlul's victory, therefore, was overwhelmingly complete.[42]

The enormous wave of support garnered by Zaghlul's rodomontade approach to politics meant that Yehya himself had been defeated, which precipitated his decision to resign immediately. On 27 January 1924, therefore, Zaghlul was sworn in as Egypt's prime minister, the first holder of the office under the country's newly adopted constitution. The inaugural session of the Egyptian Parliament would soon follow, which took place on 15 March. The scene within the Chamber of Deputies that day naturally was one of great celebration, as both the king and the prime minister were present in order to usher into being a new era of modern constitutional government for the ancient state and people of Egypt. By that time,

Allenby had returned from his gubernatorial progress through Sudan and of course he too took his place among the political worthies on the great day, well pleased that his declaration's promises of two years earlier were coming to pass in the life of the revived Egyptian polity. However, the celebratory atmosphere of mid-March that might have implied a reasonably smooth run of politics in the near future was not to be maintained. Indeed, the balance of 1924 would prove to be every bit as rocky for both Allenby and the Egyptian government as anything witnessed during the recent past.

As events in Egypt took place that spring, the British state, watching on, was undergoing its own version of a political sea change at almost the same time. In the autumn of 1922, well after the political excitement occasioned by the Allenby Declaration and Egyptian independence, the Lloyd George Coalition government of nearly six years' standing had fallen as a result of the irreparable internecine divisions caused by the Chanak Crisis. Lying in wait, the Conservatives together with their supporting Unionists had assumed the reins of power, first under the leadership of Andrew Bonar Law, and then a short time later that of Stanley Baldwin. The Conservatives were not able to remain in power beyond December 1923, however, because in that month the British general election had yielded a decisive breakthrough for the still-nascent Labour Party and its doughty leader, Ramsay MacDonald. Although having failed to win the election outright, by capturing 191 seats in the House of Commons Labour had won the highest number of seats of the three main parties. A hung parliament was the result and the sitting Conservative prime minister, Baldwin, was left clinging to power until the next month (January 1924) at which time he had no choice but to give way to MacDonald. The former prime minister and leader of the Liberals, H. H. Asquith, had long been in agreement with MacDonald over the pressing issue of free trade. Their shared stance in this regard had put them squarely in opposition to the protectionist position of the Tories, which was the issue that had precipitated the election. As Asquith put it, he 'would not lift a finger to keep the Conservative government in office'.[43] For the first time in modern British history, therefore, the two dominant political parties had been shut out of the nation's highest public office. Accordingly, for most of the balance of 1924 MacDonald as the Labour Party's first ever prime minister would be at the helm of British government policy, including of course that which pertained to affairs in Egypt.[44]

MacDonald's government had been formed on 22 January 1924, just after the Egyptian elections and in advance of the opening of Parliament in Cairo in March. In Britain, the new prime minister had decided to become his own foreign secretary, thereby displacing what Asquith had once called the Foreign Office's disdain for the 'incubus of the Archduke Curzon' – which meant that MacDonald would be involved directly in the ongoing issues of Egyptian governance.[45] For Zaghlul, the Egyptian Constitution's 'reserved subjects', especially Sudan, were at the top of his negotiating list with Britain, and shortly after assuming control of the Egyptian government he made it known that he would like to return to London in order to take up such issues that had been left unresolved by the Allenby Declaration. MacDonald resisted this overture, however, not wanting to become embroiled in a situation for the moment at least that had caused his predecessors such grief. Along with MacDonald's fellow Labour neophytes, he would spend the party's first ministry – which would last a mere nine months – working very hard to prove that they were 'fit to govern'. Accordingly, MacDonald and his colleagues were less than enamoured of having to plunge immediately into something as turbulent and politically unrewarding domestically as Egyptian affairs.[46]

As a declared internationalist with pacifist instincts, however, MacDonald might have been expected to welcome Zaghlul's overtures to come to London. They knew one another, having met during Zaghlul's earlier talks at Westminster, as well as during a visit afterwards to Egypt by MacDonald himself. At first, following Zaghlul's request for renewed negotiations, the prime minister had put him off by saying that the place for such talks should be Cairo among the people involved directly in the prevailing issues. Not liking this response, however, Zaghlul insisted instead that the nature of the issues demanded the convening of a high-level conference in London involving the Egyptian and British governments. On this point at least Allenby agreed with Zaghlul, inasmuch as he wished also to see these matters discussed away from the always-heightened and often violent political atmosphere of Egypt. Although reluctant to host such a meeting MacDonald became convinced to do so, and in due course invited Zaghlul to come to London that June.

As the spring passed, however, Zaghlul became increasingly confident in his position as prime minister because no Egyptian parliamentary or even extra-parliamentary opposition existed. His demands remained uncontested therefore, and became ever more adamantine. As always, these demands were centred on the issue of Sudan, but they encapsulated also what he said now was a considered rejection of the Allenby Declaration altogether. In short, Zaghlul had begun to push for unqualified independence for Egypt, and such independence must necessarily include Sudan. 'The Egyptian nation will never give up the Sudan,' Zaghlul had thundered in March to great acclaim in the Chamber of Deputies. Accordingly, the Egyptian government would not continue to countenance a British 'army of occupation' in Sudan headed by its English Sirdar, Sir Lee Stack. Equally galling to Zaghlul and his fellow Wafdists was that Stack also held the appointment of governor general of Sudan, thus making his rule there complete.[47] In making these points about Sudan as clearly and controversially as it could, the Zaghlul government's first budget that spring had omitted intentionally the line item covering the cost of the Egyptian Army, an action that was meant to unsettle – and it did – both Allenby and the British government.[48]

As a result of Zaghlul's provocative stance over Sudan, MacDonald – who had insisted that the London talks be held without any preconditions – chose to postpone holding the conference in June. He hoped that given time tempers in Egypt might calm down and that cooler heads would prevail.[49] In part, MacDonald was right in this calculation, although Zaghlul's uncompromising attitude angered many in the British Foreign Office, as well as in Parliament. One peer in particular, Charles Cripps, 1st Baron Parmoor and a member of the Cabinet, became especially agitated over the issue and stated firmly in a speech in the House of

Lords in June that Britain would never, ever 'abandon Sudan'. Having done so once to its everlasting shame, he said in an allusion to the saga of General Gordon at Khartoum in 1884–5, Cripps declared that Britain should never travel down that road again.[50] Cripps's belligerent words on this occasion were reported in Egypt, which had the predictable effect of sparking public protests and moving Zaghlul to threaten to resign as prime minister. Once the immediate excitement over Cripps's outburst had died down, however, which it did within a matter of days, MacDonald reissued his invitation to Zaghlul to have him come to London that autumn. Thus suitably mollified, the Egyptian prime minister arrived in the British capital in September after having spent the previous two months vacationing in France in anticipation of just such an outcome.

The promise of a meeting with the British government and Zaghlul's absence in France and London that summer and early autumn, however, did not work to quell persistent public protests in Egypt over the Sudan question. Indeed, the ongoing protests carried out in his name had turned to sustained acts of violence in August. At Khartoum, Port Sudan and Atbara, riots and acts of mutiny had been undertaken by Egyptian soldiers, bent on reinforcing the nationalists' unwavering point that Sudan belonged to Egypt and that British claims over it via the condominium therefore were illegitimate. Allenby, as usual at home in England that summer on vacation, was not able to direct the British response to the rioting, however, so in his stead the Sirdar, Lee Stack, carried the main burden and responsibility of reasserting public order. Owing to the continuing violence, Stack made the decision to withdraw Egyptian troops from Sudan in August, an action deemed necessary to quell the likelihood of serial mutinies and even further violence breaking out there. But doing so came at a cost, as Stack was seen now by many disaffected Egyptian soldiers, as well as by nationalists, as the main culprit in what they considered to be their unjustified expulsion from Sudanese territory that they considered Egypt's own.

Meanwhile, as these events caused continuing turmoil in Egypt and Sudan, in London talks with the MacDonald government got under way finally at the end of September. In the event, however, they went nowhere: 'a complete failure', as they were described later.[51] MacDonald, after several months in office during which he had handled a number of pressing Foreign Office files – the most important of which was Germany's refusal to pay war reparations as required by the terms of the Treaty of Versailles – was in no mood to be hectored by Zaghlul. Indeed, the Egyptian prime minister remained tone deaf during their few days of talks, and given MacDonald's strained state of mind he was disinclined to compromise. Accordingly, the talks broke down, and an angry and disappointed Zaghlul chose to return to Egypt in October. So too did Allenby, who had participated in the fruitless talks also but now went back to Cairo enveloped in a miasma of frustration over their failure to yield an agreement.

By then, the Egypt to which both men returned was positively seething over the issue of Sudan. Zaghlul's continuing refusal to regard the 1922 Allenby Declaration as a foundation upon which to build a civil and modern Egyptian polity meant that he had made full national independence and the expulsion of the British from both the country and Sudan the high bar he had to clear in order to satisfy the demands of his Wafd party supporters. Indeed, any and all Egyptian nationalists saw him now as their best hope to bring British rule altogether to an end. The tension-wracked atmosphere in Egypt became almost unbearable later that autumn, however, and would climax on 19 November when Lee Stack was gunned down in the streets of Cairo by politically motivated assassins. Fifty-six years old, a Sandhurst graduate, and a career soldier who had risen to the rank of major general, Stack's tenure as Egyptian Sirdar beginning in 1916 and governor general of Sudan from the following year, could not have come at a more extreme time politically. The constant demands by Zaghlul and other nationalists for Sudan to be made part of a fully sovereign Egypt had had the effect of turning Stack, as noted earlier, into a symbol of their inflamed grievances. The recent disturbances and mutinies had heightened tensions further, and had placed Stack even more squarely in the sightlines of those who believed that extreme action was the only way forward to achieve the desired political ends. As demonstrated earlier, political assassination had been a steady feature of the Egyptian nationalist campaign for a number of years, but before November 1924 no target had ever been as significant as the one chosen in that month.

On 19 November, a Wednesday, around 1.00 pm, Stack together with his driver and an aide were on their way home from Egypt's War Office to the Sirdaria, Stack's official residence, in order to have lunch. The Sirdaria was located in Zamalek, which was part of the European quarter that dominated the central part of the city, and on the way there they got caught in a typical Cairo traffic jam. In the meantime, a group of six assassins having scouted Stack's usual route home over the preceding days had chosen this moment to attack the Sirdar's unmistakable vehicle, a large black Cadillac. As the car sat motionless in heavy traffic about half way to the Sirdaria, the assassins began to shoot at its three occupants and also, like Gavrilo Princip did infamously in Sarajevo in 1914, had tossed a bomb which did not explode. In response, Stack's driver (an Australian former soldier, Fred March) gunned the Cadillac's powerful engine immediately in a bid to get away from the attack, but the assassins had hit all three of their targets, with Stack being mortally wounded. Rushing to the British Residency located nearby the scene of the attack, the wounded driver found the Allenbys about to entertain to lunch H. H. Asquith, the former British prime minister who happened just then to be on holiday in Egypt (Figure 13). The stricken Stack was taken from the car and carried into Allenby's office, bleeding badly from three gunshot wounds, all caused by exploding dum-dum bullets and therefore of the worst possible kind. Word of the shooting spread quickly, which meant that shortly thereafter Zaghlul too arrived breathless at the residency in an attempt both to express his outrage at what the assassins had done and to imply that in no way could he be held responsible for their actions. Allenby, now if ever living up to his reputation as the Bull, was reported to have yelled at Zaghlul: 'This is your doing!' In response, a duly chastened Zaghlul apparently was to have muttered in French, 'It's the end for me!'[52]

In the aftermath of the attack, both the driver and Stack's aide survived, but the Sirdar himself died late the next evening after having emergency surgery

Figure 13 The Allenbys with their pet stork in the garden of the British Residency, located alongside the Nile, Cairo, 1923.

performed at Cairo's Anglo-American Hospital. Naturally, Allenby was livid over these events, both the death of a friend and high government official, but also over the interminable nature of political assassination in nationalist Egypt and the supreme effrontery of a group of students, clerks and artisans (as he learnt later) having murdered someone who was second in rank only to himself among the resident British. In a singular way, Lee Stack's assassination would mark the (anti-) climax of Allenby's tenure as high commissioner, beginning what would turn out to be the final seven months of his proconsular career. 'Stack's murder', he would write a short time later to his sister Nell, 'surely hurried a line of action, on our part, which had been inevitable.'[53]

That hurried line of action would begin almost immediately following Stack's death and sad and solemn funeral held three days later on 22 November. The liturgy was held at All Saints Church and was attended by most of official Cairo, including Zaghlul and his Cabinet, who were reported to have said that the 'authors of the crime were scoundrels bent on the injury of Egypt'.[54] Zaghlul's words of condemnation, however, did little to appease the view of those who believed that his brand of serially confrontational politics lay at the root of Stack's assassination. Tension around the funeral proceedings therefore had been extremely high. Large crowds in the streets added to the heightened atmosphere, as did a heavy police and military presence during the procession. At the graveside within the

Old Cairo Protestant Cemetery, an obviously anguished Allenby stood sentry over Stack's coffin for some time before it was lowered slowly into the ground. He then returned directly to the residency in order to await an answer to a cable that had been sent to the Foreign Office a day earlier. The cable had contained the list of demands that Allenby intended to make of Zaghlul's government in order to extract from it due recompense for the outrage of Stack's murder.

At the receiving end in London of Allenby's sternly written cable was Austen Chamberlain, the new Conservative foreign secretary who had taken office less than three weeks earlier. On 4 November the MacDonald government had been dissolved, an event occasioned by the recent publication of an inflammatory article in the newspaper of the Communist Party of Great Britain, *Workers' Weekly*, in which British soldiers had been enjoined not to open fire on factory strikers in the North in the interests of working-class unity. The magazine's editor, J. R. Campbell, had been prosecuted for sedition, a charge that the Labour government believed was too harsh but in deciding to withdraw the prosecution the Attorney General, Sir Patrick Hastings, was accused of having succumbed to the more extreme voices of the 'Red' Labour backbench. Sensing weakness in the government – especially in the midst of a more general fear throughout British society at that time of left-wing politics – the Liberals under their leader Asquith then suggested a committee of inquiry to investigate the case but MacDonald rejected the idea, choosing instead to seek the confidence of the House of Commons. Doing so was a mistake, however, as the government lost in the House on a vote of censure prompting a general election on 29 October. The election saw the Tories win easily and thus on 4 November a new British government had been formed with Stanley Baldwin as prime minister and Chamberlain, Joseph Chamberlain's eldest son and the half-brother of Neville, installed at the Foreign Office.[55]

On the torturous afternoon of 22 November therefore, it was a reply from Chamberlain that Allenby awaited, and when it did not come with the alacrity that the clearly agitated high commissioner expected, he decided to proceed to deliver his demands to Zaghlul unilaterally. Time was of the essence in Allenby's mind because it was expected that Zaghlul would resign that very day during an emergency meeting of the Chamber of Deputies to be held following Stack's funeral at 5.00 pm. Allenby had specified to Chamberlain therefore, that he needed a reply by noon in order to prevent Zaghlul from slipping the net, as it were. When the reply did not come, however, Allenby decided that he could wait no longer and around 4.00 pm drove to the prime minister's residence in person. Accompanied by a cavalry regiment, and in order to make the point of his outrage over Stack's murder unmistakably clear dressed in a lounge suit rather than the diplomatically normative frock coat and top hat, Allenby went to confront Zaghlul. Upon his arrival, Allenby proceeded to enter the house directly with the flourish of a military fanfare, and then read out peremptorily in English his demands to an undoubtedly astonished and embarrassed Zaghlul. Knowing that he did not understand the language, Allenby then handed Zaghlul a translation of the list of demands in French (which, as an upper class Egyptian, he did understand), and then departed immediately to return to the residency.[56]

Allenby's demands, numbering seven, were harsh, but not unjustifiable given the context of the assassination. They read as follows: Zaghlul, on behalf of the Egyptian government, was to apologize unreservedly; he was to prosecute the perpetrators, as well as forbid and suppress any further popular demonstrations; compensation in the amount of L500,000 was to be paid to the British government; all Egyptian officers and units stationed in Sudan were to be withdrawn within twenty-four hours; a disputed area (Gezira) in Sudan was to be made ready for irrigation; and, finally, all opposition to the position that the British government had taken over the protection of foreign interests in Egypt was to cease immediately. The list of demands was accompanied by a tersely worded preamble in which Allenby's intense anger over events was made clear. 'His Majesty's Government', he wrote in dramatically undiplomatic language, 'consider that this murder, which holds up Egypt as at present governed to the contempt of civilized peoples, is the natural outcome of a campaign of hostility to British rights and British subjects in Egypt and Sudan.' In even more fulsome terms he laid out his understanding of how the Egyptian government had allowed 'the Governor-General of the Sudan to be murdered', and thus had proved to be 'incapable or unwilling to protect foreign lives'.[57]

Unsurprisingly, the reply by the Foreign Office to Allenby's impassioned cable, which had arrived at the residency while he was at Zaghlul's, offered a moderation of his list of demands, altering their content, and eliminating its provocatively worded preamble. Zaghlul's own promptly made reply to Allenby, meanwhile, was unequivocal in rejecting all of his original demands, except for the compensatory. The money – which the British government had wanted either eliminated or reduced to L250,000 – was duly paid, however, after which Zaghlul chose this moment to resign as prime minister. He was succeeded in office a day later on 24 November by Ahmed Ziwar. To him, therefore, it would fall to meet Allenby's six unmet demands.

Allenby pushed hard now to make his uncompromising position on Stack's assassination even clearer, and to resist the British government's attempts at moderation. Already, Allenby had called in part of the Royal Navy's Mediterranean Fleet to lie in the roads off Alexandria and Port Said, which conjured for some visions of Gladstone's similar decision made back in 1882. Quickly also, Allenby put more troops onto the streets of Cairo. Meanwhile, a trio of Wafdists was soon arrested on suspicion of their complicity in the Stack killing. Altogether, in the event, Allenby acted much more the career military commander than the latter-day diplomat in the highly tense period following Stack's assassination. But in so doing he was about to be checked hard by Austen Chamberlain as foreign secretary. Beginning on 24 November, the same day that Allenby's rigorous response to the assassination had brought about the advent of a new Egyptian government, the two men began a highly charged correspondence over the prevailing situation in the country. Alarmed by what he interpreted to be Allenby's truculent and militarist response to the assassination, Chamberlain began to move quickly to place his own representative in Egypt in order to exert greater supervision over the high commissioner. Such tergiversation, however, was seen immediately by Allenby for what it surely was intended to be: an attempt to undercut his gubernatorial authority. Allenby reacted accordingly as soon as Chamberlain had informed him on 24 November that 'I am impressed with the difficulty of putting you fully in possession of the mind and purpose of His Majesty's Government by a simple exchange of telegrams, I have therefore decided to send Mr. Nevile Henderson to Cairo'.[58] Henderson would hold the rank of minister plenipotentiary, stated Chamberlain, to which Allenby recoiled immediately, seeing the intended move as amounting to a usurpation of the authority of both himself and his existing staff. Even more worrisome to the high commissioner was that in his view the arrival of Henderson would signal to the Egyptians that he was being censured by the British government for his actions after the assassination. Allenby's conclusion was that Egyptians would interpret such actions by Britain as demonstrating a lack of confidence in his handling of the crisis. If Chamberlain were to insist upon sending Henderson, Allenby believed therefore, it would appear in Egypt to amount to 'my practical supersession', he wrote to the foreign secretary on 26 November, which would 'seriously weaken my position'.[59]

The man in question, Nevile Henderson, was an Eton-educated career diplomat who had seen postings in St. Petersburg and Rome, and currently was at the British Embassy in Constantinople. To Chamberlain, Allenby's understanding of his motivations in deciding to send Henderson to Cairo was mistaken, however – a 'construction' wholly unwarranted, he wrote. My intention, he continued to Allenby during the last week of November, is 'to give you the fullest measure of support' in order to attain a 'fuller explanation of [the] purpose and policy of His Majesty's Government'.[60] This back-and-forth correspondence, which continued in earnest for a week, shows Chamberlain to be plainly disingenuous, however, and Allenby to be rather more justified in his understanding of what the foreign secretary – despite his protestations to the contrary – was attempting to do by proposing to send out Henderson. Of course, the letters read in part as a dialogue of the deaf, although for his part Allenby's words as usual, were never less than pointed and clear. But Chamberlain's position on the matter, the result of persistent disquiet at the Foreign Office over Allenby's tenure as high commissioner that had begun under Curzon, was now reaching its zenith. Chamberlain's many futile attempts to explain his position to Allenby were met by him with variations of the reply that 'you have missed my point'.[61] Citing the 'lamentably bad effect' the announcement of Henderson's coming to Cairo had had locally already, Allenby began to hint therefore at the possibility that he might be forced to resign if the foreign secretary were to insist on sending Henderson to Egypt.[62]

In response to this thinly veiled threat, Chamberlain began now to accuse Allenby of labouring under a 'complete misapprehension' as to his motivations. Allenby rejected this charge strongly by making the point yet again to the foreign secretary that a minister plenipotentiary, as it was proposed Henderson would be, was of a high enough rank to give the impression of 'practically superseding the High Commissioner'.[63] Finally, on 28 November, Allenby had reached the limit of what he took to be Chamberlain's obfuscations. 'Either you have confidence in me or you have not,' he stated bluntly. 'Since you have made a striking appointment to my staff in the midst of a crisis without consulting me, and published it without giving me an opportunity of expressing my opinion, I presume you have not. It is therefore my duty to resign.'[64] Chamberlain replied by expressing his 'great regret' over Allenby's decision to offer his resignation, but continued to dispute with him about the nature and impact of Henderson's appointment by writing rather churlishly that 'if accepted by you in the spirit in which it was made, [it] cannot affect your position or produce any bad effects.'[65] By 1 December the die was cast, however. Henderson was coming to Cairo, which he did later that month, and Allenby was going home. When his return home would take place, however, remained unclear, and his resignation was not made public. But a return home would not be anytime soon, at least. 'I should not think of proposing to leave my post at this critical time,' he informed Chamberlain.[66]

A few days later on 3 December, and thus barely a week after Stack's funeral, Henderson arrived in Egypt and was interviewed immediately by an understandably vexed Allenby, until the tension broke finally at midnight when the exhausted high commissioner led the equally spent new minister plenipotentiary to where he would be spending the night in a room at the residency.[67] Chamberlain of course had placed Henderson in a highly uncomfortable position, which both he and Allenby recognized clearly. On 5 December, two days after his initial meeting with Allenby, Henderson wrote to Walford Selby at the Foreign Office in London: 'What is absolutely undeniable is that my appointment did create an unfortunate impression and effect here.' Selby had served Allenby well as first secretary during three years in Cairo that had come to an end in 1922, so he knew intimately the situation in which Henderson now found himself. 'What it amounts to is this,' Henderson continued. 'Lord Allenby will persist in his resignation – unless I go.' But he 'is from certain points of view, which you know a great deal better than I do, ideally suited to the post. Therefore it is in the public interest to keep him here.'[68] Henderson was certain also in reference to Allenby's handling of Zaghlul after the assassination, as he wrote to Selby on the following day, 'that the Bull did absolutely the only thing possible in the circumstances: & that in taking the responsibility he did, deserves tremendous credit. The F.O. owe him, or rather the Cabinet does.'[69]

For the moment, then, with the initial intensity of the Stack assassination crisis slackening and with the offer to resign having clarified his thinking, Allenby could spend the balance of the year and the Christmas season in calmer waters. On 23 December, as he explained to Nell, who in the aftermath of their mother's death had become one of his regular correspondents, 'the attitude of S. Zaghloul would have necessitated my ultimatum, anyhow; unless he had climbed down; wh/ he had no intention of doing. He was out for defiance; & revolution here with the same thing in the Sudan. If the British Government remain firm, we have the future in our hands.'[70]

Thus it was that Allenby would enter what he assumed now were his final few months as British high commissioner of Egypt after having spent almost six years presiding over the birth pangs of its move towards political modernity. The country's struggles over national independence and constitutional rule were very much of the kind that would come to mark many other parts of the British Empire both then and indeed right up until the era of widespread decolonization, still some forty years away in the future. In this way, Allenby had been present at the creation of modern Egypt, even if the events of the previous six weeks had caused him no end of challenges both in Cairo and London.

Having made clear his intention to resign, Allenby's future in Egypt lay more closely now in the hands of his political superiors, Chamberlain and the prime minister, Stanley Baldwin. By the New Year 1925 Allenby was suggesting to both of them that the time would be right in March for his resignation to be made public, after the Egyptian elections had taken place. Perhaps with an understandable eye on his retirement finances, he wrote to Nell in mid-January remarking that, 'I hope that Winston will do something in the way of reducing income tax, now he is Chancellor of the Exchequer.' Churchill, after twenty years in the Liberal Party, had become a Tory again – 'anyone can rat', he had remarked pithily, 'but it takes a certain amount of ingenuity to re-rat' – and Baldwin had rewarded his rediscovered loyalty with high office.[71] Already that month Allenby had sent Henderson to Sudan in his stead, having decided that his usual annual peregrinations around the country might be needlessly provocative given recent events there. In February, a report surfaced in the London press that Allenby had tendered his resignation which, while true, had not yet become official. Given the approaching Egyptian elections, as well as the upcoming court trials of the nationalists who had been arrested over Stack's assassination, Allenby wanted that information to be suppressed. Accordingly, he denied the published report of his resignation, and asked Chamberlain to do the same: 'The forces of order in Egypt at this moment', he wrote to him on 28 February, 'are largely leaning upon me. I therefore earnestly beg you to endorse my denial.'[72] Chamberlain, with whom Allenby had grown gradually to be on friendlier terms over the preceding couple of months, did so readily, after having brought the issue to Cabinet the day before.[73] But the press had begun to sniff out something about which they were not wrong, just prematurely informed, so the rumours persisted that Allenby would be leaving Egypt in the near future.

As the spring passed, Allenby became that much surer of his decision to resign. In March, the Egyptian elections were duly held in which the Wafdists won another majority of the seats in the Chamber of Deputies. King Fuad, however, refused to accept their victory and used his constitutional prerogative to dissolve parliament and bring to an immediate end the government's short-lived mandate. The continuing nature of Wafdist–Fuad animus did not bode well for Egypt's future, which Allenby was quick to recognize. At the same time, however, given the upheavals of the preceding months, Zaghlul chose wisely not to contest the dissolution. Indeed, the Stack assassination and its aftermath would mark the effective termination of Zaghlul's political career and by the summer of 1927, after having taken ill, he was dead. But Saad Zaghlul's popular memory and political legacy remained strong in Egypt, and today he continues to be revered as the *za'im al-umma*, a leader of great heroism in the early history of Egyptian nationalism.

Stack's assassins, meanwhile, were duly tried in May and June of 1925, the investigation carried out by the Egyptian police and not, at the express instruction of Allenby, by British security officials.[74] The members of the assassination gang would be convicted and most of them executed in August, well after Allenby's departure. By the beginning of May also, Allenby had written Chamberlain to say that 'I think you will agree that the time has come when my resignation, as tendered in my private telegram of November 26th, should be submitted to His Majesty. The situation in Egypt is quiescent.'[75] Allenby's final month in Egypt indeed was quiet and valedictory. On 18 May, Chamberlain informed Allenby that he had formally submitted his resignation to the king, 'in accordance with your wishes'. Allenby, meanwhile, was miffed that two days earlier the announcement of his successor's appointment had been reported publicly before having been told of it himself. 'Please inform me', he cabled Chamberlain, 'whether this is true and whether the announcement was authorized.'[76] The Foreign Office, alas, had got in one final dig, it would seem, against Allenby. Sir George Lloyd, indeed, had accepted the high commissionership, which was announced in the House of Commons on 20 May. His arrival in Egypt was timed for October. By then Allenby and Mabel would be well ensconced back in England, having left Cairo for the final time on 14 June (Figure 14). Their last weeks in the country saw a series of farewell dinners and receptions, and on the day of their departure they were cheered in the streets of Cairo en route to the railway station, from which they proceeded to Port Said and then the boat home. 'The old chief is off in a few hours,' Henderson wrote to Selby that afternoon. 'Up to the time of writing all the farewells have gone off very well,' he continued. 'Lord A. is sad to go now the time has come: & there is no doubt that most people here are sincerely sorry to see him go. ... I like him & his personality. He has the gift of winning the admiration & affection of his subordinates.'[77]

As for Selby, however, although no longer on the scene in Egypt, he would continue to feel the sting of the discord of Allenby's last months as high commissioner for a very long time. 'I shall feel miserable to the end of my days', he wrote thus years later, 'as regards the Chamberlain/Allenby incident.'[78] But as for Allenby himself, he had left the disagreement with Chamberlain behind and was exceedingly pleased to be going home permanently. Upon reaching London, he and Mabel were met with the same sort of approbation that they had experienced at the end of their tenure in Cairo a week earlier. Writing to Nell from London early in July, Allenby reported happily that we 'are deep in dissipation; luncheons, dinners; day & night'.[79]

Allenby's departure from Egypt after six years, and with it the advent of his retirement, had come at just the right moment for him. Though marred severely near the end of his tenure by Stack's assassination, as well as by the bitter disagreement with Chamberlain, the hard work of moving Egypt out from a position of imperial subservience as a British protectorate and onto the path of constitutional independence had been achieved, and would be of long-lasting value to the country. Allenby's ability to embody a reforming liberalism along with a ready willingness to do what was required to maintain public order was not understood well at the time, however, by either Egyptian nationalists or by his own

Figure 14 Allenby with Mabel in Cairo, 1922. Theirs was a long and happy marriage.

countrymen, whether in England or in Egypt. 'I believe', Henderson had written to Selby in April, 'about 50% of the British residents are anti-Bull.'[80] But Allenby had shown a clear instinct to facilitate constitutional maturation in Egypt which, even under the immediate stress of Stack's shocking assassination, had not been abandoned. In leaving Egypt when he did, Allenby had bequeathed to the country the necessary constitutional tools required to work towards a greater realization of its independence which, unfortunately in the short term under the new high commissioner Lloyd, would not occur.

'Lord Allenby in Egypt: Six Hard Years', headlined *The Times* on 20 June, as the subject of the report had been steaming across the Mediterranean on his way home for the last time.[81] Indeed, the years had been hard, especially for a career man of arms thrust unexpectedly into undertaking the proconsular duties of a polity as complicated and highly charged as nationalist-era Egypt. But Allenby had acquitted himself extremely well, having achieved a reasonable balance between irresistible Egyptian nationalist aspirations and ineluctable British imperial interests. Allenby's constitutional recipe, as we have seen, had had the effect of satisfying some while enraging others, but as a piece of imperial-era realpolitik, no other solution was likely to be found, or (for the British, at least) was desirable. In writing to A. J. ('Archie') Kerr-Clark, British counsellor at Cairo in the aftermath of Allenby's retirement, Selby articulated well the necessary ambiguity of the former high commissioner's time in Egypt: 'My own opinion is that the tributes which are now being paid to him are no more than he deserves for his many years of steadfastness and patience in one of the most difficult positions of our representation abroad. Of course, he has his critics, but how could that be otherwise in a world where criticism is the order of the day.'[82] If Allenby had been alive and active later in the 1960s, it is likely that he would have worn the laurels of a British colonial governor of the sort who had smoothed the way for independence in, for example, Ghana, Nigeria or Kenya. But in Egypt, during Allenby's tenure in the 1920s, following such a course of action was never going to be less than extraordinarily complicated, if not impossible. For the British, Egypt – much like Ireland – had been always a very difficult geopolitical conundrum to solve, as the next thirty years of its history would demonstrate clearly. For Allenby therefore, having been a key part of the constitutional solution in Egypt during six years at the helm, his time there can be described only as a feat of high proconsular skill combined with dogged perseverance.

Chapter 8

ALLENBY IN REPOSE, 1925–36, AND IN RETROSPECT

Upon reaching London on 25 June 1925, Allenby had been met both by his family and by a highly approving press, of which *The Spectator*, which praised him as one of the two 'most distinguished of our public men' (the other, it said, George Bernard Shaw), is typical.[1] Nevile Henderson, acting high commissioner in Egypt until the arrival of Sir George Lloyd in October, had expressed concern to Walford Selby at the Foreign Office about the circumstances of Allenby's resignation, hopeful that 'no controversy will arise as to why he went'.[2] As it turned out, Henderson need not have worried. Allenby was greeted by no such queries, nor did he wish himself to re-plough in any way the ground churned up recently by his rocky relations with the foreign secretary, Austen Chamberlain. Still, it was becoming clear that Stanley Baldwin's Conservative government would not be making any further use of Allenby's talents. To be sure, in his sixty-fifth year, Allenby was set fair to retire. But he remained in excellent health, was 'strikingly handsome, of the determined chin order, standing well over six feet ... Bull' of public acquaintance, as *The Daily Mail* had once described him, and thus he appeared ideally suited to take on another significant governmental appointment.[3] However, such an appointment did not, and would not, come. Perhaps Allenby's demonstrated determination not to be reined in by the controlling hand of either bureaucratic or political masters figured into this outcome. In retirement Allenby would never allude to having been sidelined by the government in 1925 in this way, and therefore it cannot be known with any degree of certainty whether he felt underused in an official capacity once he had returned home permanently to England. As it transpired therefore, Allenby would enjoy a fulfilling retirement that lasted for over a decade.

Even though the British government of the day may have moved beyond believing it is necessary to honour Allenby's long military and proconsular service further, the always-admiring King George – in an act of thanks and patronage coming just the year before he died – offered to him Deal Castle as a home. Located on the Kent coast, and dating from the time of Henry VIII, Deal was an impressive medieval structure comprised of a keep and six inner and outer bastions. But by twentieth-century standards it no longer served a purpose either for defence or as a barracks, and was being used instead as a royal grace and favour private residence. Allenby accepted the king's offer, and he and Mabel lived there briefly, but the 'funny little Tudor fort, on the beach at Deal; partly modernized', as he described it to his sister Nell, ultimately was not to their taste.[4] Accordingly, they occupied it only for a few months before returning to London and fairly directly settling on the purchase of the lease of a townhouse in South Kensington just off Gloucester Road, at 24 Wetherby Gardens. Here Allenby would remain for the rest of his life, and from it he would begin now a robust retirement of travel, charitable engagements, public speaking and recreation.

As 1st Viscount Allenby he sat in the House of Lords. But Westminster was never his favourite place to be and he addressed his peers only very infrequently in the years of his retirement. Allenby had never been a natural public speaker, or a professional politician as we have seen, but he took seriously his position as a peer of the realm, seeing in it a continuation of the high social position occupied by his long-dead father. Travel abroad continued to come easily and frequently to Allenby and his wife, and during their first year of living in London they took an extended journey to Australia, New Zealand and Canada. Travelling Down Under, he was met by headlines such as 'Liberator of Palestine', 'Digger Allenby' and the 'Great Soldier'. His closely covered progress through Australia and New Zealand proved a ringing success, part of which he declared was because 'I have never felt more strongly … how wide and how united is the British Empire. … These great young nations are bound to the Mother Country by indissoluble ties.'[5] Moreover, any residual ill-feeling the Anzacs may have had stemming from the controversial incident at Surafend in 1918, by then had dissipated. The invitation to visit the antipodes had come from his old military colleague from the Middle East campaign, General Harry Chauvel, with whom Allenby was happy to reacquaint himself. On their return journey to England the Allenbys travelled across most of 'the great Dominion of Canada' in winter by rail from Vancouver to Montreal, stopping off at various provincial capitals, including an eye-wateringly cold and snowy Winnipeg (Figure 15). Just as had happened in Australia and New Zealand he was greeted enthusiastically throughout Canada by large crowds also.[6]

The next year the Allenbys journeyed to South Africa and Southern Rhodesia (today's Zimbabwe), visiting Victoria Falls, and then returned home via Nairobi and Cairo. During the autumn of 1928 they then chose to visit the United States, where there had long been a keen interest in him as the conqueror of Jerusalem, especially among the prominent American Jewish community. In an interview for the *New York Herald Tribune*, for example, Allenby was asked about how he had felt upon entering the Holy City in 1917 and had replied in characteristically phlegmatic fashion: 'I am not a sentimental person, but the taking of Jerusalem afforded me great satisfaction.' When questioned later about fighting at Megiddo, or 'Armageddon' as it was better known, Allenby answered with a smile that 'it would be hard for all the nations to meet there, really. The plain is so very narrow.'[7] Indeed, his reputation preceded him wherever he went. A few years earlier, for example, the rising American author, F. Scott Fitzgerald – who would go on to enjoy great and lasting fame – had named one of the characters in his debut novel, *This Side of Paradise* (1920), after him. 'Allenby', he had called the impressively drawn Princeton University football captain, 'slim and defiant', in an homage to the victor of Jerusalem.[8]

Figure 15 Allenby in Winnipeg amid the January snows during a railway journey across Canada in 1926.

During the years that followed, the Allenbys continued to travel regularly, especially during the winter months. India, Jamaica, Brazil, Malaya, they visited them all in the early 1930s. So too did they make a return trip to Palestine in the spring of 1933, which would continue as a British Mandate for a further fifteen years. While there, at the opening of the new YMCA building in Jerusalem, Allenby spoke about international harmony and cooperation, an idea that he would develop more clearly in the years to come. Warming to his theme, he remarked in a speech to an appreciative gathering of the city's Muslims, Jews and Christians that 'nationalism is generally accepted as a high virtue, while internationalism is often regarded as almost criminal. Why should this be? There is no sane reason for so narrow a view. We have to live together. ... The fruits of victory are perishable; and, at their best, are unsatisfying.'[9]

Sporadically, during these years, he kept in touch with the most famous of his wartime associates, T. E. Lawrence, who by then had rejected the fame first thrust upon him by the American promoter Lowell Thomas. The 'Lawrence of Arabia' stage name that had brought its own brief appeal to him in the early 1920s had ever since become an intolerable burden. Having changed his name twice in order to enjoy a semblance of anonymity, Lawrence had settled on the name T. E. Shaw and was living semi-reclusively in a Dorset cottage, Clouds Hill, near the village of Moreton. Earlier, in January of 1927, Allenby had written to Lawrence in order to express his thanks for having received from him a copy of *Seven Pillars of Wisdom*. Calling the book a 'fit record of your splendid achievements in the War', Allenby went on to say that he was 'grateful for the kind way in which you refer to my part in our collaboration, and am happy to think that to our unity of thought and intention can be attributed, in great measure, the success obtained'.[10]

Allenby and Lawrence of course would be linked permanently by their shared experience of the Arab Revolt in the desert, and their esteem remained mutual, long-lasting and almost unbroken. The only negative comment Allenby ever uttered about his universally famous former military subordinate was to say that 'I had a dozen chaps who could have done the job better'.[11] But this remark, albeit with a sting in the tail, was made by him as a throwaway. Conversely, Allenby's considered view of Lawrence is captured by a comment attributed to him and used by the screenwriter Robert Bolt in David Lean's, *Lawrence of Arabia*: 'people would have to visit a war museum to learn of him', Allenby observed, 'but that T.E. Lawrence would be remembered and become a household name.' Later, at the time of Lawrence's early death in 1935, just a year before his own, Allenby would speak about him again and do so fulsomely, as we shall see.

For Lawrence's part, the awe in which he had held Allenby from their first meeting in Cairo in July of 1917 never really left him. In a letter written to his friend and correspondent Charlotte Shaw in May of 1927, a few months after receiving the one from his former commander-in-chief cited earlier, he wrote at length:

> Allenby sent me a very pleasant letter. ... This relieves me, for it has been a fear of mine that his sense of proportion (a very sober and stern quality in him) somehow associated my person with the ridiculous reputation raised about it by the vulgar. You see, my campaign and fighting efforts were entirely negligible, in his eyes. ... He is a very large, downright and splendid person, and being publicly yoked with a counter-jumping opportunist like me must often gall him deeply. You and G.B.S. [George Bernard Shaw] live so much with poets and politicians and artists that human oddness attracts you, almost as much as it repels. Whereas with the senior officers of the British army conduct is a very grave matter.[12]

Lawrence was too self-deprecating here, however, in thinking that Allenby considered his efforts in the Arab Revolt to have been merely a 'negligible' part of the campaign in the Middle East. As Neil Faulkner has reinforced recently, the contribution made by Lawrence's leadership and by the Sharifian forces altogether, especially in the run-up to the fall of Damascus, were significant, even decisive, something that Allenby himself understood at the time.[13] Indeed, in September of 1933 on the occasion of Faisal's death, Allenby would pay tribute to Lawrence's partner in the desert war over the BBC by saying that he had been 'a good soldier, an able politician and – what many politicians are not – honest with it. His sense of duty was great.'[14]

Churchill, another of Lawrence's champions, meanwhile, was typically effusive in his praise of Lawrence's *Seven Pillars*. 'What a tale!' he exclaimed in a letter to its author in May 1927. 'I think your book will live with Gulliver's Travels and Robinson Crusoe.' Having many years earlier tried his own hand – quite successfully it should be added – at a similar brand of writing in *The River War* (1899), his account of Kitchener's re-conquest of the Sudan, Churchill's admiration (envy?) was genuine. So too was his desire that he might be informed soon by Lawrence that the 'long holiday is finished, and that your appetite for action has returned. Please do not wait till the Bolshevik Revolution entitles me to summon you to the centre of strife by an order "from the Imperial Stirrup".'[15] Such a 'holiday' of course, despite the fact that along with Allenby Lawrence always had considered Churchill to be one of his 'gallery of chiefs', would never come to an end.[16]

In 1934, Allenby received the last of his many royal honours when he was appointed Knight Grand Cross of the Royal Victorian Order (GCVO), a mark of singular favour for showing distinguished personal service to the monarch. By this time Allenby's life had settled into a steady routine of travel, occasional forays into the public eye and a small number of service activities. One of these was acting as president of the British National Cadet Association. But his great passion for the outdoors and for the natural world remained at the centre of his retirement life, and would never flag. Tending his aviary at Wetherby Gardens was a regular part of Allenby's daily routine, for example, as was angling as often as he could. Whether it be on the River Tay in Scotland, the longest in the country, or nearer to home on the gentler Avon, he loved the rhythmic casting of the angler's line. Accordingly, in the autumn of 1935 he would venture to South America in order to fish the waters of Patagonia, his visit there having been smoothed by the arrangements made by a happy-to-oblige Nevile Henderson, the newly arrived British ambassador to Argentina. After the passage of ten years, the tensions between the two men that had surrounded Henderson's appointment to Cairo had long since passed.

Earlier, in the late spring of that year, and a few months before his journey to Argentina, Allenby – along with the whole country – had been shocked and saddened to learn of Lawrence's untimely death as a result of an accident while riding a motorcycle on the Dorset road leading to his Clouds Hill cottage. The accident had rendered Lawrence comatose, a state from which he did not emerge. After six days remaining in this way he had died on 19 May. After having been informed of Lawrence's death later that day, Allenby was interviewed on the radio and offered an encomium to his former colleague, calling him 'a good friend and valued comrade', who had been 'the mainspring of the Arab Movement' and had showed 'a genius for leadership'. Indeed, Allenby eulogized Lawrence at some length, concluding his remarks with, 'he has left, to us who knew and admired him, a beloved memory; and to all his countrymen, the example of a life well-spent in service'.[17] A short while later in July, Allenby followed up his remarks on the radio with a written tribute to Lawrence that was published in the *Journal of the Central Asian Society*. In it, he said much the same thing as he had done over the air, although having had time to ruminate awhile on the legacy of his deceased friend was able to offer a measured but greatly admiring summing up of his life: 'T.E. Lawrence has left a name that will live,' Allenby wrote. 'He was perhaps the most interesting product of the Great War; yet, withal, a character difficult to know'.[18] Allenby, of whom Lawrence had remarked once in error did not understand the nature of the Arab Revolt, 'and for whose success his instinct had little sympathy', nonetheless praised his fallen comrade for having offering inspired leadership and 'fiery energy' to the Arabs, which had 'amazed and delighted them'.[19] Altogether, Allenby – in no less a way than did Churchill – held Lawrence in extremely high regard and genuinely mourned his death. Indeed, Churchill would be a pallbearer at Lawrence's funeral and share in the anguish of another of its famous attendees, the trailblazing first woman elected to Parliament, Nancy Astor, who cried out to him at the time, 'Oh, Winnie, Winnie, we've lost him'.[20]

Following Lawrence's death in what would prove to be Allenby's own final year of life, he was appointed rector of the University of Edinburgh. In April of 1936, therefore, he travelled north in order to give the traditional annual rectorial address to students and faculty. Having been promoted as a candidate by a large number of undergraduates who had championed Allenby as 'the man who never starts a job he cannot finish', in advance of his address he was carried ceremonially by them to the meeting hall on an open sedan chair amid much cheering.[21] In his address, Allenby spoke with evident passion about a theme, as noted earlier, that had been of growing importance to him during his retirement years. In an age when the League of Nations was floundering and the Western democracies were under a strong challenge by the surging dictatorships of Germany and Italy, Allenby spoke up firmly for the virtues of representative government and cooperative internationalism. In a pointed disquisition on the need for structured internationalism – indeed, for 'World Police for World Peace', he called it – Allenby emphasized the fact that in his experience 'war is not a satisfactory method of settling disputes. Ordeal by battle brings no lasting benefit to either combatant.' The impact that his animated, though measured, anti-war speech had on the assembled academic worthies and students, coming as it did from one of the great British imperial military figures of the modern era, is impossible to know. But clearly, Allenby's appeal was one made to those ideals embodied by the embattled League of Nations, although such ideals should be mediated at all times, he insisted, by the following principle: 'steadfastly maintain your own national rights; but recognize the similar rights of other nations, as bound up with yours'.[22]

A few days after giving his address in Edinburgh, Allenby received a letter of commendation for it from Sir Herbert Samuel, his old friend and former administrative colleague in the Middle East. Samuel's five-year term as high commissioner for Palestine had ended back in 1925, the same year as Allenby had returned from Egypt, and just then he was out of Parliament after having lost his seat as a Liberal in the 1935 general election, which had been won overwhelmingly by Baldwin's Conservatives. Allenby expressed his thanks to Samuel for having written to him, and for the ready approval of his internationalist message given to the students.[23] The letter to Samuel, as it turned out, written on 2 May, would be almost the last one ever written by Allenby. Less than two weeks later, on 14 May, he died, after returning home to Wetherby Gardens from a short excursion on foot in order to make a purchase for his aviary. He collapsed while seated at the desk in his study. The cause of Allenby's death was deemed to have been a burst blood vessel in his brain, from which he had died immediately. Five days later his cremated remains were interred at Westminster Abbey near the Tomb of the Unknown Warrior, today called St. George's Chapel.[24] Allenby had just passed his seventy-fifth birthday on 23 April. 'I can but thank God, he went like that & was spared pain or suffering,' wrote Mabel to a friend. 'Never had I seen him so well, so full of vigour. We had had such a happy time in Edinburgh.'[25]

The deceased Allenby was well- and widely mourned. First of course by his wife, Mabel, Lady Allenby, and then by his remaining three siblings: Elizabeth, Nell and Alfred. His older sister Catherine (Kitty) had died just a year earlier, and his younger brother Claude, the year before that in 1934. The late Claude's elder son, Dudley, then thirty-three years of age, inherited the peerage as 2nd Viscount Allenby, a line that continues today, the current holder of the title being Henry Jaffray Hynman Allenby, 4th Viscount Allenby. The parliamentary grant of L50,000 that had come with Allenby's ennoblement in 1919 had ensured his financial position, just over L30,000 of which he left to Mabel in his will.[26] She would live on for almost six more years before dying in March of 1942.

The nation shared fully also in Allenby's loss. His death and funeral were covered by the BBC and by all the major newspapers. Allenby's death notice in *The Times* – 'A Great Soldier and Administrator' – was shaped by Sir Walford Selby, as he had become in 1931, who was asked especially to give assistance in its writing (Figure 16).[27] In Cairo, a memorial service for Allenby was held at St. Mary's Pro-Cathedral, on the same day, 19 May, as his funeral took place in London. The *Egyptian Gazette* headlined Allenby as 'Great', but (or perhaps because) he had always displayed 'Patience, Honesty & Simplicity'.[28] In Jerusalem, he was honoured likewise amid widespread public recognition of his death. A few of the obituaries that ran in the press departed from the irenic, however, and adopted a militaristic tone, such as the one in London which praised Allenby for having been 'the hammer of the Turks'.[29]

Poetically, perhaps, Allenby's death had occurred just a few months before the 1936 Anglo-Egyptian Treaty was signed in August. Negotiated by the Baldwin government, it required the British to withdraw all its troops from Egypt except for those deemed necessary to protect the Suez Canal. As Selby noted in his *Times* obituary, it had been Allenby in 1922 who had 'laid the secure foundations' of this treaty, a view shared by the then Egyptian ambassador to Britain, Hafez Afifi, who commented that 'the declaration of 28 February 1922 had a very important influence on the present result'.[30] In this way, it may be argued, a clear line can be seen to run from Allenby's actions in 1922, to the Anglo-Egyptian Treaty of 1936, to its twenty-year expiration in 1956 and the culmination of Egyptian nationalism

Figure 16 Allenby in 1931: Well into retirement and long out of uniform.

under the regime of Gamal Abdel Nasser. 'My name is current coin from Cairo to Khartoum,' Allenby had said once to Curzon during their intense discussions over Egypt's future back in 1921.[31] The diplomatic history of Egypt for more than thirty years following Allenby's departure in 1925 would ensure that his name would long continue to be understood in much the same way.

*   *   *

Today, however, well into the twenty-first century, prominent figures of the age of European empire such as Allenby are most emphatically not 'current coin'; or if they are, it is mainly because of their being pointed to retrospectively as leading examples of a discredited imperial past. Men of arms like Allenby especially, it would seem, who supported the British imperial project with military force, are prone to denigration and ridicule in a time when empire as both political ideology and international organizational principle are seen as equally reprehensible. However, the 'Imperial Idea' in human history, as A. P. Thornton wrote many years ago, has never been less than strangely ambiguous and terminally resilient, defiant of easy explanation and resistant to rote categorization.[32] After all, how does one square, for example, an international system that in the nineteenth century at once was responsible for the gradual abolition of the brutal and centuries-old Atlantic Slave Trade, while at the same time permitting the devastating Bengal Famine? These kinds of incongruities in the history of empire are indeed almost countless, and when taken as individual events call rightly for empire's opprobrium. But there is a problem with this sort of approach to the history of empire – that is, of examining a single horrific event and extrapolating from it a general denigration of the phenomenon. All history, as is clear to anyone who takes the discipline seriously, is integrative, inconsistent and firmly resistant to reductionism. The result of this reality for a figure like Allenby, for example, who was praiseworthy in his own age but, for the most part, is a despised relic in ours, is that he is dismissed easily as having accomplished nothing of lasting value. But not only that. He and others like him are seen as having been little more than instruments of empire, useful to their political masters but otherwise simply the purveyors of indefensible social and cultural destruction.[33] This biography has attempted to demonstrate that in the story of Allenby's imperial life such a view is simply not true.

That Allenby was considered to be heroic as the term was understood generally in his own day is beyond question. The contemporaneous cultural reception accorded him throughout the Western world alone following the defeat of the Turks at Jerusalem in December of 1917 was almost unparalleled for a figure in British imperial history. Certainly, one searches in vain for another event in the long history of the British Empire that was lionized in an equally laudatory way. To be sure, Nelson's victory at Trafalgar in 1805 was of surpassing importance to Britain's physical security and was celebrated accordingly. But Allenby's taking of Jerusalem had brought together a millennium's worth of history as it bore on the medieval Crusades, the renewed sense of both Jewish and Arab national purpose, and the modern ethic of pluralistic accommodation (Muslim, Jewish, and Christian) in a manner that yielded great international approbation. What then might be the proper way historically in which to view Allenby and his signal achievements in the Middle East?

In recent years, historians have spent much time re-evaluating national heroes in ways that far surpass earlier post-colonial attempts merely to de-bunk or to denigrate those heroes of long-standing seen by moderns to be anachronistic, offensive, or both. Max Jones is one such historian. His important essay, 'What Should Historians Do with Heroes? Reflections on Nineteenth- and Twentieth-Century Britain', published in 2007, has done more perhaps than any other piece of work to shape contemporary debate on the nature and understanding of heroism, especially as it applies to the traditional heroes of the British Empire.[34] Jones does not include Allenby by name in his appraisal of such heroes, but much of what he suggests applies well to him when seeking to understand the manner in which Allenby was received and celebrated – most especially his victory at Jerusalem – by the British nation, and indeed by much of the Western world.

As we have seen, the response to Allenby's taking of Jerusalem in December 1917 was one of almost overwhelming approbation, with barely a discordant note to be heard. The trope of Allenby as a 'Modern Crusader' or 'The Greatest of the Crusaders', of having fulfilled the unfinished work of Richard Lionheart, was the most widespread response to his victory over the Ottomans in Palestine and was presented widely in British and other English-language newspapers.[35] But of high significance too was the idea that Allenby was a liberator of over half-a-million Palestinian Arabs from the despised grip of Turkish control: 'Heroic leader and dispenser of victory', wrote Sharif Faisal to Allenby in the autumn of 1917, summing up in six words what he thought of him. Additionally, of course, Allenby was seen also as the deliverer of a recovered Jewish homeland: 'the name of Allenby, a son of Great Britain, whose dogma is the freedom of nations,' wrote one breathless Jewish admirer in December 1917. 'That name to-day is imprinted in the hearts of all Israelites.'[36]

Then came too, the equally celebrated routing of the Turkish-German forces in Syria and the establishment there – if temporarily, at least – of Arab control. Allenby's insistence on Arab independence, even if it meant initially a supervised form of it by the British and then the French, marked him out as something other than simply a military conqueror.[37] Rather, altogether, he had become one of those 'gallant men' of empire, as the *Sunday Times* would enthuse about him, whose form of heroism was timeless and therefore stretched well beyond Britain to resonate with other nations and peoples.[38]

As widely celebrated as Allenby's achievement was, not every account of his military victories and what they had wrought in the Middle East was of the brass band variety. For example, he may have been 'To-day's Hero', as the *Westminster Gazette* called him, but its editorialist then went on to question the unremitting adulation that he had received in the aftermath of the Palestine campaign. As stated in October of 1919, on the occasion of Allenby being awarded the freedom of the City of London, his welcome as 'the last and greatest of the Crusaders was a blunder and gives offence to millions of our fellow-[Muslim] subjects in the Empire'.[39] The reference here mainly was to India's vast population of Muslims, so at the time and given Allenby's standing among the Arabs such perceived offence to Islam was ignored. But the *Gazette* had a point. On the other hand, as we have seen, Allenby had severe misgivings about the Zionist Organization's demand for a Jewish national homeland in Palestine and what its establishment there would mean for its Arab inhabitants.

Allenby's contemporary heroism therefore was nothing less than complex and of a type that transcended conventionally useful military victories, as signal and liberating as those victories had been under his command in 1917–18. To Allenby, the war against the Ottomans was a traditionally just war in that its goals were to free an oppressed people (the Arabs), as well as to open up the possibility for another oppressed people (the Jews) to taste freedom also, and like the Arabs potentially to form their own modern nation state.[40] Allenby must therefore, it seems to me, be seen as representing something beyond simply a conventional (Christian), imperial hero.[41] Allenby's own religious faith was traditional, as we have seen, in that he had been baptized in the Church of England as an infant and thereafter was raised in its contemporary religio-social verities and milieu. As an adult, however, he did not attend church regularly and was not demonstrably devout. But that he understood himself to be Christian is axiomatic. To that end, when visiting Jerusalem later in 1933, for example, he spoke thus: 'Believing in life beyond the tomb, we cannot but feel that in this Land of ancient strife, myriad spirits are about and around us; souls of friends and of enemies, now united, in mutual comprehension and full wisdom; free from the toils of the flesh, and willing and able to help us mortals on the upward path.'[42] Moreover, earlier, in the period around Jerusalem's fall in 1917, he had stayed in touch with all the religious leaders in the city ensuring that the rights and prerogatives of the various faith communities they represented, and which his Proclamation had pledged to protect, would be respected. Understandably, he was closest in this regard to Rennie MacInnes, the Anglican bishop of Jerusalem, but his stance towards all of the religions represented in the Holy City was essentially irenic.[43]

That some saw Allenby simply as a 'Christian Crusader' is indisputable nonetheless. But it is worth noting that he himself rejected such an interpretation of what he had accomplished in Palestine. Initially, in June of 1917, it will be recalled that Allenby had not been pleased at being sent from France to the Middle East. Indeed, his old friend and colleague, Sir Henry McMahon, recalled later having had to cheer up Allenby by saying that fighting in Palestine presented a 'unique opportunity' much unlike anything found on the Western Front.[44] Moreover, Allenby was firm in disputing the charge that 'our object was to deliver Jerusalem from the Moslem. Not so. Many of my soldiers were Moslem. The importance of Jerusalem lay in its strategical position.'[45] Finally, Allenby's military victories in Syria, and later his proconsular work in Egypt, had nothing whatsoever to do with the 'Christian Crusader' or 'Lionheart' motif.

Allenby's accomplishments in fulfilling both command and gubernatorial roles of course make him as one among many in British imperial history. Other examples of the same duality, such as Lord Kitchener or General Gordon, abound. But in wrestling mightily with the emergent reality of twentieth-century political nationalism, Allenby was one of the first to do so, and his approach to the phenomenon was notably progressive, if tempered always by his acceptance of the primacy of British imperial interests. Only seldom did he ever articulate what might be viewed as a philosophy or an ethic of empire. But one such moment came in 1930 when Allenby wrote the following words in the appropriately named magazine, *John Bull*: 'Our Empire came out of the ordeal of the World War triumphant in achievement, proud in statesmanship and exalted in prestige. ... The Empire is in good case, and Britain, heart of the Empire, pulsates with life.'[46] As unsophisticated and propagandistic as this particular rendering of the British Empire's purpose may read, Allenby's view of it as being essentially a force for good in international affairs cannot be doubted. Whether it be soldiers, administrators, traders, jurists, physicians or missionaries, Allenby's view of the work of the British overseas was that regardless of location, at their best they engendered the lineaments of holistic civil society and a respect for the rule of law.[47] In this way, it may be suggested, he saw the British Empire in much the same light as did that long-time pro-empire publicist and Cabinet minister, Leo Amery, who believed firmly that the British had an exalted destiny to fulfil internationally.[48] Still, as we saw earlier, in his Edinburgh rectorial address of a few years later, Allenby had begun by then to give voice to a more developed idea of internationalism, the logical end of which – had he lived – would likely have transcended seeing the British Empire as an absolutely necessary organizing component of the modern international order.

The historian Stephen Heathorn has written recently of British imperial heroes. In Heathorn's book, Allenby remains un-named, but his inclusion in the author's roster of 'anachronistic' heroes, as he calls them, could be imagined easily.[49] Heathorn's definition of anachronistic heroes, however, while helpful, is not satisfying ultimately in that many of the things for which such heroes were celebrated come to us today as essential features of the modern nation state or, indeed, political entities of any sort. In Allenby's case, for example, his understanding of Arab nationalism – as limited as it may have been, and as subservient as it was to British war aims in the Middle East – nevertheless was entirely modern and progressive in acknowledging that the Arab desire (or at least that of Hussein and Faisal) was to create a unified Arab state. So too, despite his more moderate approach to it, was Allenby's support for the creation of a Jewish national homeland in Palestine. Similarly, Allenby's six years in Egypt were an exercise in large part in state-building, albeit according to the constitutional gradualist model that had long defined the British Empire's approach to colonial 'independence', and which would continue to prevail through to the end of the decolonization era in the 1960s. Such features of Allenby's approach to both military command and civil governance, it is therefore reasonable to suggest, are not captured well by the term 'anachronistic'. The fact that for many colonial nationalists, notably for Saad Zaghlul in Egypt, British constitutional gradualism meant little more than interminable and incomprehensible delays might be a legitimate criticism of Allenby's record there, but it is not necessarily so if the goal was to achieve political independence without the ineluctable violence and human hardships inherent in a continuous cycle mass civil disorder.

Allenby's falling within the category of 'soldier-hero', a friendlier term used by Graham Dawson in yet another attempt to understand traditional figures of empire, means that his reputation over time has diminished nevertheless in an age in which the accomplishments of such figures are no longer celebrated in the culturally approved ways engaged in by earlier generations.[50] In the 1920s, for example, Allenby's name was honoured regularly by its being attached to a number of schools, parks, streets, suburbs and even to a town. This kind of approbation occurred in Palestine and England, as well as in the various dominions of the British Empire.[51] Today, these vestiges of broad societal respect for the soldier-hero are to be seen still, despite campaigns in some places to have such agents of perceived military subjugation erased from public memory. Allenby's own position as one of the sword arms of the British Empire is leavened by the fact that he also was a liberator, which may account in part why these attempts have not touched (yet?) his memorialization in any overt way. Hence, implying that Allenby's form of heroism is simply of another time and place does not quite explain the man's enduring legacy, especially at this particular moment in history when the 100th anniversary of the First World War is being marked in many countries around the world, including Israel where Allenby remains traditionally heroic. Of course, in some important respects Israel is a special case. But the country's modern period that began with Allenby's victory in 1917 is not so unlike that of other post-colonial states as to disqualify it from this sort of analysis.[52] Thus it would appear to be Allenby's heroic duality that makes his reputation and legacy more demonstrably modern, and therefore more readily acceptable, than that of some of his contemporaries and forebears.

The supreme comparator in this regard of course is T. E. Lawrence, whose own version of heroism has retained, for various reasons, much more cultural currency and attendant popular interest than has Allenby's. Accordingly, Lawrence has been, and continues to be, the subject of a great many books, articles, films, symposia, museum exhibitions and plays, easily outstripping Allenby's fame in a way that he himself predicted, as noted earlier.[53] Still, in one of the most recent of these offerings – a stage play, Howard Brenton's *Lawrence after Arabia*, performed in London for the first time in 2016 to celebrate the centenary of the beginning of the Arab Revolt – the playwright has Allenby occupy a vital role in Lawrence's story. At the end of an attempt to write Allenby's biography, therefore, one might be justified in saying that for him such a contemporary restorative balance is only right.

AFTERWORD
ALLENBY AND THE MIDDLE EAST TODAY

As I write, the events described in this book that relate directly to the Middle East occurred almost exactly 100 years ago. The centenary of the First World War carries with it a clear recognition of its shaping impact on the modern Middle East. For most historians, a hundred years is not a very long period of time; and when considered in relation to the age-old lands and peoples of the Middle East, a century seems very brief indeed. That said, in the region's 7,000 years of recorded history, it may be argued that the past 100 of them have been as full of change and controversy as almost any that have come before.

Certainly, the eight-year period from 1917 to 1925 during which Allenby was engaged in winning military campaigns and crafting administrative policy in the Middle East left an indelible mark on the geopolitics of the region. The impact of those years continues to be felt by generations of Egyptians, Israelis, Palestinians, Iraqis and Saudi Arabians, the successor modern political nationalities of the 400-year-old Ottoman Empire that crumbled in the face of the Allenby-led Allied onslaught of the First World War. In this way, military paramountcy shaped the Middle East in the early twentieth century no less than it had under the Romans; or as it had during the period of the three major medieval Islamic caliphates culminating in the Abbasids; or under the Crusaders; or during the four centuries of Turkish rule.[1] Indeed, operating as they did during the First World War, the Western Allies acted exactly in keeping with the military traditions bequeathed to them by all those who have sought always to control and shape the destiny of the cradle lands of Western Civilization. In this regard, therefore, Allenby is understood best to have been the chief military arm of a congeries of powerful external forces determined once again to bend the region to its bidding. In other words, Allenby's story in the Middle East reads in most respects like a very old one, but with a contemporary face. *Plus ça change*.

At the time of Allenby's retirement to England in 1925, he departed a region in which the necessary military upheavals of war had begun to be flattened out into political and administrative arrangements that sought to achieve in the Middle East at once both civil society and the long-term maintenance of imperial interests. In short, the timeless bargain of the periphery and metropole that constitutes collaborative imperialism continued to prevail, a state of affairs given its classic definition in the 1950s by the Oxbridge historians, Ronald Robinson and John Gallagher.[2] Mandatory Palestine, the forerunner of the modern state of Israel, would remain under British control until 1948, two years after a domestic Jewish terrorist campaign had culminated in the bombing of the King David Hotel in Jerusalem, the site of Britain's administrative headquarters. Almost 140 people were either killed or wounded in that devastating bomb blast, and the shock of it helped both to hasten Britain's departure from Israel, and to bring about the country's concomitant independence two years later.

Undoubtedly, had Allenby been alive to witness the descent of Palestine into anti-British terrorism at the hands especially of the Irgun Zvai Leumi (National Military Organization), which was responsible for the King David Hotel bombing in 1946, and of its splinter-group, the so-called Stern Gang, he would have been outraged. So too would he have been appalled by the shabby treatment accorded Israel's Palestinian minority ever since. In our own day it has become normative to decry the impact of the Sykes–Picot Agreement – 'Why a 100-year-old pact is still hated in the Mideast' – headlined a typical newspaper column, for example, in 2016 in Canada's *Globe and Mail* marking the agreement's centenary.[3] However, it should be recognized that the agreement as it was envisaged in 1916, and then enacted in part two years later, has nothing to do with today's Middle East, notwithstanding the murderous protestations demanding its 'overthrow' by the so-called Islamic State of Iraq and the Levant (ISIL), or Daesh as its Arabic acronym would have it.

Sykes–Picot was superseded long ago by the actions of the independent or semi-independent states of the Middle East. 'Decolonisation has finished', notes the Dutch historian of empire, H. L. Wesseling, in words that apply equally to all parts of the formerly imperialized world. 'It definitely belongs to the past. Yet somehow it has refused to become history.'[4] Hence, it might be said that continuing to call into question Sykes-Picot's perceived iniquities in the formation of the modern Middle East is a bit like blaming Charlemagne for the fact that the historic capital of the Franks at Aachen would become later part of modern-day Germany, rather than of France. The claim made in 2014 by ISIL, therefore, that it wishes to re-establish a caliphate that would usurp 'the legality of all emirates, groups, states and organizations' in the Middle East is nothing more than a contemporary jihadist–imperialist one and carries with it far less legitimacy and likely no more longevity than did the claims made by Britain and France in 1916.[5] The key difference, of course, is that the Sykes–Picot vision of the modern Middle East was a temporary one, and certainly did not prescribe the wanton murder of Muslims and non-Muslims alike as a necessary prescription to bring about a new political order. Rather, it was made to sponsor post-Ottoman state-building, principally for nationalist Muslim Arabs committed to moving beyond the long-time imperial suzerainty of the Turks. That this vision came to include a Jewish national homeland was much more a function of the Balfour Declaration of 1917, as we have seen, than it was of Sykes–Picot. But even in promulgating the Balfour Declaration it was never the intention of the British government for such a proposed Jewish homeland to develop into a state that would progressively marginalize the historic Palestinian Arab population found within its borders. Allenby himself, it will be recalled, was absolute in holding this position and would have found wholly unacceptable the increasingly rigid interpretation of the nature and scope of Mandatory Palestine in the later 1930s and 1940s, not to mention that of the independent state of Israel in which Arab rights were and are severely restricted. As Allenby had reiterated to Chaim Weizmann in the spring of 1918, 'We have to be extremely careful not to hurt the sensibilities of the [Arab] population.'⁶ Such advice, it may be argued, was never followed very assiduously, either then or later.

Not only was it Allenby who took an irenic position in thinking about how best to accommodate the two claims for emergent statehood in Palestine, however, so too did Prince Faisal. In 1919, for instance, he wrote to Felix Frankfurter, a prominent member of the American delegation at the Paris Peace Conference, an ardent Zionist, and a future justice of the US Supreme Court, to say that 'we are working together for a reformed and revived Near East, and our two movements complete one another. The Jewish movement is national and not imperialist. ... Indeed I think that neither can be a real success without the other.'⁷ The fact that this capaciously inclusive vision for the post-Ottoman Middle East did not prevail is one of the great political and social tragedies of our time. But to blame Sykes–Picot for the way in which the various national actors came to operate in the Middle East during the years after 1916, and continue to operate today, is both myopic and unhistorical.

Beyond an evaluation of the creation of Israel alone, a similar stance of blaming the architects of the post–First World War regional settlement despite the near-universal contemporary desire to expel the Ottoman Turks remains strong. In books such as Peter Mangold's *What the British Did: Two Centuries in the Middle East* and *Winston's Folly: How Winston Churchill Created Modern Iraq*, by Christopher Catherwood, to name just two, the point of view they adopt is one of relentless criticism, leading to the culminating position that British (and French) actions in the wartime Middle East were meddlesome, their impact baleful and their legacy shameful.⁸ Arguments of this sort remain curiously unhistorical, however, in that such authors tend to assume that governments and individuals, whether they be the British and French states or leading figures like Allenby, Lawrence, Lloyd George, Bell, Churchill, Faisal, Weizmann and many others, were either free agents able to act in any way that they chose, or the circumstances in which they acted were uniquely without precedent and therefore could be shaped in any direction that they desired. Such utopias, however, have never been the real world of history, and they certainly did not prevail in the Middle East during the First World War and its aftermath.

In his outstanding study of Lawrence as a man of arms during the Arab Revolt published recently, Neil Faulkner draws the conclusion ultimately that the 'Arab Revolt had been', in fact, 'a mirage in the desert ... a false hope'.⁹ Like all revolutions, putative or fulfilled, the outcome of the revolt in the desert of course was unpredictable. In the same way, and simultaneously, those Russians who had put their unadulterated faith in the Bolshevik Revolution in 1917 only to find their lives blighted by decades of autocratic tyranny far exceeding that to which they had been subjected by the unseated Tsars, would doubtless concur. So too, a century and more earlier, the majority of Anglo-American colonists in 1775 who had opposed the revolt against the British only to find themselves marginalized quickly, persecuted viciously, their property confiscated and their future reduced to exile by an assertively intolerant American revolutionary elite. Hence, it may be suggested that Faulkner is too confident in seeing the Arab Revolt as a failure.

What, indeed, was the alternative for concerted Arab action in 1917, besides doing nothing? History had yielded to the various Arab tribal groups not much more than continued stagnation under the oppressive and divisive hand of the Ottoman Turks unless something were to happen that shook up the ground upon which they stood. For Sharif Hussein first, and then for Faisal in earnest, the only real alternative to such terminal stasis, as we have seen clearly, was to join forces with the British, defeat the Turks and work for the realization of a modern and unified Arab national state. The fact that the achievement of such a new Pan-Arab state – or what did develop instead in the form of the smaller Arab states of Syria, Iraq, Saudi Arabia and (Trans-) Jordan – was far less than perfect, says almost nothing about what the real historical choices were at the time, and therefore what the measurement of contemporary success should be. The deep irony of course, which Faulkner points out, is that it was the defeated Ottoman Turks, rather than the Arabs, who were able to move quickly after the war to form a modern, post-imperial nation state in a way that none of the infant Arab states was able to do.[10]

For Allenby, outside of his direct military and early administrative impact on Palestine, Arabia and Syria, it is in Egypt, of course, that we can see his main proconsular legacy. To this end, the Declaration of 1922 that paved the way for Egyptian independence, and which bears his name, was at once both far-reaching and imperfect. But in its very promulgation Egyptian politics were re-calibrated in such a way as to make it almost impossible for political regression to occur, at least in theory. Even though British imperial interests – in the form chiefly of the Suez Canal – would continue to dominate the Anglo-Egyptian relationship, after 1922 Egypt was on course to achieve much more than what had been granted formally by the declaration of that year. Allenby's persistence in demanding of the British government a negotiated change in Egypt's status was essential to bringing about this constitutional advance. That Wafd nationalists under Saad Zaghlul's leadership thought the pace of change in this regard to be glacial, responding to it therefore with street violence and ultimately political assassination, says much more about their own impatience and lack of foresight than it does about Allenby's inability to marshal the right way forward during an extraordinarily tense time politically in Egypt.

Did Allenby overreact in his authoritarian response to the assassination of Sir Lee Stack in November of 1924? Arguably no, the firm hand he displayed both then and afterwards helped to reduce the probability of further violence while allowing Zaghlul the opportunity to exert control over his more extreme Wafdist supporters. In the end, with Allenby's long-contemplated resignation taking effect in June of 1925, he departed Egypt having moved it from a place of dependency as a British protectorate to one of independent status, complete with a relatively liberal constitution and an elected parliament. These achievements, regardless of the failure of later generations of British administrators and politicians, along with Egyptian nationalist leaders, to oversee permanent constitutional maturation, cannot be laid at Allenby's feet. Indeed, the further one travels from the 1920s in viewing the modern political history of Egypt, the more significant does Allenby's achievement appear to be in retrospect. There's no doubt that Egypt's independence in 1922 coming about as it did under his purview, although limited in scope, had marked an irreversible and firmly progressive sea change in the country's modern constitutional development.

Today, a century later, the Arab Spring that took place in various parts of the Middle East in 2011 showed clearly how resistant to the democratic constitutional trajectory inaugurated by the 1922 Allenby Declaration were the Egyptian regimes that took power afterwards in the significant years of 1936, 1952, 1956 and 1981. So too it must be said, for the earlier part of that time, had been the British themselves. To borrow from John Darwin's comprehensive study of the rise and fall of global empires, *After Tamerlane*, in the 1920s the British had reached the 'limit' of their empire in Egypt, although most of those resident in the imperial centre in London had not yet realized it.[11] Allenby, for one, however, had been clear-eyed in recognizing this reality. Hence his insistence on the adoption of the Declaration of 1922 and, in his view, the necessary incrementalism of its approach to both Egyptian political independence and the concomitance of British imperial withdrawal. That a succeeding generation of British imperialists refused to allow this view of the need for decolonization to proceed at pace in Egypt was a policy failure of the highest order. The sharp shock of the nationalization of the Suez Canal in 1956 by the regime of Gamal Nasser would prove to be the event that slammed-shut the door on Britain's too-slow realization of its imperial vulnerability in Egypt, and indeed across the entire Middle East. As Darwin observes succinctly, 'Suez signalled the end of British ambition to manage the politics of the whole Arab world.'[12] However, back in the early 1920s, Allenby had come already to the inescapable and prescient conclusion that such a realization should be at the centre of British policy towards Egypt and the Middle East. If such a view had been more widespread among his peers then and during the years that followed, a compelling argument can be made that much of the civil instability, political radicalism, terrorist violence and human suffering that has blighted both Egypt and the wider Arab world ever since might have been mitigated, or perhaps even avoided altogether.

CHRONOLOGY

1861   Edmund Henry Hynman Allenby, born 23 April, Brackenhurst Hall, near Southwell, Nottinghamshire

1871   Educated privately, Ashbocking vicarage, Suffolk

1875   Enters Haileybury College

1881   Enters Royal Military Academy Sandhurst

1882   Gazetted lieutenant, 6th (Inniskilling) Dragoons, and sent to South Africa

1886   Returns to England

1887   Promoted captain

1888   Goes back to South Africa; promoted adjutant

1890   Returns to England and garrison duty

1896   Enters Staff College, Camberley; marries Adelaide Mabel Chapman, 30 December

1897   Promoted major

1898   Horace Michael Hynman, son and only child, born 11 January

1899   Sees service in the Second South African War

1902   Promoted brevet lieutenant colonel; created Companion of the Bath (CB)

1903   Promoted colonel

1905   Promoted brigadier general

1909   Promoted major general

1910   Appointed inspector general of cavalry

1914   Assumes command of Cavalry Division at the outbreak of war in August

1915   Created Knight Commander of the Bath (KCB)

1917   Battle of Arras; transferred to Middle East as commander of the Egyptian Expeditionary Force; Third Battle of Gaza (Beersheba); capture of Jerusalem, 9 December; created Knight Grand Cross of the Most Distinguished Order of Saint Michael and Saint George (GCMG)

1918   Battle of Megiddo; created Knight Grand Cross of the Bath (GCB)

1919   Appointed (special) high commissioner for Egypt; created 1st Viscount Allenby of Megiddo and Felixstowe; promoted field marshal

1925   Retires to London

1934   Created Knight Grand Cross of the Royal Victorian Order (GCVO)

1936   Dies, 14 May

NOTES

Preface

1 Quoted in Jeremy Wilson, *Lawrence of Arabia: The Authorized Biography of T.E. Lawrence* (New York: Atheneum, 1990), p. 937.
2 Saki (Hector Hugh Munro). Quoted in the *Times Literary Supplement*, 12 December 2018, p. 14.
3 Peter Mangold, *What the British Did: Two Centuries in the Middle East* (London: I.B. Tauris, 2016), p. 111.
4 Archibald Wavell, *Allenby: A Study in Greatness*, 2 vols (London: George G. Harrap, 1940–43); Lawrence James, *Imperial Warrior: The Life and Times of Field-Marshal Viscount Allenby 1861–1936* (London: Weidenfeld & Nicolson, 1993).

Chapter 1

1 The biographical information about the Allenby family has been gleaned essentially from H. C. G. Matthew and Brian Harrison, eds, *Oxford Dictionary of National Biography*, vol. 1 (Oxford: Oxford University Press, 2004), p. 837.
2 Today, Allenby Park occupies the former site of Felixstowe Hall, which was razed in the years following Catherine Allenby's death in 1922.
3 Quoted in James, *Imperial Warrior*, p. 4.
4 Rudyard Kipling, *The Islanders* (1902): 'flannelled fools at the wicket or the muddied oafs at the goals.'
5 Quoted in Archibald Wavell, *Allenby: A Study in Greatness*, vol. 1 (London: George G. Harrap, 1940), pp. 31–2.
6 Lytton Strachey, *Eminent Victorians* (London: Chatto & Windus, 1918).
7 John Bew, *Citizen Clem: A Biography of Attlee* (London: Riverrun, 2016), pp. 34–6.
8 See Thomas Hughes, *Tom Brown's School Days*, published originally in 1857. See also, J. R. De S. Honey, *Tom Brown's Universe: The Development of the Public School in the 19th Century* (London: Millington, 1977).
9 Quoted in Wavell, *Allenby*, p. 32.
10 Quoted in James, *Imperial Warrior*, p. 7.
11 See Clive Dewey, *Anglo-Indian Attitudes: The Mind of the Indian Civil Service* (London: Hambledon Continuum, 1993).
12 Wavell, *Allenby*, p. 35.
13 AP, 6/1/20.
14 AP, 6/1/21.
15 AP, 6/1/22. See also, Brian Gardner, *Allenby* (London: Cassell, 1965), p. 6.
16 AP, 6/1/33.
17 See R. H. Thoumine, *Scientific Soldier: A Life of General Le Marchant, 1766–1812* (Oxford: Oxford University Press, 1968).

18 Quoted in Raymond Savage, *Allenby of Armageddon: A Record of the Career and Campaigns of Field-Marshal Viscount Allenby* (Indianapolis: Bobbs-Merrill, 1926), p. 25.

19 AP, 6/1/31.

20 Wavell, *Allenby*, p. 38.

21 AP, 6/1/33! Richard Cannon, *Historical Record of the Sixth, or Inniskilling Regiment of Dragoons: Containing an Account of the Formation of the Regiment in 1689, and of Its Subsequent Services to 1846* (London: Parker, Furnivall, & Parker, 1847).

22 See Martin Meredith, *Diamonds, Gold, and War: The British, the Boers, and the Making of South Africa* (New York: Public Affairs, 2007), pp. 13–21.

23 John Darwin, 'Unlocking the World: Port Cities and Globalisation, 1830–1930', a public lecture given on 7 July 2015, University of Konstanz.

24 See Donald Harman Akenson, *God's Peoples: Covenant and Land in South Africa, Israel and Ulster* (Montreal and Kingston: McGill-Queen's University Press, 1991).

25 See Ian Knight, *Zulu Rising: The Epic Story of Isandlwana and Rorke's Drift* (London: Pan Books, 2010).

26 See Ron Lock and Peter Quantrill, *Zulu Vanquished: The Destruction of the Zulu Kingdom* (London: Greenhill, 2005).

27 See John Laband, *The Transvaal Rebellion: The First Boer War, 1880–1881* (New York: Longman/Pearson, 2005).

28 AP, 6/2/10.

29 Christopher Saunders and Iain R. Smith, 'Southern Africa, 1795 – 1910', in Andrew Porter (ed.), *The Oxford History of the British Empire, vol. III, The Nineteenth Century* (Oxford: Oxford University Press, 1999), pp. 607–8.

30 See John Mackenzie, *Austral Africa: Losing It or Ruling It: Being Incidents and Experiences in Bechuanaland, Cape Colony, and England* (London: Sampson Low, Marston, Searle & Rivington, 1887).

31 See Robert I. Rotberg, *The Founder: Cecil Rhodes and the Pursuit of Power* (Oxford: Oxford University Press, 1988).

32 Wavell, *Allenby*, p. 48.

33 Jeffrey Butler, 'The German Factor in Anglo-Transvaal Relations', in Prosser Gifford and Wm. Roger Louis (eds), *Britain and Germany in Africa: Imperial Policy and Colonial Rule* (New Haven, CT: Yale University Press, 1967), p. 185.

34 Quoted in H. C. G. Matthew, *Gladstone 1809–1898* (Oxford: Clarendon Press, 1997), p. 596.

35 See C. Brad Faught, *Gordon: Victorian Hero* (Washington DC: Potomac, 2008), pp. 75–92.

36 Wavell, *Allenby*, p. 50.

37 James, *Imperial Warrior*, p. 19.

38 AP, 6/4/48.

39 See John S. Galbraith, *Crown and Charter: The Early Years of the British South Africa Company* (Berkeley: University of California Press, 1974).

40 AP, 1/1/6.

41 AP, 1/1/4.

42 AP, 1/1/8.

43 See H. C. G. Matthew, *The Liberal Imperialists: The Ideas and Politics of a Post-Gladstonian Elite* (Oxford: Oxford University Press, 1973).

44 AP, 1/1/7.

45 AP, 6/3/24.

46   AP, 6/3/9, 26.
47   AP, 6/2/35.
48   AP, 6/3/7, 24.
49   AP, 1/1/15.

Chapter 2

1   Quoted in Keith Terrance Surridge, *Managing the South African War, 1899–1902: Politicians V. Generals* (Woodbridge: Boydell, 1998), p. 17.
2   Quoted in Mark Weber, 'The Boer War Remembered', *The Journal of Historical Review*, 18, no. 3 (May–June 1999): 15.
3   Quoted in Antony Thomas, *Rhodes: The Race for South Africa* (New York: St. Martin's Press, 1997), p. 284.
4   J. A. Hobson, *The War in South Africa: Its Causes and Effects* (London: James Nisbet & Co., 1900), and *Imperialism: A Study* (London: Constable, 1902).
5   AP, 1/1/22.
6   Ibid.
7   AP, 1/2/1.
8   AP, 1/2/2.
9   AP, 1/2/1.
10   AP, 1/2/6.
11   C. Brad Faught, *Kitchener: Hero and Anti-Hero* (London: I.B. Tauris, 2016), p. 107.
12   Ibid., pp. 107–11.
13   AP, 1/2/7.
14   AP, 1/2/9.
15   AP, 1/2/20.
16   AP, 1/2/9; 1/2/16.
17   AP, 1/2/9.
18   AP, 1/2/16.
19   AP, 1/2/11.
20   AP, 1/2/16.
21   AP, 1/2/10.
22   Rudyard Kipling, *Bridge-Guard in the Karroo* (1901).
23   AP, 1/2/6.
24   AP, 1/2/17.
25   Ibid.
26   Ibid.
27   AP, 1/2/20.
28   AP, 1/2/26.
29   Quoted in Denis Judd and Keith Surridge, *The Boer War* (New York: Palgrave Macmillan, 2003), p. 150.
30   AP, 1/2/26.
31   AP, 1/2/27.
32   AP, 1/2/30.
33   Ibid.
34   Faught, *Kitchener*, p. 110.
35   AP, 1/2/28.

36 AP, 1/2/27.
37 AP, 1/2/28.
38 AP, 1/2/31.
39 Ibid.
40 AP, 1/2/41.
41 AP, 1/2/42.
42 AP, 1/2/135.
43 AP, 1/2/109.
44 Thomas Pakenham, *The Boer War* (New York: Perennial, 2001), p. 467.
45 Quoted in John Pollock, *Kitchener: Architect of Victory, Artisan of Peace* (New York: Carroll & Graf, 2001), pp. 189–92.
46 Quoted in Faught, *Kitchener*, p. 118.
47 AP, 1/2/95.
48 AP, 1/2/114.
49 Quoted in Trevor Royle, *The Kitchener Enigma* (London: Michael Joseph, 1985.), p. 72.
50 AP, 1/2/114.
51 AP, 1/2/121.
52 AP, 1/2/120.
53 AP, 1/2/121.
54 AP, 1/2/120; 1/2/135.
55 See Faught, *Kitchener*, pp. 118–22.
56 Ibid.
57 Niall Ferguson, *Empire: The Rise and Demise of the British World Order and the Lessons of Global Power* (New York: Basic Books, 2002), p. 235.
58 AP, 1/2/143.
59 AP, 1/2/120.
60 AP, 1/2/132.
61 AP, 1/2/95.
62 AP, 1/2/135.
63 AP, 1/12/20.
64 AP, 1/2/143; 1/2/150.
65 AP, 1/4/28.
66 AP, 1/2/164.
67 AP, 1/4/29.
68 AP, 1/2/164.
69 AP, 1/4/27.
70 AP, 1/2/160.
71 AP, 6/5/5.
72 Rudyard Kipling, *The Lesson* (1901); see Spencer Jones, *From Boer War to World War: Tactical Reform of the British Army, 1902–1914* (Norman: University of Oklahoma Press, 2012).
73 AP, 1/4/33.
74 AP, 1/4/37.
75 AP, 1/4/34.
76 See Ian F. W. Beckett, *The Army and the Curragh Incident 1914* (London: Bodley Head, 1986).
77 Byron Farwell, *Queen Victoria's Little Wars* (New York: Norton, 1985).

78 Viscount Grey of Fallodon, *Twenty-Five Years 1892–1916* (New York: Frederick A. Stokes, 1925), p. 20.

Chapter 3

1   A tension-wracked period of time rendered superbly on-screen, for example, in the BBC Two drama, *37 Days*, broadcast appropriately in August of 2014, exactly 100 years after it had occurred.
2   AP, 6/6/1.
3   AP, 1/5/94.
4   AP, 1/5/1–2.
5   'Kaiser Wilhelm II and the Contemptible Little Army, 19 August 1914', firstworldwar. com.
6   AP, 1/5/3–5.
7   Martin Gilbert, *First World War* (Toronto: Stoddart, 1994), p. 56.
8   See David Lomas, *Mons 1914: The BEF's Tactical Triumph* (Wellingborough: Osprey, 1997).
9   George Gordon, *The Retreat from Mons* (London: Houghton Mifflin, 1917), p. 40.
10 James, *Imperial Warrior*, pp. 61–2.
11 Matthew Hughes, 'Edmund Allenby', in Ian F. W. Beckett and Steven Corvi (eds), *Haig's Generals* (Barnsley: Pen & Sword, 2006), p. 17. See also, Nikolas Gardner, *Trial by Fire: Command and the British Expeditionary Force in 1914* (Westport: Praeger, 2003), pp. 54–5.
12 Ibid.
13 AP, 1/5/6.
14 See David Clarke, *The Angel of Mons: Phantom Soldiers and Ghostly Guardians* (London: Wiley, 2005); Faught, *Kitchener*, pp. 202–3.
15 See Holger H. Herwig, *The Marne, 1914: The Opening of World War I and the Battle that Changed the World* (New York: Random House, 2009).
16 Faught, *Kitchener*, p. 197.
17 AP, 1/5/11.
18 AP, 1/5/13.
19 AP, 1/5/16; 6/1/39.
20 AP, 1/5/26.
21 AP, 1/5/12.
22 Wavell, *Allenby*, p. 144.
23 AP, 1/5/18.
24 AP, 1/5/21, 16.
25 AP, 1/5/37.
26 AP, 1/5/38.
27 AP, 1/5/29. Prince Maximilian of Hesse-Kassel (1894–1914) was the son of Princess Margarete of Prussia (1872–1954), who was a granddaughter of Queen Victoria and sister to Kaiser Wilhelm II.
28 AP, 1/5/28.
29 AP, 1/5/48.
30 Gilbert, *First World War*, p. 99.
31 Faught, *Kitchener*, p. 193.

32 AP, 1/5/57, 61, 68.

33 AP, 1/5/57.

34 AP, 1/5/28.

35 AP, 1/6/4.

36 See Malcolm Brown, ed., *No Man's Land: Christmas 1914 and Fraternization in the Great War* (London: Constable, 2007).

37 AP, 1/6/2.

38 J. E. Edmonds and G. C. Wynne, *Official History of the Great War: Military Operations, France and Belgium 1915, Volume I, Winter 1914–15: Battle of Neuve Chapelle, Battle of Ypres* (London: Macmillan, 1927), p. 310.

39 AP, 6/6/27. Porter was the husband of Allenby's youngest sister Helen (Nell).

40 Edmonds and Wynne, *Official History, Volume I*, p. 340.

41 Quoted in James, *Imperial Warrior*, p. 74.

42 Ibid., p. 75.

43 Ibid.

44 AP, 1/6/8.

45 C. S. Forester, best known for his series of *Horatio Hornblower* novels of life in the Royal Navy during the Napoleonic Wars, published *The General* in 1936. The novel is highly critical of the way in which most British generals commanded their troops during the First World War, the extremely high casualty figures being the result of wooden thinking, Forester believed. In his title character, General Sir Herbert Curzon (an unsubtle conflating of Kitchener with Curzon), he attempted to besmirch the reputations of two dead men and then extended the attempt even further by nicknaming another fictional character in the book, General Wayland-Leigh, 'the Buffalo', thereby also implicating Allenby. It is not known whether Allenby read the book, which was published just before he died.

46 Quoted in Wavell, *Allenby*, p. 159.

47 Prov. 15.1.

48 AP, 1/6/7.

49 AP, 1/6/17.

50 J. E. Edmonds, *Official History of the Great War: Military Operations, France and Belgium, Battles of Aubers Ridge, Festubert, and Loos* (London: Macmillan, 1928), pp. 392–3.

51 Faught, *Kitchener*, pp. 217–18.

52 AP, 1/6/16.

53 AP, 1/7/1.

54 AP, 1/6/14.

55 AP, 1/7/6.

56 Wavell, *Allenby*, p. 161.

57 J. E. Edmonds, *Official History of the Great War: Military Operations, France and Flanders, 1916, Volume I: Sir Douglas Haig's Commander to the 1st July: Battle of the Somme* (London: Macmillan, 1932), p. 474.

58 Wavell, *Allenby*, p. 163.

59 AP, 1/7/9.

60 Gilbert, *First World War*, p. 324.

61 See David Murphy, *Breaking Point of the French Army: The Nivelle Offensive of 1917* (Barnsley: Pen & Sword, 2015).

62 C. B. Falls, *Official History of the Great War: Military Operations, France and Flanders, 1917: The German Retreat to the Hindenburg Line and the Battles of Arras, Volume I* (London: Macmillan, 1940), p. 178.

63 *The London* Gazette, 13 February 1917.

64 G. C. Wynne; Robert T. Foley, ed., *If Germany Attacks: The Battle in Depth in the West* (London: Tom Donovan Editions, 2008), p. 173.

65 AP, 1/8/1.

66 AP, 1/8/2.

67 AP, 1/8/4.

68 Jonathan Nicholls, *Cheerful Sacrifice: The Battle of Arras 1917* (Barnsley: Pen & Sword, 2005), pp. 210–11.

69 Hughes, 'Edmund Allenby', pp. 26–8.

70 J. P. Harris, *Douglas Haig and the First World War* (Cambridge: Cambridge University Press, 2008), pp. 324–7.

71 Gary Sheffield and John Bourne, eds, *Douglas Haig: War Diaries and Letters 1914-1918* (London: Weidenfeld & Nicolson, 2006), p. 495.

72 See Tim Cook, *Vimy: The Battle and the Legend* (Toronto: Penguin, 2017).

73 Harris, *Douglas Haig*, p. 327.

74 AP, 6/7/56.

Chapter 4

1 'With Allenby in Palestine and Lawrence in Arabia' was the title given by Lowell Thomas to the multimedia show that he presented in New York and London in 1919. The show proved to be enormously popular, propelling both Allenby and especially Lawrence to great fame.

2 Quoted in Gilbert, *First World War*, p. 303.

3 Gardner, *Allenby*, p. 113.

4 Quoted in ibid., pp. 111, 114.

5 First published in 1894, it remains a standard reference work and is in print today.

6 AP, 1/8/6.

7 C. R. Koppes, 'Captain Mahan, General Gordon and the Origin of the Term "Middle East"', *Middle East* 12 (1976): 95–8.

8 See Christopher Simon Sykes, *The Man Who Created the Middle East: A Story of Empire, Conflict and the Sykes-Picot Agreement* (London: William Collins, 2016).

9 Quoted in Michael D. Berdine, *Redrawing the Middle East: Sir Mark Sykes, Imperialism and the Sykes-Picot Agreement* (London: I.B. Tauris, 2018), p. 10.

10 See Corelli Barnett, *The Collapse of British Power* (Stroud: Sutton, 1997).

11 Faught, *Gordon*, pp. 75–92, and *Kitchener*, pp. 78–100.

12 Especially, Doughty's *Travels in Arabia Deserta* (Cambridge: Cambridge University Press, 1888).

13 See Peter Hopkirk, *The Great Game: On Secret Service in High Asia* (London: John Murray, 1990).

14 See Eugene Rogan, *The Fall of the Ottomans: The Great War in the Middle East* (New York: Basic Books, 2015).

15 Quoted in Matthew, *Gladstone 1809-1898*, p. 389.

16 See Roger Owen, *Lord Cromer: Victorian Imperialist Edwardian Proconsul* (Oxford: Oxford University Press, 2004).

17 Rob Johnson, *The Great War & the Middle East* (Oxford: Oxford University Press, 2016), p. 62.

18 CP, PP/MCR/C1, 'Notes on Palestine Campaign', by Lieutenant General Sir Philip Chetwode, 15 February 1918.

19 Quoted in Martin Gilbert, *Churchill: A Life* (London: Heinemann, 1991), p. 291.

20 See Faught, *Kitchener*, chs. 7–8.

21 Quoted in George H. Cassar, *Kitchener's War: British Strategy from 1914 to 1916* (Washington DC: Potomac, 2004), p. 119.

22 Lord M. Hankey, *The Supreme Command, 1914-1918*, vol. I (London: George Allen and Unwin, 1961), p. 262.

23 Quoted in Berdine, *Redrawing the Middle East*, p. 20.

24 KP, PRO 30/57/91.

25 Quoted in Polly A. Mohs, *Military Intelligence and the Arab Revolt: The First Modern Intelligence War* (New York: Routledge, 2007), p. 34.

26 Sir Arnold Wilson quoted in Rogan, *The Fall of the Ottomans*, p. 325.

27 Ali A. Allawi, *Faisal I of Iraq* (New Haven and London: Yale University Press, 2014), pp. 3–8.

28 Hussein's fourth and youngest son, Zeid, born in 1898, had a negligible role in these discussions but later during the revolt would command the Arab Northern Army.

29 Allawi, *Faisal I of Iraq*, p. 60.

30 Elie Kedourie, *In the Anglo-Arab Labyrinth: The McMahon-Husayn Correspondence and Its Interpretations, 1914–1939* (New York: Cambridge University Press, 1976), p. 3.

31 See G. F. Clayton; Robert O. Collins, ed., *An Arabian Diary* (Berkeley: University of California Press, 1969), and Ronald Storrs, *The Memoirs of Sir Ronald Storrs* (New York: G.P. Putnam's Sons, 1937), chs. 7–8.

32 *HMSO Correspondence between Sir Henry McMahon and the Sherif Hussein of Mecca*, Command Papers 5957, 1939.

33 Ibid.

34 Allawi, *Faisal I of Iraq*, p. 61.

35 Storrs, *Memoirs*, p. 163.

36 Ibid., p. 166.

37 Neil Faulkner, *Lawrence of Arabia's War: The Arabs, the British and the Remaking of the Middle East in WWI* (New Haven and London: Yale University Press, 2016), p. 173.

38 Malcolm Brown, ed., *The Letters of T.E. Lawrence* (London: J.M. Dent & Sons, 1988), p. 83.

39 Quoted in ibid., p. 17.

40 Quoted in Georgina Howell, *Daughter of the Desert: The Remarkable Life of Gertrude Bell* (London: Macmillan, 2006), p. 133. See also, Lisa Cooper, *In Search of Kings and Conquerors: Gertrude Bell and the Archaeology of the Middle East* (London: I.B. Tauris, 2016), pp. 51–2.

41 Brown, ed., *The Letters of T.E. Lawrence*, pp. 36–7.

42 Printed privately in 1926. First published in Britain by Jonathan Cape in 1935.

43 Quoted in Malcolm Brown, *Lawrence of Arabia: The Life the Legend* (London: Thames & Hudson, 2005), p. 27.

44 Brown, ed., *The Letters of T.E. Lawrence*, p. 68.

45 Quoted in Wilson, *Lawrence of Arabia*, p. 168. Brown, ed., *The Letters of T.E. Lawrence*, p. 75.

46 Quoted in Wilson, *Lawrence of Arabia*, p. 169.

47 Ibid., p. 174.

48 T. E. Lawrence, 'Syria, The Raw Material, 1915', *Arab Bulletin*, 12 March 1917, telstudies.org.

49 Brown, ed., *The Letters of T.E. Lawrence*, p. 72.
50 Ibid., p. 79.
51 T. E. Lawrence, *Seven Pillars of Wisdom: A Triumph* (London: Penguin, 1962), p. 57.
52 Quoted in Wilson, *Lawrence of Arabia*, p. 212.
53 Brown, ed., *The Letters of T.E. Lawrence*, p. 79.
54 See James Barr, *A Line in the Sand: Britain, France and the Struggle that Shaped the Middle East* (London: Simon & Schuster, 2011), chs. 1–2.
55 Quoted in ibid., p. 12.
56 Ibid.
57 Robert H. Lieshout, *Britain and the Arab Middle East: World War I and Its Aftermath* (London: I.B. Tauris, 2016), pp. 102–13.
58 Quoted in Wilson, *Lawrence of Arabia*, p. 259.
59 Brown, ed., *The Letters of T.E. Lawrence*, p. 81.
60 Lady Bell, ed., *The Letters of Gertrude Bell*, vol. I (London: Ernest Benn, 1927), p. 372.
61 Quoted in P. P. Graves, *The Life of Sir Percy Cox* (London: Hutchinson, 1941), p. 202.
62 Ibid., p. 203.
63 Brown, ed., *The Letters of T.E. Lawrence*, p. 82.
64 See Paul K. Davis, *Ends and Means: The British Mesopotamian Campaign and Commission* (London: Associated University Presses, 1994).
65 Quoted in Wilson, *Lawrence of Arabia*, p. 273.
66 See Faught, *Kitchener*, ch., 10.
67 Quoted in Faulkner, *Lawrence of Arabia's War*, p. 174.
68 Brown, ed., *The Letters of T.E. Lawrence*, p. 84.
69 Storrs, *Memoirs*, p. 186.
70 Quoted in Faulkner, *Lawrence of Arabia's War*, p. 189.
71 Storrs, *Memoirs*, p. 204.
72 Prince Zeid was also present, but his young age (eighteen) precluded him as an appropriate choice for leader.
73 Quoted in Wilson, *Lawrence of Arabia*, p. 310.
74 Lawrence, *Seven Pillars of Wisdom*, p. 92.
75 Quoted in Allawi, *Faisal I of Iraq*, p. 78.
76 Allawi, *Faisal I of Iraq*, p. 79.
77 Quoted in Wilson, *Lawrence of Arabia*, p. 326.
78 Brown, ed., *The Letters of T.E. Lawrence*, p. 102.
79 Quoted in Wilson, *Lawrence of Arabia*, p. 346.
80 Brown, ed., *The Letters of T.E. Lawrence*, p. 97; quoted in Faulkner, *Lawrence of Arabia's War*, p. 212.
81 Ibid., p. 95.
82 Quoted in Wilson, *Lawrence of Arabia*, p. 355. Vickery worked closely for a time with Lawrence, but they never got on well with one another.
83 Brown, ed., *The Letters of T.E. Lawrence*, pp. 103–4.
84 Quoted in Wilson, *Lawrence of Arabia*, p. 358.
85 Lawrence, *Seven Pillars of Wisdom*, p. 684.
86 Brown, ed., *The Letters of T.E. Lawrence*, pp. 104–5.
87 Ibid., p. 103.
88 Quoted in Barr, *A Line in the Sand*, p. 37.
89 Quoted in Wilson, *Lawrence of Arabia*, p. 381.
90 Lawrence, *Seven Pillars of Wisdom*, pp. 186–7.
91 Quoted in Wilson, *Lawrence of Arabia*, p. 382.

92 Brown, ed., *The Letters of T.E. Lawrence*, p. 101.

93 Lawrence, *Seven Pillars of Wisdom*, p. 233.

94 Ibid., p. 230.

95 Ibid., p. 233.

96 Ibid., p. 24.

97 Brown, ed., *The Letters of T.E. Lawrence*, p. 111.

98 Lawrence, *Seven Pillars of Wisdom*, p. 283.

99 See Faulkner, *Lawrence of Arabia's War*, pp. 273–7.

100 Lawrence, *Seven Pillars of Wisdom*, p. 311.

101 Ibid., p. 320.

102 CP, PP/MCR/C1.

103 AP, 1/8/6.

104 Lawrence, *Seven Pillars of Wisdom*, p. 329.

105 RP, 8/1/63.

106 Lawrence, *Seven Pillars of Wisdom*, p. 330.

107 Ibid., p. 392.

108 Matthew Hughes, ed., *Allenby in Palestine: The Middle East Correspondence of Field Marshal Viscount Allenby June 1917–October 1919* (Stroud: Sutton, 2004), p. 36.

109 RP, 7/5/71.

110 Lawrence, *Seven Pillars of Wisdom*, p. 331.

111 Hughes, ed., *Allenby in Palestine*, p. 38.

112 Ibid., p. 42.

113 AP, 6/8.

114 AP, 1/8/7.

115 AP, 1/8/8.

116 RP, 8/1/68.

117 Brown, ed., *The Letters of T.E. Lawrence*, p. 113.

118 AP, 1/8/10.

119 Brown, ed., *The Letters of T.E. Lawrence*, p. 124.

120 See Faulkner, *Lawrence of Arabia's War*, pp. 222–3.

121 A full delineation of Lawrence's guerrilla military strategy is contained in Chapter 33 of *Seven Pillars of Wisdom*.

122 AP, 1/8/15.

123 RP, 8/1/64.

124 RP, 8/1/73.

125 Hughes, ed., *Allenby in Palestine*, p. 68.

126 RP, 4/5/6.

127 RP, 4/4/97.

128 RP, 8/1/69–70.

129 CP, PP/MCR/CI.

130 RP, 8/1/75.

131 AP, 1/8/21.

132 See Alan H. Smith, *Allenby's Gunners: Artillery in the Sinai & Palestine Campaigns 1916–1918* (Barnsley: Pen & Sword, 2017), pp. 117–52.

133 See John D. Grainger, *The Battle for Palestine 1917* (Woodbridge: Boydell, 2017), ch. 6. See also, Anthony Bruce, *The Last Crusade: The Palestine Campaign in the First World War* (London: John Murray, 2002), ch. 5.

134 CP, PP/MCR/C1. See Richard Meinertzhagen, *Middle East Diary, 1917–1956* (London: Cresset, 1959). See also, Mark Cocker, *Richard Meinertzhagen: Soldier,*

Scientist and Spy (London: Secker & Warburg, 1989), ch. 7, and Yigal Sheffy, *British Military Intelligence in the Palestine Campaign 1914–1918* (London: Frank Cass, 1998), pp. 169–73.

135 As recorded in Gen. 21.25 and 26.25.

136 AP, 1/8/17.

137 RP, 8/1/79.

138 AP, 1/8/22.

139 AP, 1/8/18; RP, 4/4/103; WL, MS Hardinge 35/166.

140 AP, 1/8/24.

141 AP, 1/8/22, 23, 28.

142 AP, 1/8/17.

143 AP, 3/7.

144 AP, 1/8/32. See Rachel Lev, 'Chronicles of a Surrender: December 9, 1917: The Story of the American Colony Photo Department Surrender Photographs', in Shimon Lev (ed.), *A General and a Gentleman—Allenby at the Gates of Jerusalem* (Jerusalem: Tower of David/ Museum of the History of Jerusalem, 2017), pp. 52–74.

145 AP, 2/5/3; 6/8/36.

146 RP, 8/1/82; Hughes, ed., *Allenby in Palestine*, p. 103.

147 Lawrence, *Seven Pillars of Wisdom*, p. 462.

Chapter 5

1 Hughes, ed., *Allenby in Palestine*, p. 104.

2 Eitan Bar-Yosef, 'The Last Crusade? British Propaganda and the Palestine Campaign, 1917–18', *Journal of Contemporary History*, 36, no. 1 (January 2001): 87–109.

3 AP, 2/1/7.

4 AP, 1/8/33.

5 AP, 1/8/32.

6 AP, 1/8/33.

7 AP, 1/8/34.

8 AP, 1/8/36.

9 Lawrence, *Seven Pillars of Wisdom*, p. 464.

10 Quoted in Michael Korda, *Hero: The Life and Legend of Lawrence of Arabia* (New York: HarperCollins, 2010), p. 354. The quote is right but the date of their meeting, which Korda places in December 1917 rather than in February 1918, is wrong. See Fred D. Crawford and Joseph A. Berton, 'How Well did Lowell Thomas know Lawrence of Arabia?', *English Literature in Translation, 1880–1920*, 39, no. 3 (1996): 299–318.

11 Lawrence, *Seven Pillars of Wisdom*, p. 56.

12 Wilson, *Lawrence of Arabia*, p. 490.

13 Faulkner, *Lawrence of Arabia's War*, pp. 366–7. Lawrence, *Seven Pillars of Wisdom*, pp. 450–6.

14 See Said's interview in *T.E. Lawrence and Arabia*, BBC, 1986.

15 Lawrence, *Seven Pillars of Wisdom*, p. 456.

16 Brown, ed., *The Letters of T.E. Lawrence*, pp. 261–2. Lawrence's epistolary and personal relationship with both Charlotte and George Bernard Shaw developed in the early 1920s and soon became deep and sustaining. In 2016, to mark the 100th anniversary

of the start of the Arab Revolt, their friendship was dramatized by Howard Brenton in his play *Lawrence after Arabia*, which ran at the Hampstead Theatre in London.

17 Ibid., p. 134.
18 BL, 2003-02-250/5.
19 Hughes, ed., *Allenby in Palestine*, p. 123.
20 Wilson, *Lawrence of Arabia*, pp. 465–6.
21 Brown, ed., *The Letters of T.E. Lawrence*, p. 132.
22 Ibid., 135. For a full explication of the 'king-making' idea, see Karl E. Meyer and Shareen Blair Brysac, *Kingmakers: The Invention of the Modern Middle East* (New York: W.W. Norton, 2009).
23 His capture and rape at Deraa does not seem to have been motivated, however, by anything other than the violent lust of the Ottoman commandant, Nahi the Bey. Faulkner, *Lawrence of Arabia's War*, p. 367. Lawrence, *Seven Pillars of Wisdom*, pp. 450–6.
24 Lawrence, *Seven Pillars of Wisdom*, p. 474.
25 Ibid., p. 475.
26 John Mordike, 'General Sir Edmund Allenby's Joint Operations in Palestine, 1917–18' (Canberra: Royal Australian Air Force, Air Power Development Centre, 2008), p. 4.
27 Quoted in Matthew Hughes, *Allenby and British Strategy in the Middle East 1917–1919* (London: Frank Cass, 1999), p. 66.
28 RP, 8/5/98.
29 AP, 2/5/7.
30 To this end, see, for example, his telegram to Robertson on 3 January 1918. Hughes, ed., *Allenby in Palestine*, pp. 124–6.
31 Lawrence, *Seven Pillars of Wisdom*, p. 491.
32 Brown, ed., *The Letters of T.E. Lawrence*, p. 139, 141.
33 Quoted in Wilson, *Lawrence of Arabia*, pp. 482.
34 Lawrence, *Seven Pillars of Wisdom*, p. 514.
35 RP, 7/5/84.
36 RP, 8/1/81; 8/1/84.
37 Lawrence, *Seven Pillars of Wisdom*, p. 515.
38 Ibid.
39 Brown, ed., *The Letters of T.E. Lawrence*, pp. 144–5. He was officially promoted temporary lieutenant colonel on 12 March. The Distinguished Service Order was awarded for his conduct at Tafila.
40 Allawi, *Faisal I of Iraq*, p. 77.
41 See Hughes, *Allenby and British Strategy*, ch. 5.
42 Hughes, ed., *Allenby in Palestine*, p. 132.
43 Ibid., p. 133.
44 BL, 2003-02-250/7. The new Bolshevik government had just finished negotiating with Germany the Treaty of Brest-Litovsk, the provisions of which took Russia out of the war.
45 For this narrative of the First Transjordan Raid, I have relied mainly on Cyril Falls and A. F. Becke, *Official History of the Great War: Military Operations Egypt & Palestine from June 1917 to the End of the War, Part I* (London: HMSO, 1930), pp. 328–49.
46 See, for example, Hughes, *Allenby and British Strategy*, pp. 75–8.
47 Hughes, ed., *Allenby in Palestine*, p. 133.
48 BL, 2003-02-250/8–9.
49 Hughes, ed., *Allenby in Palestine*, p. 138.

50 Ibid., p. 139.
51 BL, 2003-02-250/9.
52 From the Jordanian side of the river, it is known now as the King Hussein Bridge.
53 Hughes, ed., *Allenby in Palestine*, p. 142.
54 Brown, ed., *The Letters of T.E. Lawrence*, p. 146.
55 Ibid.
56 Lawrence, *Seven Pillars of Wisdom*, p. 529.
57 Quoted in Wilson, *Lawrence of Arabia*, pp. 497–8.
58 Faulkner, *Lawrence of Arabia's War*, p. 393.
59 Wilson, *Lawrence of Arabia*, pp. 499–500.
60 Brown, ed., *The Letters of T.E. Lawrence*, p. 146.
61 WP, 2/33A/2.
62 In narrating the events of the Second Transjordan Raid, I have relied mainly on Falls and Becke, *Official History of the Great War, Part I*, pp. 364–94.
63 See Smith, *Allenby's Gunners*, pp. 211–21.
64 Hughes, ed., *Allenby in Palestine*, p. 148, 152.
65 Quoted in Field-Marshal Viscount Wavell, *Allenby: Soldier and Statesman* (London: White Lion, 1974), p. 215.
66 WP, 2/33A/3A.
67 WP, 2/33A/4.
68 Quoted in Wilson, *Lawrence of Arabia*, p. 501.
69 WP, 2/33A/4.
70 Allawi, *Faisal I of Iraq*, p. 131.
71 Quoted in ibid.
72 Quoted in Faulkner, *Lawrence of Arabia's War*, p. 403.
73 Lawrence, *Seven Pillars of Wisdom*, p. 541.
74 Quoted in Wilson, *Lawrence of Arabia*, p. 506.
75 Ibid.
76 See, for example, Lawrence's letter to Hussein dated 25 June 1918. Brown, ed., *The Letters of T.E. Lawrence*, pp. 147–9.
77 Allawi, *Faisal I of Iraq*, pp. 238–9.
78 Quoted in Timothy J. Paris, *Britain, the Hashemites, and Arab Rule, 1920–1925: The Sherifian Solution* (London: Frank Cass, 2003), p. 50. See, also, Allawi, *Faisal I of Iraq*, p. 115.
79 Allawi, *Faisal I of Iraq*, p. 116.
80 Quoted in Wilson, *Lawrence of Arabia*, p. 514.
81 Hughes, ed., *Allenby in Palestine*, p. 153.
82 WP, 2/33A/14.
83 The site of the nearby Qumran Caves where the Dead Sea Scrolls were discovered in 1946–7.
84 WP, 2/33A/14.
85 WP, 2/33A/17. See, also, Allenby to General Reginald Wingate, 5 August 1918. WL, MS Hardinge 38/162.
86 WP, 2/33A/18.
87 WP, 2/33A/20.
88 Faulkner, *Lawrence of Arabia's War*, pp. 415–19.
89 Quoted in Wilson, *Lawrence of Arabia*, p. 527.
90 Lawrence, *Seven Pillars of Wisdom*, pp. 553–4.
91 BL, 2003-02-250/14.

92 Quoted in Faulkner, *Lawrence of Arabia's War*, p. 419.
93 Lawrence, *Seven Pillars of Wisdom*, p. 555.
94 WP, 2/33A/18.
95 BL, 2003-02-250/12.
96 Lawrence, *Seven Pillars of Wisdom*, p. 555.
97 WP, 2/33A/22.
98 WP, 2/33A/21.
99 CP, PP/MCR/CI.
100 WP, 2/33A/22A.
101 Brown, ed., *The Letters of T.E. Lawrence*, p. 150.
102 Quoted in Wilson, *Lawrence of Arabia*, p. 534.
103 Lawrence, *Seven Pillars of Wisdom*, p. 603.
104 AP, 1/9/1.
105 Faulkner, *Lawrence of Arabia's War*, p. 431.
106 Wavell, *Allenby*, p. 226.
107 WP, 2/33A/20.
108 Quoted in Rogan, *The Fall of the Ottomans*, p. 375.
109 AP, 1/9/2.
110 A. J. Hill, *Chauvel of the Light Horse: A Biography of General Harry Chauvel, GCMG, KCB* (Carlton: Melbourne University Press, 1978), p. 173.
111 Quoted in David R. Woodward, *Hell in the Holy Land: World War I in the Middle East* (Lexington: University Press of Kentucky, 2006), p. 195.
112 Quoted in Hughes, ed., *Allenby in Palestine*, p. 180.
113 Quoted in Wilson, *Lawrence of Arabia*, p. 549.
114 Ibid., 550.
115 Lawrence, *Seven Pillars of Wisdom*, pp. 611–12.
116 WP, 2/33A/23.
117 AP, 1/9/3; 1/9/4.
118 In narrating the events of the Battle of Megiddo, I have relied mainly on Falls and Becke, *Official History of the Great War, Part II*, pp. 468–594.
119 CP, PP/MCR/CI.
120 WP, 2/33A/24.
121 Hughes, ed., *Allenby in Palestine*, p. 189.
122 AP, 1/9/9.
123 AP, 1/9/4.
124 Lawrence, *Seven Pillars of Wisdom*, pp. 651–8; see, also, Wilson, *Lawrence of Arabia*, p. 557.
125 AP, 1/9/10.
126 Quoted in Wilson, *Lawrence of Arabia*, p. 555.
127 Quoted in Allawi, *Faisal I of Iraq*, p. 137.
128 Hughes, ed., *Allenby in Palestine*, p. 191.
129 Ibid.
130 Quoted in Wilson, *Lawrence of Arabia*, p. 558.
131 Rogan, *The Fall of the Ottomans*, p. 378.
132 Quoted in Wilson, *Lawrence of Arabia*, p. 561.
133 AP, 1/9/11.
134 Ibid.
135 AP, 2/1/11.
136 Quoted in Wilson, *Lawrence of Arabia*, p. 562.

137 Lawrence, *Seven Pillars of Wisdom*, p. 666.
138 Allawi, *Faisal I of Iraq*, p. 146.
139 Wilson, *Lawrence of Arabia*, p. 564.
140 Lawrence, *Seven Pillars of Wisdom*, p. 683.
141 AP, 2/5/17.
142 AP, 1/9/12; Lawrence, *Seven Pillars of Wisdom*, p. 683.
143 LL, MS.Eng.d.3341, f. 7.
144 Brown, ed., *The Letters of T.E. Lawrence*, p. 155.
145 AP, 1/9/12.
146 Faulkner, *Lawrence of Arabia's War*, pp. 457–8. See also, John D. Grainger, *The Battle for Syria 1918–1920* (Woodbridge: Boydell, 2013), ch. 13.
147 AP, 2/1/12.

Chapter 6

1 Hughes, ed., *Allenby in Palestine*, p. 199.
2 Ibid.
3 Ibid., 201.
4 AP, 1/9/15.
5 Hughes, ed., *Allenby in Palestine*, p. 202.
6 AP, 1/9/14.
7 Ibid., p. 212.
8 Ibid.
9 WP, 2/33A/28.
10 WP, 2/33A/29.
11 Ibid.
12 AP, 1/9/17.
13 Hughes, ed., *Allenby in Palestine*, p. 215.
14 Wilson, *Lawrence of Arabia*, p. 571.
15 Quoted in Barr, *A Line in the Sand*, p. 69.
16 Brown, ed., *The Letters of T.E. Lawrence*, p. 161.
17 Quoted in Allawi, *Faisal I of Iraq*, p. 157.
18 Wilson, *Lawrence of Arabia*, p. 571.
19 Quoted in Allawi, *Faisal I of Iraq*, pp. 167–8.
20 Quoted in D. Hunter Miller, *My Diaries of the Conference of Paris*, vol. 15 (New York: Appeal, 1924), pp. 507–8.
21 WP, 2/33A/28.
22 Quoted in Allawi, *Faisal I of Iraq*, pp. 170–1.
23 Quoted in Berdine, *Redrawing the Middle East*, p. 221.
24 WP, 2/33A/29.
25 WP, 2/33B/1.
26 WP, 2/33B/4.
27 AP, 2/1/57.
28 AP, 2/1/46.
29 Hughes, ed., *Allenby in Palestine*, p. 220.
30 See James, *Imperial Warrior*, pp. 183–4. Also, Hughes, ed., *Allenby in Palestine*, p. 227.
31 Hughes, ed., *Allenby in Palestine*, pp. 222–3.

32 AP, 1/10/3.

33 AP, 1/10/4.

34 Hughes, ed., *Allenby in Palestine*, p. 224.

35 Wavell, *Allenby*, pp. 258–9.

36 Berdine, *Redrawing the Middle East*, p. 230.

37 PKP, GD40/17/37, f. 30.

38 Quoted in Wavell, *Allenby*, p. 259.

39 PKP, GD40/17/1234.

40 Margaret MacMillan, *Paris 1919: Six Months that Changed the World* (New York: Random House, 2001), p. xxv.

41 AP, 1/10/7.

42 Ibid.

43 Quoted in James, *Imperial Warrior*, p. 185.

44 MacMillan, *Paris 1919*, p. 394.

45 Hughes, ed., *Allenby in Palestine*, pp. 229, 232.

46 Ibid., p. 228.

47 Ibid., p. 232.

48 Quoted in John Darwin, *Britain, Egypt and the Middle East: Imperial Policy in the Aftermath of War 1918–1922* (London: Macmillan, 1981), p. 83.

49 Ibid.

50 AP, 1/10/7.

51 Selma Botman, *Egypt from Independence to Revolution, 1919–1952* (Syracuse: Syracuse University Press, 1991), pp. 26–9.

52 See Owen, *Lord Cromer*.

53 See M. W. Daly, *The Sirdar: Sir Reginald Wingate and the British Empire in the Middle East* (Philadelphia: American Philosophical Society, 1997).

54 WL, MS Hardinge, 38/154.

55 WL, MS Hardinge, 40/143–6.

56 Ibid.

57 E. W. Polson Newman, *Great Britain in Egypt* (London: Cassell, 1928), p. 219. Hughes, ed., *Allenby in Palestine*, pp. 240–1.

58 AP, 1/10/8.

59 Darwin, *Britain, Egypt and the Middle East*, p. 42.

60 David Gilmour, *Curzon: Imperial Statesman 1859–1925* (London: John Murray, 2003), p. 523.

61 AP, 1/10/11.

62 WL, MS Hardinge, 40/143–6; emphasis in original.

63 AP, 1/10/10.

64 Quoted in Lanver Mak, *The British in Egypt: Community, Crime and Crises 1882–1922* (London: I.B. Tauris, 2012), p. 221.

65 Hughes, ed., *Allenby in Palestine*, p. 237.

66 Newman, *Great Britain in Egypt*, p. 224.

67 AP, 1/10/9.

68 AP, 1/10/10; Allawi, *Faisal I of Iraq*, p. 219.

69 Brown, ed., *The Letters of T.E. Lawrence*, p. 164.

70 PKP, GD40/17/38, f. 142.

71 WP, 2/33B/16.

72 KP, GD40/17/38, f. 115.

73 WP, 2/33B/23.

74 KP, GD40/38, f. 132.

75 KP, GD40/38, f. 134.

76 Hughes, ed., *Allenby in Palestine*, p. 266.

77 Allawi, *Faisal I of Iraq*, p. 243.

78 Quoted in ibid., p. 244.

79 Hughes, ed., *Allenby in Palestine*, p. 278.

80 Ibid., 275.

81 David Fromkin, *A Peace to End all Peace: The Fall of the Ottoman Empire and the Creation of the Modern Middle East* (New York: Avon, 1989), p. 397. For the broader, long-range implications of American policy in the Middle East see James Barr, *Lords of the Desert: Britain's Struggle with America to Dominate the Middle East* (London: Simon & Schuster, 2018).

82 AP, 1/10/2.

83 Ibid.

84 AP, 11/14/19A.

85 AP, 2/5/27.

86 AP, 1/10/14.

87 AP, 1/10/15.

88 PKP, GD40/17/1343, f. 4.

89 Ibid., ff. 5–7.

90 PKP, GD40/17/1343/f. 10.

91 *The Times*, 25 July 1925.

92 See John Marlowe, *Milner: Apostle of Empire* (London: Hamish Hamilton, 1976).

93 AP, 1/10/21.

94 Ibid.

95 AP, 1/10/20.

96 AP, FO 141/434/1, 4.

97 AP, FO 141/499/2.

98 Darwin, *Britain, Egypt and the Middle East*, p. 87.

99 LGP, F/59/11/2.

100 While on tour in Sudan, Allenby maintained a wide correspondence. One of those to whom he sent a letter was Mrs Bertha Vester. Together with her husband Frederick, they shared in the ownership of the American Colony Hotel in Jerusalem. During the war the hotel had served as a hospital for the wounded and sick, 'without distinction of creed or nationality', praised Allenby in his letter. During Allenby's long stay in Palestine he had visited the American Colony on a number of occasions during which he was photographed. Today, the ACH holds an extensive archive of these and other photos of the period, as well as letters. Allenby to Mrs B. Vester, 24 January 1920, American Colony Archive Collections, American Colony Hotel, Jerusalem.

101 As contained, for example, in Milner's book, *England in Egypt* (London: Edward Arnold, 1882).

102 This idea received its most thorough elaboration at the hands of Ronald E. Robinson, 'Non-European Foundations of European Imperialism: Sketch for a Theory of Collaboration', in Roger Owen and Robert B. Sutcliffe (eds), *Studies in the Theory of Imperialism* (London: Longman, 1972), pp. 117–42.

103 John Darwin, *The Empire Project: The Rise and Fall of the British World-System, 1830–1970* (Cambridge: Cambridge University Press, 2009), p. 380.

104 WP, 2/33B/12A.

105 AP, 1/11/10.

106 James, *Imperial Warrior*, p. 206.
107 Faught, *Kitchener*, pp. 186–7.
108 Quoted in John Darwin, 'Imperialism in Decline? Tendencies in British Imperial Policy between the Wars', *The Historical Journal*, 23, no. 3 (1980): 669.
109 AP, 1/11/15.
110 Quoted in Richard Toye, *Churchill's Empire: The World that Made Him and the World that He Made* (London: Pan, 2011), p. 149.
111 Quoted in Deirdre McMahon, 'Ireland and the Empire-Commonwealth, 1900–1948', in Judith M. Brown and Wm. Roger Louis (eds), *The Oxford History of the British Empire: Volume IV, The Twentieth Century* (Oxford: Oxford University Press, 1999), p. 146.
112 Ibid.
113 AP, 1/11/16.
114 WP, 2/33B/16.
115 LGP, F/12/3/32(b).
116 LGP, F/49/13/2.
117 WP, 2/33B/30.
118 FO/800/156/50.
119 LGP, F/12/3/32(d).
120 WP, 2/33B/31.
121 AP, 1/11/20.
122 AP, 1/11/22.
123 Allawi, *Faisal I of Iraq*, p. 294.
124 AP, 1/11/44.
125 For a comprehensive treatment of the history of the Permanent Mandates Commission, see Susan Pedersen, *The Guardians: The League of Nations and the Crisis of Empire* (New York: Oxford University Press, 2015).
126 FO/141/624/1.
127 LGP, F/59/10.
128 Ibid.
129 KP, GD/40/17, f. 320.
130 AP, 1/11/22.
131 Mak, *The British in Egypt*, p. 230.
132 See E. R. J. Owen, *Cotton and the Egyptian Economy, 1820–1914: A Study in Trade and Development* (Oxford: Clarendon Press, 1969).
133 AP, 1/11/40.
134 AP, 1/12/4, 18.
135 AP, 1/11/35–6.
136 AP, 1/11/41.
137 Ibid.
138 AP, 1/11/41.
139 Quoted in Toye, *Churchill's Empire*, p. 142.
140 Brown, ed., *The Letters of T.E. Lawrence*, p. 184.
141 Ibid.
142 Warren Dockter, *Churchill and the Islamic World* (London: I.B. Tauris, 2015), pp. 140–2.
143 Brown, ed., *The Letters of T.E. Lawrence*, p. 185.
144 AP, 1/12/5.
145 AP, 1/12/13.

146 AP, 1/12/16.

147 Brown, ed., *The Letters of T.E. Lawrence*, p. 185.

148 Ibid.

149 WP, 2/33D/9.

150 Quoted in Howell, *Daughter of the Desert*, p. 399.

151 AP, 1/12/19.

152 Quoted in Janet Wallach, *The Desert Queen: The Extraordinary Life of Gertrude Bell* (London: Weidenfeld & Nicolson, 1996), p. 300.

153 As a book such as Christopher Catherwood's *Churchill's Folly: How Winston Churchill Created Modern Iraq* (New York: Carroll & Graf, 2004), one among many, demonstrates.

154 AP, 1/12/19.

155 Brown, ed., *The Letters of T.E. Lawrence*, pp. 185–6.

156 AP, 1/12/20.

157 Wavell, *Allenby*, p. 291.

158 AP, 1/12/21.

159 AP, 1/12/22.

160 AP, 1/12/20.

161 AP, 1/12/29.

162 AP, 1/12/30, 31B.

163 AP, 1/12/33.

164 BL, 2003-02-250/15.

165 WP, 2/33C/9.

Chapter 7

1 WP, 2/33C/8.

2 LGP, F/13/3/6.

3 Ibid.

4 AP, 2/5/28.

5 FO/800/153/35, f. 140.

6 AP, 2/5/11.

7 Quoted in Wavell, *Allenby*, pp. 302–3.

8 Darwin, *Britain, Egypt and the Middle East*, p. 127.

9 James, *Imperial Warrior*, p. 210.

10 LGP, F/13/3/6.

11 LGP, F/13/3/5(a).

12 AP, 1/13/1D.

13 Brown, ed., *The Letters of T.E. Lawrence*, p. 193.

14 LL, MS.Eng.d.3341, f. 254.

15 Derek Hopwood, *Tales of Empire: The British in the Middle East, 1880–1952* (London: I.B. Tauris, 1989), p. 23.

16 SP, MS.Eng.d.3224, f. 520; ff. 27–8.

17 SP, MS.Eng.c.6581, ff. 10–11.

18 Quoted in Mak, *The British in Egypt*, p. 240.

19 Quoted in James, *Imperial Warrior*, p. 210.

20 Darwin, *Britain, Egypt and the Middle East*, p. 269.

21 AP, 1/13/1D.

22 Quoted in James, *Imperial Warrior*, p. 214.

23 AP, 2/5/12.

24 AP, 1/13/11, 14.

25 AP, 5/22.

26 AP, 1/13/24.

27 AP, 1/11/14.

28 AP, 1/13/26.

29 AP, 1/13,28B.

30 See J. G. Darwin, 'The Chanak Crisis and the British Cabinet', *History*, 65, no. 213 (February 1980): 32–48.

31 See C. P. Stacey, *Canada and the Age of Conflict, Volume 2: 1921–1948, The Mackenzie King Era* (Toronto: University of Toronto Press, 1981), pp. 17–27.

32 AP, 1/13/33.

33 Donald M. Reid, 'Political Assassination in Egypt, 1910–1954', *The International Journal of African Historical Studies*, 15, no. 4 (1982): 625–6.

34 AP, 2/5/12.

35 See C. Brad Faught, 'An Imperial Prime Minister? W.E. Gladstone and India, 1880–1885', *The Journal of the Historical Society*, 6, no. 4 (December 2006): 567–70.

36 AP, 1/14/4.

37 FO/141/516/6.

38 Ibid.

39 Mak, *The British in Egypt*, p. 240.

40 FO/141/516/6.

41 Ibid.

42 See Abdeslam M. Maghraoui, *Liberalism Without Democracy: Nationhood and Citizenship in Egypt, 1922–1936* (Durham: Duke University Press, 2006).

43 Quoted in T. O. Lloyd, *Empire, Welfare State, Europe: English History 1902–1992*, 4th edn (Oxford: Oxford University Press, 1993), p. 129.

44 Roy Jenkins, *Asquith* (London: Collins, 1964), pp. 483–502.

45 Ibid., p. 501.

46 Lloyd, *Empire*, p. 131.

47 Quoted in James, *Imperial Warrior*, p. 215.

48 Newman, *Great Britain in Egypt*, p. 243.

49 *Parliamentary Debates* (23 June 1924).

50 Ibid.

51 Wavell, *Allenby*, p. 330.

52 This narrative is drawn mainly from Henry Keown-Boyd, *The Lion and the Sphinx: The Rise and Fall of the British in Egypt, 1882–1956* (Spennymoor: The Memoir Club, 2002), pp. 99–101.

53 AP, 1/14/4.

54 *The New York Times*, 23 November 1924.

55 Lloyd, *Empire*, p. 133.

56 Allenby himself did not provide an account of his movements during these hours, but others did, which I have used as found in Wavell, *Allenby*, pp. 334–6; James, *Imperial Warrior*, p. 220; and Keown-Boyd, *The Lion and the Sphinx*, pp. 101–3.

57 Quoted in Wavell, *Allenby*, pp. 336–7.

58 AP, 2/3/1.

59 AP, 2/3/4.

60 AP, 2/3/5.
61 AP, 2/3/7.
62 Ibid.
63 AP, 2/3/9.
64 AP, 2/3/12.
65 AP, 2/3/15.
66 AP, 2/3/16.
67 Keown-Boyd, *The Lion and the Sphinx*, p. 105.
68 SP, MS.Eng.c.6581, f. 41.
69 SP, MS.Eng.c.6581, f. 45.
70 AP, 1/14/4.
71 Quoted in Kay Halle, ed., *Irrepressible Churchill: A Treasury of Winston Churchill's Wit* (London: World, 1966), pp. 52–3.
72 AP, 2/3/23.
73 AP, CAB/23/49, f. 20.
74 Keown-Boyd, *The Lion and the Sphinx*, p. 112.
75 FO/794/13.
76 FO/141/741/7.
77 AP, 2/5/14–15.
78 AP, 7/1/10.
79 AP, 1/14/6.
80 SP, MS.Eng.c.6581, f. 97.
81 *The Times*, 20 June 1925.
82 SP, MS.Eng.c.6581, f. 105.

Chapter 8

1 AP, 4/4.
2 AP, 2/5/14.
3 AP, 4/3.
4 AP, 1/14/6.
5 AP, 4/5.
6 AP, 5/25.
7 AP, 3/10.
8 F. Scott Fitzgerald, *This Side of Paradise* (Oxford: Oxford University Press, 2009), p. 41.
9 AP, 3/5. The YMCA building had been constructed directly opposite the well-known King David Hotel, which itself had been built just two years earlier.
10 LL, MS.Eng.d.3341, ff. 6–7.
11 Quoted in James, *Imperial Warrior*, p. 237.
12 Brown, ed., *The Letters of T.E. Lawrence*, pp. 320–1.
13 Faulkner, *Lawrence of Arabia's War*, p. 449.
14 Quoted in Allawi, *Faisal I of Iraq*, p. xxviii.
15 LL, MS.Eng.d.3341, ff. 255–6.
16 Brown, ed., *The Letters of T.E. Lawrence*, p. 391.
17 Printed in *The Listener*, 22 May 1935.
18 AP, 3/6.
19 Brown, ed., *The Letters of T.E. Lawrence*, p. 320; AP, 3/6.

20 Quoted in Korda, *Hero*, p. 680.

21 AP, 4/6–8.

22 AP, 3/86.

23 HSP, A/155(IX)/53a.

24 Matthew and Harrison, eds, *Oxford Dictionary of National Biography*, vol. 1, p. 841.

25 AP, 7/2/1.

26 Matthew and Harrison, eds, *Oxford Dictionary of National Biography*, vol. 1, p. 841.

27 SP, MS.Eng.d.3225, f. 61.

28 AP, 4/8.

29 SP, MS.Eng.d.3225, f. 62.

30 Ibid.

31 Ibid.

32 A. P. Thornton, *The Imperial Idea and Its Enemies: A Study in British Power* (London: St. Martin's Press, 1959). The scholarly, as well as popular, debate over the impact of (British) imperialism continues apace. See, for example, Dane Kennedy's recent book, *The Imperial History Wars: Debating the British Empire* (London: Bloomsbury, 2018).

33 'Useful' was the word used pejoratively by a reviewer in *The Times Literary Supplement* a few years ago to describe Kitchener in a review of my biography of him. In a review that chose essentially not to engage the book, it nonetheless demonstrates my point of imperial figures such as Kitchener and Allenby being seen simply as one-dimensional instrumentalists. See Faught, *Kitchener*, p. 31.

34 Max Jones, 'What Should Historians Do With Heroes? Reflections on Nineteenth- and Twentieth-Century Britain', *History Compass*, 5, issue 2 (2007): 439–5.

35 *The Globe*, 8 October 1919; *The Tatler*, 24 September 1919.

36 AP, 2/5/1, 4.

37 AP, 2/5/8.

38 *Sunday Times*, 12 October 1919.

39 *Nottingham Evening News*, 16 September 1919; *The Westminster Gazette*, 11 October 1919.

40 For this interpretation of the war in the Middle East, I have found helpful Nigel Biggar's, *In Defence of War* (Oxford: Oxford University Press, 2013).

41 See Olive Anderson, 'The Growth of Christian Militarism in Mid-Victorian Britain', *English Historical Review*, 86, no. 338 (1971): 46–72.

42 AP, 3/5.

43 Allenby's correspondence with Bishop MacInnes is housed at the Middle East Centre Archive, St. Antony's College, Oxford.

44 AP, 6/8/68.

45 AP, 6/8/70.

46 AP, 3/12.

47 Although such a view fell out of favour quickly as nationalism and independence gathered irresistible strength within the British Empire after the Second World War, recent scholarship on the impact of colonial-era Christian missionaries provides a very strong correlation between their presence in a given colony and its long-range political stability, gender equality and economic prosperity later once having become a sovereign country. See Robert D. Woodberry, 'The Missionary Roots of Liberal Democracy', *American Political Science Review*, 106, issue 2 (May 2012): 244–74.

48 See, for example, W. R. Louis, 'Leo Amery and the Post-war World, 1945-55', *Journal of Imperial and Commonwealth History*, 30 (2002): 71–90. Also, AP, 6/9/5.

49 Stephen Heathorn, *Haig and Kitchener in Twentieth-Century Britain: Remembrance, Representation and Appropriation* (Farnham: Ashgate, 2013).

50 The eponymous title of an excellent piece of cultural history by Graham Dawson, *Soldier Heroes: British Adventure, Empire and the Imagining of Masculinities* (London and New York: Routledge, 1994).

51 Leading examples are Allenby Garden in Be'er Sheva, Israel, which includes his memorial bust, as well as the Allenby Bridge that links Israel with Jordan, and Allenby Street in Tel Aviv; Allenby Primary School in Ealing, London; Allenby Gardens in Adelaide, Australia; Allenby Park in Auckland, New Zealand; and the (tiny) town of Allenby in the Canadian province of British Columbia, which, alas, has been abandoned. Finally, my children attended Allenby Junior Public School, located within the neighbourhood of Allenby, in Toronto.

52 See, for example, 'Jerusalem Celebrates a Century since Allenby Entered the Capital', *The Jerusalem Post*, 11 December 1917.

53 Among the many examples that could be included here I will mention only the T. E. Lawrence Society's highly popular biennial three-day conference held in Oxford, which over time has shown itself devoted to probing almost every aspect of Lawrence's life, war record and writings.

Afterword

1 See Hugh Kennedy, *Caliphate: The History of an Idea* (New York: Basic Books, 2016).

2 See Ronald Robinson and John Gallagher, with Alice Denny, *Africa and the Victorians: The Official Mind of Imperialism*, 2nd edn (London: Macmillan, 1985). See also, Robinson, 'Non-European Foundations of European Imperialism', pp. 117–42.

3 *The Globe and Mail*, 9 May 2016.

4 Quoted in Anthony Kirk-Greene, 'Decolonisation in British Africa', *History Today* (January 1992), p. 50.

5 As described, for example, in the *Los Angeles Times*, 2 July 2014.

6 Quoted in Chaim Weizmann, *Trial and Error: The Autobiography of Chaim Weizmann* (New York: Harper, 1949), p. 274.

7 KP, GD40/17/40, f. 347.

8 Mangold, *What the British Did*; Catherwood, *Churchill's Folly*.

9 Faulkner, *Lawrence of Arabia's War*, p. 467.

10 Ibid.

11 John Darwin, *After Tamerlane: The Rise & Fall of Global Empires 1400–2000* (London: Penguin, 2008), ch. 6.

12 Ibid., p. 456.

BIBLIOGRAPHY

Primary sources

Archives

Allenby Papers (FM Edmund Allenby, 1st Viscount Allenby of Megiddo), Liddell Hart Centre for Military Archives, King's College London (AP)

American Colony Archive Collections, American Colony Hotel, Jerusalem (AC)

C. W. Battine Letters, National Army Museum, London (BL)

Chetwode Papers, Imperial War Museum, London (CP)

Foreign Office records related to Lord Allenby, National Archives, Kew, London (FO)

Kitchener Papers, National Archives, Kew, London (KP)

T.E. Lawrence Letters, Bodleian Library, Oxford (LL)

Lloyd George Papers, Parliamentary Archives, London (LGP)

Bishop Rennie MacInnes Letters, Middle East Centre Archive, St Antony's College, Oxford (ML)

Philip Kerr, 11th Marquess of Lothian Papers, National Records of Scotland, Edinburgh (PKP)

Sir William Robertson Papers, Liddell Hart Centre for Military Archives, King's College London (RP)

Sir Herbert Samuel Papers, Parliamentary Archives, London (HSP)

Sir Walford Selby Papers, Bodleian Library, Oxford (SP)

Sir Henry Wilson Papers, Imperial War Museum, London (WP)

Sir Reginald Wingate Letters, Hardinge Collection, Cambridge University Library (WL)

Secondary Sources

Books

Akenson, Donald Harman. *God's Peoples: Covenant and Land in South Africa, Israel and Ulster* (Montreal and Kingston, McGill-Queen's University Press, 1991).

Allawi, Ali A. *Faisal I of Iraq* (New Haven and London, Yale University Press, 2014).

Barnett, Corelli. *The Collapse of British Power* (Stroud, Sutton, 1997).

Barr, James. *A Line in the Sand: Britain, France and the Struggle that Shaped the Middle East* (London, Simon & Schuster, 2011).

Barr, James. *Lords of the Desert: Britain's Struggle with America to Dominate the Middle East* (London, Simon & Schuster, 2018).

Beckett, Ian F. W. *The Army and the Curragh Incident 1914* (London, Bodley Head, 1986).

Beckett, Ian F. W. and Steven J. Corvi, eds. *Haig's Generals* (Barnsley, Pen & Sword, 2006).

Bell, Lady, ed. *The Letters of Gertrude Bell*, vol. I (London, Ernest Benn, 1927).

Berdine, Michael D. *Redrawing the Middle: Sir Mark Sykes, Imperialism and the Sykes-Picot Agreement* (London, I.B. Tauris, 2016).

Bew, John. *Citizen Clem: A Biography of Attlee* (London, Riverrun, 2016).

Biggar, Nigel. *In Defence of War* (Oxford, Oxford University Press, 2013).

Botman, Selma. *Egypt from Independence to Revolution, 1919–1952* (Syracuse, Syracuse University Press, 1991).

Brown, Malcolm, ed. *The Letters of T.E. Lawrence* (London, J.M. Dent & Sons, 1988).

Bruce, Anthony. *The Last Crusade: The Palestine Campaign in the First World War* (London, John Murray, 2002).

Cannon, Richard. *Historical Record of the Sixth, Or Inniskilling Regiment of Dragoons: Containing an Account of the Formation of the Regiment in 1689, and of Its Subsequent Services to 1846* (London, Parker, Furnivall, & Parker, 1847).

Cassar, George H. *Kitchener's War: British Strategy from 1914 to 1916* (Washington DC, Potomac, 2004).

Catherwood, Christopher. *Churchill's Folly: How Winston Churchill Created Modern Iraq* (New York, Carroll & Graf, 2004).

Clayton, G. F. *An Arabian Diary*, ed. Robert O. Collins (Berkeley, University of California Press, 1969).

Cocker, Mark. *Richard Meinertzhagen: Soldier, Scientist and Spy* (London, Secker & Warburg, 1989).

Cooper, Lisa. *In Search of Kings and Conquerors: Gertrude Bell and the Archaeology of the Middle East* (London, I.B. Tauris, 2016).

Daly, M. W. *The Sirdar: Sir Reginald Wingate and the British Empire in the Middle East* (Philadelphia, American Philosophical Society, 1997).

Darwin, John. *After Tamerlane: The Rise & Fall of Global Empires 1400–2000* (London, Penguin, 2008).

Darwin, John. *Britain, Egypt and the Middle East: Imperial Policy in the Aftermath of War 1918–1922* (London, Macmillan, 1981).

Darwin, John. *The Empire Project: The Rise and Fall of the British World-System, 1830–1970* (Cambridge, Cambridge University Press, 2009).

Davis, Paul K. *Ends and Means: The British Mesopotamian Campaign and Commission* (London, Associated University Presses, 1994).

Dawson, Graham. *Soldier Heroes: British Adventure, Empire and the Imagining of Masculinities* (London and New York, Routledge, 1994).

De S. Honey, J. R. *Tom Brown's Universe: The Development of the Public School in the 19th Century* (London, Millington, 1977).

Dewey, Clive. *Anglo-Indian Attitudes: The Mind of the Indian Civil Service* (London, Hambledon Continuum, 1993).

Dockter, Warren. *Churchill and the Islamic World* (London, I.B. Tauris, 2015).

Doughty, Charles M. *Travels in Arabia Deserta* (Cambridge, Cambridge University Press, 1888).

Fallodon, Viscount Grey of. *Twenty-Five Years 1892–1916* (New York, Frederick A. Stokes, 1925).

Falls, Cyril and A. F. Becke, *Official History of the Great War: Military Operations Egypt & Palestine from June 1917 to the End of the War, Parts I & II* (London, HMSO, 1930).

Farwell, Byron. *Queen Victoria's Little Wars* (New York, Norton, 1985).

Faught, C. Brad. *Gordon: Victorian Hero* (Washington DC, Potomac, 2008).

Faught, C. Brad. *Kitchener: Hero and Anti-Hero* (London, I.B. Tauris, 2016).

Faulkner, Neil. *Lawrence of Arabia's War: The Arabs, the British and the Remaking of the Middle East in WWI* (New Haven and London, Yale University Press, 2016).

Ferguson, Niall. *Empire: The Rise and Demise of the British World Order and the Lessons for Global Power* (New York, Basic Books, 2002).

Fieldhouse, D. K. *Western Imperialism in the Middle East 1914–1958* (Oxford, Oxford University Press, 2006).

Fromkin, David. *A Peace to End all Peace: The Fall of the Ottoman Empire and the Creation of the Modern Middle East* (New York, Avon, 1989).

Galbraith, John S. *Crown and Charter: The Early Years of the British South Africa Company* (Berkeley, University of California Press, 1974).

Gardner, Brian. *Allenby* (London, Cassell, 1965).

Gardner, Nikolas. *Trial by Fire: Command and the British Expeditionary Force in 1914* (Westport, Praeger, 2003).

Gilbert, Martin. *Churchill: A Life* (London, Heinemann, 1991).

Gilbert, Martin. *First World War* (Toronto, Stoddart, 1994).

Gilmour, David. *Curzon: Imperial Statesman 1859–1925* (London, John Murray, 2003).

Grainger, John D. *The Battle for Palestine 1917* (Woodbridge, Boydell, 2017).

Grainger, John D. *The Battle for Syria 1918–1920* (Woodbridge, Boydell, 2013).

Graves, P. P. *The Life of Sir Percy Cox* (London, Hutchinson, 1941).

Halle, Kay, ed. *Irrepressible Churchill: A Treasury of Winston Churchill's Wit* (London, World, 1966).

Hankey, Lord M. *The Supreme Command, 1914–1918* (London, George Allen and Unwin, 1961).

Harris, J. P. *Douglas Haig and the First World War* (Cambridge, Cambridge University Press, 2008).

Heathorn, Stephen. *Haig and Kitchener in the Twentieth-Century Britain: Remembrance, Representation and Appropriation* (Farnham, Ashgate, 2013.)

Hill, A. J. *Chauvel of the Light Horse: A Biography of General Harry Chauvel, GCMG, KCB* (Carlton, Melbourne University Press, 1978.)

Hobson, J. H. *Imperialism: A Study* (London, Constable, 1902).

Hobson, J. H. *The War in South Africa: Its Causes and Effects* (London, James Nisbet & Co., 1900).

Hopkirk, Peter. *The Great Game: On Secret Service in High Asia* (London, John Murray, 1990).

Hopwood, Derek. *Tales of Empire: The British in the Middle East, 1880–1952* (London, I.B. Tauris, 1989).

Howell, Georgina. *Daughter of the Desert: The Remarkable Life of Gertrude Bell* (London, Macmillan, 2006).

Hughes, Matthew, ed. *Allenby in Palestine: The Middle East Correspondence of Field Marshal Viscount Allenby June 1917–October 1919* (Stroud, Sutton, 2004).

James, Lawrence. *Imperial Warrior: The Life and Times of Field-Marshal Viscount Allenby 1861–1936* (London, Weidenfeld & Nicolson, 1993).

Jenkins, Roy. *Asquith* (London, Collins, 1964).

Johnson, Rob. *The Great War & the Middle East: A Strategic Study* (Oxford, Oxford University Press, 2016).

Jones, Spencer. *From Boer War to World War: Tactical Reform of the British Army, 1902–1914* (Norman, University of Oklahoma Press, 2012).

Judd, Denis and Keith Surridge. *The Boer War* (New York, Palgrave Macmillan, 2003).

Kedourie, Elie. *In the Anglo-Arab Labryrinth: The MacMahon-Husayn Correspondence and its Interpretations, 1914–1939* (New York, Cambridge University Press, 1976).

Kennedy, Dane. *The Imperial History Wars: Debating the British Empire* (London, Bloomsbury, 2018).

Kennedy, Hugh. *Caliphate: The History of an Idea* (New York, Basic Books, 2016).

Keown-Boyd, Henry. *The Lion and the Sphinx: The Rise and Fall of the British in Egypt, 1882–1956* (Spennymoor, The Memoir Club, 2002).

Knight, Ian. *Zulu Rising: The Epic Story of Isandlwana and Rorke's Drift* (London, Pan Books, 2010).

Korda, Michael. *Hero: The Life and Legend of Lawrence of Arabia* (New York, HarperCollins, 2010).

Laband, John. *The Transvaal Rebellion: The First Boer War, 1880–1881* (New York, Longman/Pearson, 2005).

Lawrence, T. E. *Seven Pillars of Wisdom: A Triumph* (London, Penguin, 1962).

Lev, Shimon, ed. *A General and a Gentleman – Allenby at the Gates of Jerusalem* (Jerusalem, Tower of David/Museum of the History of Jerusalem, 2017).

Lieshout, Robert H. *Britain and the Arab Middle East: World War I and Its Aftermath* (London, I.B. Tauris, 2016).

Lloyd, T. O. *Empire, Welfare State, Europe: English History 1902–1922*, 4th edn (Oxford, Oxford University Press, 1993).

Lock, Ron and Peter Quantrill. *Zulu Vanquished: The Destruction of the Zulu Kingdom* (London, Greenhill, 2005).

Mackenzie, John. *Austral Africa: Losing It or Ruling It: Being Incidents and Experiences in Bechuanaland, Cape Colony, and England* (London, Sampson Low, Marston, Searle & Rivington, 1887).

MacMillan, Margaret. *Paris 1919: Six Months that Changed the World* (New York, Random House, 2001).

Maghraoui, Abdeslam M. *Liberalism Without Democracy: Nationhood and Citizenship in Egypt, 1922–1936* (Durham, Duke University Press, 2006).

Mak, Lanver. *The British in Egypt: Community, Crime and Crises 1882–1922* (London, I.B. Tauris, 2012).

Mangold, Peter. *What the British Did: Two Centuries in the Middle East* (London, I.B. Tauris, 2016).

Marlowe, John. *Milner, Apostle of Empire* (London, Hamish Hamilton, 1976).

Matthew, H. C. G. *Gladstone 1809–1898* (Oxford, Clarendon Press, 1997).

Matthew, H. C. G. *The Liberal Imperialists: The Ideas and Politics of a Post-Gladstonian Elite* (Oxford, Oxford University Press, 1973).

Meinertzhagen, Richard, *Middle East Diary, 1917–1956* (London, Cresset, 1959).

Meredith, Martin. *Diamonds, Gold, and War: The British, the Boers, and the Making of South Africa* (New York, Public Affairs, 2007).

Meyer, Karl E. and Shareen Blair Brysac, *The Kingmakers: The Invention of the Modern Middle East* (New York, W.W. Norton, 2009).

Miller, D. Hunter. *My Diaries of the Conference of Paris*, vol. 15 (New York, Appeal, 1924).

Milner, Alfred. *England in Egypt* (London, Edward Arnold, 1882).

Mohs, Polly A. *Military Intelligence and the Arab Revolt: The First Modern Intelligence War* (New York, Routledge, 2007).

Newman, E. W. Polson. *Great Britain in Egypt* (London, Cassell, 1928).

Owen, Roger. *Cotton and the Egyptian Economy, 1820–1914: A Study in Trade and Development* (Oxford, Clarendon Press, 1969).

Owen, Roger. *Lord Cromer: Victorian Imperialist Edwardian Proconsul* (Oxford, Oxford University Press, 2004).

Pakenham, Thomas. *The Boer War* (New York, Perennial, 2001).

Paris, Timothy J. *Britain, the Hashemites, and Arab Rule, 1920–1925: The Sherifian solution* (London, Frank Cass, 2003).

Pedersen, Susan. *The Guardians: The League of Nations and the Crisis of Empire* (New York, Oxford University Press, 2015).

Pollock, John. *Kitchener: Architect of Victory, Artisan of Peace* (New York, Carroll & Graf, 2001).

Robinson, Ronald and John Gallagher with Alice Denny. *Africa and the Victorians: The Official Mind of Imperialism*, 2nd edn (London, Macmillan, 1985).

Rogan, Eugene. *The Fall of the Ottomans: The Great War in the Middle East* (New York, Basic Books, 2015).

Rotberg, Robert I. *The Founder: Cecil Rhodes and the Pursuit of Power* (Oxford, Oxford University Press, 1988).

Royle, Trevor. *The Kitchener Enigma* (London, Michael Joseph, 1985).

Savage, Raymond. *Allenby of Armageddon: A Record of the Career and Campaigns of Field-Marshal Viscount Allenby* (Indianapolis, Bobbs-Merrill, 1926).

Sheffy, Yigal. *British Military Intelligence in the Palestine Campaign 1914–1918* (London, Frank Cass, 1998).

Smith, Alan H. *Allenby's Gunners: Artillery in the Sinai & Palestine Campaigns 1916–1918* (Barnsley, Pen & Sword, 2017).

Stacey, C. P. *Canada and the Age of Conflict, Volume 2: 1921–1948, The Mackenzie King Era* (Toronto, University of Toronto Press, 1981).

Storrs, Ronald. *The Memoirs of Sir Ronald Storrs* (New York, G.P. Putnam's Sons, 1937).

Strachey, Lytton. *Eminent Victorians* (London, Chatto & Windus, 1918).

Surridge, Keith Terrance. *Managing the South African War, 1899–1902: Politicians V. Generals* (Woodbridge, Boydell, 1998).

Sykes, Christopher Simon. *The Man Who Created the Middle East: A Story of Empire, Conflict and the Sykes-Picot Agreement* (London, William Collins, 2016).

Thomas, Antony. *Rhodes: The Race for South Africa* (New York, St. Martin's Press, 1997).

Thornton, A. P. *The Imperial Idea and Its Enemies: A Study in British Power* (London, St. Martin's Press, 1959).

Thoumine, R. H. *Scientific Soldier: A Life of General Marchant, 1766–1812* (Oxford, Oxford University Press, 1968).

Toye, Richard. *Churchill's Empire: The World that made Him and the World that He Made* (London, Pan, 2011).

Wallach, Janet. *The Desert Queen: The Extraordinary Life of Gertrude Bell* (London, Weidenfeld & Nicolson, 1996).

Wavell, Archibald. *Imperial Warrior: The Life and Times of Field-Marshal Viscount Allenby, 1861–1936*, 2 vols (London, George G. Harrap, 1940–43). Re-issued in one volume, Field-Marshal Viscount Wavell, *Allenby: Soldier and Statesman* (London, White Lion, 1974).

Weizmann, Chaim. *Trial and Error: The Autobiography of Chaim Weizmann* (New York, Harper, 1949).

Wilson, Jeremy. *Lawrence of Arabia: The Authorized Biography of T.E. Lawrence* (New York, Atheneum, 1990).

Woodward, David R. *Hell in the Holy Land: World War I in the Middle East* (Lexington, University Press of Kentucky, 2006).

Journal Articles/Chapter Contributions

Anderson, Olive. 'The Growth of Christian Militarism in Mid-Victorian Britain', *English Historical Review*, vol. 86, no. 338 (1971), pp. 46–72.

Bar-Yosef, Eitan. 'The Last Crusade? British Propaganda and the Palestine Campaign, 1917–18', *Journal of Contemporary History*, vol. 36, no. 1 (January 2001), pp. 87–109.

Butler, Jeffrey. 'The German Factor in Anglo-Transvaal Relations', in Prosser Gifford and Wm. Roger Louis, eds, *Britain and Germany in Africa: Imperial Policy and Colonial Rule* (New Haven, Yale University Press, 1967), pp. 167–93.

Coppes, C. R. 'Captain Mahan, General Gordon and the Origin of the Term "Middle East"', *Middle East*, vol. 12 (1976), pp. 95–8.

Crawford, Fred D. and Joseph A. Berton, 'How Well Did Lowell Thomas know Lawrence of Arabia?', *English Literature in Translation, 1880–1920*, vol. 39, no. 3 (1996), pp. 299–318.

Darwin, John. 'The Chanak Crisis and the British Cabinet', *History*, vol. 65, no. 213 (February 1980), pp. 32–48.

Darwin, John. 'Imperialism in Decline? Tendencies in British Imperial Policy between the Wars', *The Historical Journal*, vol. 23, no. 3 (1980), pp. 657–79.

Faught, C. Brad, 'An Imperial Prime Minister? W.E. Gladstone and India, 1880–85', *The Journal of the Historical Society*, vol. 6, no. 4 (December 2006), pp. 567–80.

Jones, Max. 'What Should Historians Do With Heroes? Reflections on Nineteenth- and Twentieth-Century Britain', *History Compass*, vol. 5, iss. 2 (2007), pp. 439–554.

Louis, W. R. 'Leo Amery and the Post-war World, 1945–55', *Journal of Imperial and Commonwealth History*, vol. 30 (2002), pp. 71–90.

McMahon, Deirdre, 'Ireland and the Empire-Commonwealth, 1900–1948', in Judith M. Brown and Wm. Roger Louis, eds, *The Oxford History of the British Empire: Volume IV, The Twentieth Century* (Oxford, Oxford University Press, 1999).

Reid, Donald M. 'Political Assassination in Egypt, 1910–54', *The International Journal of African Historical Studies*, vol. 15, no. 4 (1982), pp. 625–51.

Robinson, Ronald E., 'Non-European Foundations of European Imperialism: Sketch for a Theory of Collaboration', in Roger Owen and Robert B. Sutcliffe, eds, *Studies in the Theory of Imperialism* (London, Longman, 1972), pp. 117–42.

Saunders, Christopher and Iain R. Smith. 'Southern Africa, 1795–1910', in Andrew Porter, ed., *The Oxford History of the British Empire, vol. III, The Nineteenth Century* (Oxford, Oxford University Press, 1999), pp. 597–623.

Weber, Mark. 'The Boer War Remembered', *The Journal of Historical Review*, vol. 18, no. 3 (May–June 1999), pp. 14–27.

Woodberry, Robert D. 'The Missionary Roots of Liberal Democracy', *American Political Science Review*, vol. 106, iss. 2 (May 2012), pp. 244–74.

Government Documents

Arab Bulletin (12 March 1917)

HMSO Correspondence between Sir Henry McMahon and the Sherif Husayn of Mecca, Command Papers 5597, 1939.

The London Gazette
Mordike, John. 'General Sir Edmund Allenby's Joint Operations in Palestine, 1917–18' (Canberra, Royal Australian Air Force, Air Power Development Centre, 2008).
Parliamentary Debates

Newspapers and Periodicals

The Globe (London)
The Globe and Mail (Toronto)
History Today
The Jerusalem Post
The Listener
Los Angeles Times
The New York Times
Nottingham Evening News
Sunday Times (London)
The Tatler
The Times (London)
The Times Literary Supplement
The Westminster Gazette

Reference

Matthew, H. C. G. and Brian Harrison, eds. *Oxford Dictionary of National Biography* (Oxford, Oxford University Press, 2004).

Novels

Fitzgerald, F. Scott. *This Side of Paradise* (Oxford, Oxford University Press, 2009).
Mahfouz, Naguib. *Palace Walk* (New York, Anchor Books, 1990).

Poetry

Kipling, Rudyard. *Bridge-Guard in the Karroo* (1901).
Kipling, Rudyard. *The Islanders* (1902).
Kipling, Rudyard. *The Lesson* (1901).

Public Lectures

Darwin, John. 'Unlocking the World: Port Cities and Globalisation, 1830–1930', 7 July 2015, University of Konstanz (online).

Websites

firstworldwar.com
telstudies.org

Films/Documentaries

General Allenby's Entry into Jerusalem (Imperial War Museum, 1917).
Lawrence of Arabia (1962).
T.E. Lawrence and Arabia (BBC, 1986).
The Legacy of Lawrence of Arabia (BBC, 2017).
The Lighthorsemen (1987).
'With Allenby in Palestine and Lawrence in Arabia' (1919).

Theatrical Plays

Lawrence after Arabia (2016), by Howard Brenton.

INDEX